Praise for *Practically Still a Virgin*

With a refreshingly honest voice, Monica shares her colorful and tumultuous life in Alaska, where one tragedy begets another. As both an adoptee and birth mother, she unfolds the complexities and losses of adoption with stark honesty, revealing the ways adoption intricately weaves itself into the fabric of her life and highlighting the intergenerational impact of adoption trauma.

—Amy Seek, *God and Jetfire: Confessions of a Birth Mother*

Monica Hall was a self-described "badass" teenager, struggling with alcohol and drugs and making bad choices in boyfriends—not unusual behaviors in kids who are abandoned, or adopted, when very young. At fifteen, and pregnant, she promised herself and her unborn child that when her daughter turned eighteen, she would find her. Before fulfilling that promise, in her early twenties Monica reunited with her own birth families, an experience that changed her profoundly. *Practically Still a Virgin* sparkles with honesty, wit, and passion. We are with the author every step of the way as she struggles to become her best self, and to understand and draw meaning from the unusual events of her life. This memoir is a powerful addition to the literature of adoption and reunion.

—Patricia Moffat, *She Turned Her Head Away*

This book takes readers on a both harrowing and heartwarming journey through the author's past. A gutsy story about overcoming loss and triumphing over pain, hers is a courageous, riveting story that is ultimately about love. The 1970s were heady times in Alaska, and like many of her generation, as a teen Hall rebelled, and she became pregnant at fifteen. Like her biological mother before her, Hall placed her own baby for adoption. It is a must read for anyone with personal ghosts they wish to vanquish.

—Kim Rich, *Johnny's Girl: A Daughter's Memoir of Growing Up in Alaska's Underworld* and *A Normal Life.*

Practically Still a Virgin was a fascinating read! Monica's adoption story is a testament to the strength and tenacity of the human spirit. The journey of this brave girl as she moves towards womanhood and through the profound experience of her trauma is powerful, heartwarming, and absolutely inspiring!

—Mary Youngblood (Chugach Alutiiq, Cherokee, Seminole), adoptee, two-time Grammy winner: 2002 and 2006 (Best Native American Music Album)

PRACTICALLY STILL A VIRGIN

An Adoption Memoir

MONICA HALL

PRISM
PROSE PRESS

ISBN: 979-8-9896451-0-7 (Paperback)
ISBN: 979-8-9896451-1-4 (Digital)
ISBN: 979-8-9896451-2-1 (Audio)

From the author: This book is a memoir, a true account based on my best recollections of events I personally experienced. I consulted my journals, diaries, and appointment books, along with those of my mother. To ensure accuracy and help with my memories, I made multiple trips to Canada and Alaska, visiting locations, conducting research. I collaborated with many individuals; several are featured in the book. The dialogue has been recreated to match my best recollections of those exchanges. In some cases, I have compressed events and time periods in service of the narrative. It's important to note that the memories of others represented here may differ from mine. The names and identifying characteristics of certain people mentioned have been changed to protect their privacy.

Interior design and photo editing by Sharon K. Miller, www.buckskinbooks.com.

BirdingInSpain, CC BY-SA 3.0 via Wikimedia Commons, Creative Commons, Attribution, Share-Alike 3.0.

For Mary

FIRST BLUSH

It was a cloudy afternoon in Anchorage. I exited sixth period at Wendler Junior High and crossed the street, skirting mud puddles as I headed toward a cluster of stringy-haired girls in peacoats. I always met my friends at the corner store to smoke after school.

A man who was much younger than my father stood behind the building like he was waiting for someone. He was a carrottop in a dark-beige trench coat and wore unlaced Tuffy boots. I'd just lit up when he opened the coat and flashed his fluorescent-white body. My friends and I laughed and turned away, as if to say, "How boring—another pervert." We were used to it. It was 1970, and Anchorage was a weird place.

Two years earlier, a full seventy years after Alaska's gold rush, black gold had been discovered on the North Slope in Prudhoe Bay. I was in fifth grade when brothels began popping up like smallpox, loosely disguised as "massage parlors." With two military bases, an influx of pipeline workers, and lots of rich oil executives, there were plenty of patrons for prostitutes, gambling dens, and strip clubs.

This culture wasn't new to our town. According to the *Anchorage Daily News*, a 1944 essay contest asked, "What's wrong with Anchorage?" The winner noted the spread of gambling and prostitution, along with a "lack of civic pride."[1] Alaska really was the Last Frontier. Even before the oil boom, it attracted a different kind of soul—people, like my parents, who were looking for a change or a new start. Others needed a place to hide.

In the late '60s, I was barely a tween and unaware of what was happening outside my little world. I was excited to make friends when I started junior high, so I didn't care where all the new kids and cute boys came from. I didn't know their parents had recently moved up from the Lower 48 because of the oil boom, nor did I know Daddy's real estate speculation business was taking off because of oil. I had no idea the mob and Hells Angels were on their way.

My early days were simpler. I'm nearly four months old in my first photo and look happy to have been rescued from a crowded foster home. The black-and-white Polaroid commemorates the day I arrived home with my adoptive parents. Scalloped white edges frame the photo, and faint white lines mark where it was pulled from the camera while wet. I'm in my birthday suit, bald as a cue ball, lying in the center of their bed on my belly, arms straight and head held high. It was 1957, two years before statehood and nearly a decade before the oil discovery that changed me—and our small town—forever.

Our first home, which we fondly called the Little House, was a pale green shoebox with two bedrooms, a one-car garage, and clapboard siding. We lived on Snowcap Drive in Anchorage's quaint Rogers Park neighborhood. Had Robert

---

1. David Reamer, "A 1944 Contest Asked the Question: 'What's Wrong with Anchorage?' This Was the Winning Response." *Anchorage Daily News*, Sept. 6, 2020, https://www.adn.com/alaska-life/2020/09/06/a-1944-contest-asked-the-question-whats-wrong-with-anchorage-this-was-the-winning-response/.

Frost come calling, he would have surely named us in a verse. The city eventually changed our poetic street name to East 27th, but we were gone by then, and so was my seemingly idyllic childhood.

Anchorage sits deep inside the Cook Inlet on a knuckle of land protected from the Pacific Ocean. Across the Knik Arm is a mountain the locals call Sleeping Lady. Her silhouette resembles a woman lying down, long hair stretched behind her. On summer nights, she's backlit by twilight pastels, the same cotton candy glow that guided me when, as a teenager, I snuck from my window after midnight.

I cut my first tooth before my fourth month and started walking at month nine, a glimmer of the independence and freedom I'd pursue throughout my life. My first three years were the best, before my brother came along, because I was the center of Mama's universe.

Every night after kneeling for prayers, I eagerly awaited a bedtime story. My favorite was the story of how Mary Monica came to be. It began with my Catholic parents' prayer that God would bring them a little girl. Then they flew on a big airplane far, far away to get their new baby. I was special because they picked me.

It was in the fall of 1957 when the thrilled couple flew from Anchorage to Edmonton, Alberta, to choose a daughter. The social worker took them to a home where a foster mother cared for ten babies. I must have been the one who stood out.

My second-favorite story was one Mama made up. It was about Forbes, a baby elephant with the same name as my gray stuffed toy. One day, Forbes became upset at his parents and ran away from the circus. Once it got dark, he was lost and frightened, and he desperately missed his mama and daddy. Finally, some nice kids found him crying and wandering the streets. Together, they took a taxi back to the circus. The mama elephant was so happy, she hugged and kissed Forbes while crying huge tears of relief.

Mama emphasized the mother elephant's worry and terror at thinking she might have lost her precious Forbes forever. She reiterated her worry of losing me throughout my upbringing.

For my first three years, I had Mama to myself while Daddy sold houses. I had her sweet, undivided attention for coloring and story time. Sometimes I sat beside her at the piano to sing nursery rhymes. We also played together in our cozy living room, which had a single-paned picture window that frosted up in winter. Our dark sofa was flanked by lamps that wore ruffled skirts and sat atop colonial maple end tables. A black oval colonial-style rug braided with faded primary colors closed in the small room.

When I was three, Mama had exciting news: "Honey, you're getting a new baby brother and you're going to be a big sister!" I was over the moon. Being big was everything I aspired to.

Soon we were on a plane to Edmonton to pick up my three-week-old brother. The social worker drove us to a house where Mama later told me the foster lady gushed about how "this one" slept through the night without waking for feedings. She said this as if my parents were getting a good baby, a not-so-high-maintenance infant.

After we brought him home, everything centered on the gangly alien child who took away my mommy. My parents named him Timothy. It turned out he was starving to death, needed fattening up with increased feedings, had digestive issues and allergies, and was so sensitive that every noise woke him, especially if it involved Mama and me having fun. I resented him. Eventually, Daddy would, too.

Practically Still a Virgin

When Tim came along, the lazy days of song and piano playing evaporated. "Not today, honey," Mama would say. "We don't want to disturb your brother."

Anchorage winters are relentless stretches of darkness with just five hours of light on the shortest day. At age four, bundled in a blue snowsuit, suspenders, red wool cap, and matching mittens—and rustling like the bag inside a cereal box—I trudged through the snow toward the fence corner that offered the best view of the street. Pressed against the steel fence post, I pushed my nose through the wire grid and watched for the big kids who would soon turn the corner on their way home from Lake Otis Elementary. Even though I'd been warned not to, I thought it wouldn't hurt to give the post a little lick. The moment my tongue touched the frozen metal, frost grabbed it—I couldn't get away without ripping off my taste buds. I was horrified and felt foolish knowing the big kids would see how stupid I'd been.

I don't recall how long I stood there or how I got free. Maybe Mama rescued me, or perhaps my breath warmed the metal enough to release me. Either way, this is my first memory of caring how others perceived me—perhaps the first blush of an ego. Maybe I feared being unlovable because I'd been abandoned twice by the age of four. More likely, I was born a show-off.

My fondest childhood memories involve making Daddy proud. He marveled when I beat all the boys in races at the park. He was also impressed that I could swallow a handful of horse-sized vitamins in one gulp and down a tablespoon of castor oil without complaint. I loved his praise.

One evening, Daddy and I sat at the kitchen table making Little Thérèse Good Deed Beads using directions from a Catholic magazine. I was on my knees watching him weave the red cord in and around ten grape-sized wooden beads so they'd stay in place when pulled to the end of a strand. He hung a silver Saint Thérèse medal encased in mother-of-pearl at one end and a crucifix at the other.

I pulled a bead every time I did something for God, just like he showed me. I can still hear Daddy's soft voice, the one he reserved just for me: "That's it, sweetheart. Hold on to it. Now pull it to the end. That's a good girl." I loved it when Daddy called me sweetheart, and I made sure to pull all ten beads every day so he'd be proud of me. Decades later, Mama said she and Daddy had high hopes for me because I was so good.

My Little Thérèse Good Deed Beads were so special that I've kept them all these years, but the thread disintegrated with age, just like my relationship with Daddy.

Portage Glacier, fifty miles south of Anchorage

APPLAUSE

When Mama was nine, she'd steal away in the rumble seat while her drunk parents drove steep mountain roads from Reno to bars in Virginia City. She said, "I thought if I went along, I could keep them from killing themselves. If they crashed, I could die with them and wouldn't be an orphan." When they fought, she and her brother hid the knives.

Daddy first spied Mama in 1940, a month after she turned fifteen. They were in his hometown of Crescent Mills, a Northern California community located in the Indian Valley. It was a small town of only one hundred people, surrounded by pines, lakes, and valleys. It was also where Mama's poor-as-church-mice family landed during the Depression. Shortly after arriving in town, her father tired of his wife's dallying and moved to San Francisco and joined the merchant marines. After that, her often-intoxicated mother had many male callers. Mama had been in Crescent Mills less than a year when Daddy saw her walking into a store.

He'd grown up in the town's biggest house but was a man of the world by 1940 and returned after traveling the country. He'd come to visit his grandmother, who raised him.

Daddy wasn't tall but had Anglo-Spanish good looks and was never without a comb in his back pocket, which he reflexively whipped out to run through his slicked-back hair. He was twenty-five when he saw the Irish beauty and asked a friend to introduce them.

The next morning, Mama woke to voices in the front room, where she saw Daddy visiting with her mother and some locals. Company was common, and after they were briefly introduced, she returned to her room to finish her book.

When Daddy visited, he was determined to get to know the brown-haired, green-eyed beauty with full lips and straight white teeth, but she didn't emerge. When he returned that evening, she eventually surfaced, announcing that she was going for a walk. He jumped up. "Do you mind if I join you?" She shrugged, and off they went.

After that walk, Daddy extended his visit for two weeks. He finally convinced Mama to elope in Reno, where they lied about her age. She was only fifteen—ten years younger

Mama and Daddy in love, Anchorage, 2 a.m., 1947

than him. Mama felt guilty leaving her mother and her five-year-old brother, whom she'd practically raised.

Daddy joined the navy and was stationed at Treasure Island. After the war, they traveled the Pacific Northwest and headed up the Alcan Highway to the Alaska territory in 1947. Later, in 1956, they settled into the Little House, and Daddy suggested that they adopt a baby girl.

As far back as I can remember, priests and nuns visited our house and often stayed for dinner. Sister Solange was a wrinkled French nun in her seventies who wore a white habit and couldn't have weighed more than ninety pounds. When I was five, I showed her my Little Thérèse Good Deed Beads and told her I loved to do things for God: "I put away my toys and help Mama, too." She patted my head, and said in her French accent, "Mary Monica, someday you're going to be a saint." I beamed and vowed to be a nun like her when I grew up.

My attraction to less-than-saintly boys began soon thereafter, when I showed off for Toby O'Toole. He lived across the road and was a feisty, rough-and-tumble five-year-old with freckles, red hair, and a ginger personality. Toby did shocking things like tossing my swings over the top bar so Mama had to unwind them. But the time he held a water-filled dish soap bottle to his jeans and pretended to pee on me was the nastiest thing I'd ever seen. I've liked bad boys ever since.

We were in his front yard one afternoon, attempting to pound a waist-high rebar stake into the ground. During this super important project, I seized the opportunity to one-up Toby. My pulse quickened while I surveyed his stance and the force with which he hit it. On my turn, I got into position, aimed, and swung even harder and faster. In my fervor, I underestimated the arc of my backswing and slammed the claw of the hammer into the crown of my head. I pushed down tears without even wincing to continue my impressive swing, then handed the hammer to Toby.

While he took his turn, I touched my wet scalp. An hour later, I got stitches. Toby never let on that he was impressed, nor did he notice my blunder—he surely would've mocked me. Toby eventually died of an overdose.

This was the beginning of my need to compete, prove my strength, and gain applause. Even at five, the drive to be cool was so crucial that I accepted the pain rather than being viewed as weak.

I chalked it up to a tomboy's healthy ego. Eventually, I realized I was born this way because I needed strength for what I'd have to endure.

The Hall Family Photo, 1963

THE ROAR

I had my IQ tested when my kindergarten teacher suggested it. I scored high, so my parents expected me to do well in school—but that didn't happen. Daddy tried to help me write my numbers in first grade, but I stumbled when transitioning to double digits. I can still remember the panic I felt in my stomach when my mind went blank and he became impatient. It was crushing to lose his praise.

Mama also tried to help me over the years, but she'd get frustrated, smack her pencil down, shove her chair away from the table, and huff, "Howard, you help her!" This replayed over and over until I stopped bringing work home.

"Honey, do you have any homework tonight?"

"No, Mama. I finished it in class."

Maybe I had difficulty in school because I'd had a good share of trauma. Whatever the reason, I felt stupid and was constantly afraid of being a disappointment.

When I was in first grade, we moved to the Midtown neighborhood and I transferred to North Star Elementary. We affectionately called our new home the Big House. I imagined I was a princess living in a mansion with a grand staircase, large picture windows spanning two floors, and an open rock fireplace tall as the sky.

In actuality, it was a two-story, three-bedroom, one-bath home. It sat on a corner lot near a commercial area. Our only close neighbors lived in an A-frame just a few steps from our back door. The mother occasionally invited me to stay for dinner, but I don't remember much about the family except they had a younger boy and a girl around my age. They also drank powdered milk, which tasted like dirt. Apart from that house, our only other neighbors lived in a trailer park across the street. In the other direction sat a barren ten-acre lot. Playmates were scarce at the Big House, so I felt isolated and lonely.

Most of my memories from that house feel gray, except for the evening of March 27, 1964, when I was a few months shy of seven. At 5:30 p.m., Daddy was still at work. Mama was in the kitchen preparing a bite to eat before Good Friday church services. The groceries we'd collected for the needy were on the counter. I sat next to my brother at the dining room table and looked through the wall of windows at our snow-covered yard, the trailer park, and the empty lot.

All the other neighborhood kids had been invited to a birthday party. Because I wasn't there, I was sure they didn't like me. The party was at a log home behind some trees on the other side of the snow-covered lot.

We were eating when the earthquake started. It was slow at first, with a gentle rocking that was oddly alarming. As the shaking escalated, it felt like we were trapped in a rock tumbler. Mama grabbed our hands while we stumbled through a minefield to the front doorway. Cupboard doors banged, dishes crashed, and the television fell on its face. The earth made a deafening roar, like a freight train was at our back door. That sound is still stuck in my head today.

As the earth shook, we braced ourselves under the stability of the door jamb. Mama's arm held me close while we rode the waves, but it didn't comfort me.

Soon after the shaking started, the neighbor lady appeared in our yard. She was trying to get to her children at the coveted birthday party. Her coat flapped open and she fell face-first in the snow with every step. Up and down she went while an invisible monster threw her around the yard, keeping her from her children.

Mama waved her arms and shouted, "Come inside!" But the woman couldn't hear over the earth's deep rumbling. She saw us, though. With every fall, her wild, panicked eyes begged us to help her reach her children.

In horror, we watched the movie happening outside our theater-sized windows. The trunk of our birch tree whipped to the ground like a willow switch. Telephone poles wagged and the trailers across the street rolled around like my little brother's Matchbox cars.

After five long minutes, it stopped. When I looked up again, the neighbor lady was gone. We didn't move because we didn't trust the stillness, which seemed louder than the roar.

We felt aftershocks into the night, eleven of them with a magnitude greater than 6. I'd brace myself every time the shaking started, waiting for it to increase like it had in the big one, but it never did. Nine more aftershocks struck over the next three weeks. In the following months, there were thousands. I got used to them after a while.

Years later, Mama told me my face turned gray and three-and-a-half-year-old Timmy whimpered, "Oh, God, please help us. Oh, God, please help us."

The megathrust quake was 9.2 in magnitude, the second largest ever recorded in the world and the biggest in North

America. There were 139 lives lost, mostly due to tsunamis, including 16 deaths on Oregon and California shorelines.

I'm not sure how Daddy made it home so fast with all the broken-up streets, but shortly after it stopped, he leapt up the steps and threw open the door. Out of breath, he yelled, "Honey, is everyone okay?" The sturdy house was a fortress. Others weren't so lucky.

The Turnagain Heights neighborhood, located along a bluff line, had magnificent sunset views of Sleeping Lady. During the quake, the clay ground liquefied, causing waves of earth to roll seventy-five homes as far as 2,000 feet into the bay. The 130-acre landslide was a jumble of trees, telephone poles, rooftops, and snow-covered earth scrambled together.

Fourth Avenue fell 10 or more feet in places, trapping cars and making businesses inaccessible. Our town was a mess, like God had shaken us up in a Yahtzee cup and left us where we landed.

NOAA photo crews help ground-truth disaster damage at Turnagain Arm. Damage caused by 1964 Good Friday Earthquake. (Photo courtesy of NOAA Photo Library via Wikimedia Commons)

Practically Still a Virgin

We stood in line for disaster-relief rations and immunizations and collected snow from the lot across the street. We boiled it in the fireplace, just like real Alaskan pioneers. We also ate the Easter food we'd planned to donate to the needy because the grocery stores were a mess—all the boxes and cans had been shaken off the shelves and into the isles.

I no longer felt bad about missing that damn party.

Thank God it was Good Friday because schools were closed, and damage to one elementary school was catastrophic. Even though our well-built home had kept us safe, we moved to a cul-de-sac in a kid-friendly neighborhood six months later.

CENSUS

In second grade, I was proud to move up a couple of reading levels. But that pride reversed when my class took an official test where we could use only our number 2 pencils.

I filled in the dots until I came to a question that asked if I was living with my real parents. Mama and Daddy were my real parents, but not my *real* parents. This was my introduction to how confusing the word "real" would become later in life.

I panicked. I didn't want to get in trouble by leaving the questions blank, nor did I want my teacher and classmates to see that I was defective, which the test seemed to prove. I wanted to crawl under my desk, like we did during earthquake and nuclear threat drills.

Confused, I told Mama about the test when I got home from school. When she told Daddy that evening, he jumped from the couch like his seat was on fire. "Who do those lousy so-and-sos think they are?" Nobody explained that the problem was with the test and not with me. Daddy was too angry to explain, angry at the powers that be for prying into our personal lives.

Practically Still a Virgin

I lay awake listening to his angry tone while they discussed what felt like the error of my being. Prior to the census questionnaire, I hadn't yet noticed that I resembled no one and had no behavioral or physical similarities to my parents, unlike the other kids and their "real" families. Besides, my classmates' existence didn't cause trouble.

After that day, I stopped focusing on academics—I was too busy trying to still the jumping beans in my chest by constantly measuring my place in the world.

The next morning, we drove the half block to school. I went to class while my parents marched into the office. Moments later, the wooden intercom squawked, "Mrs. Blue, can you please come to the office?"

I never again shared my worries, concerns, or troubles with my parents.

CAROL

At our new house, Tim's bedroom window was small and high on the wall, but mine was low and large enough to climb through. Within a few years, the cedar siding would develop a worn spot where I'd place my foot to hoist myself through my window in the wee morning hours.

Our court in City View contained twelve houses, and there were fifteen kids to play doorbell ditch, red light–green light, and hide-and-seek. At age eleven, I began babysitting for two boys who lived at the end of the court and played with my brother. Their father was a hunter, pilot, and guide with a museum of dead stuffed animals in the den—bearskin rugs and antlers with marble eyes.

Most of the three-bedroom, one-bath homes had the same layouts: the same basements, cedar-shingled siding, and one-car garages. Ours was painted pinkish beige and was three houses in on the left. When I was in fifth grade, Mama started taking art classes and made one of the basement rooms into an art studio where she could disappear for hours.

A window over the kitchen sink looked down on the flat backyard, where Daisy, our cairn terrier, spent most of her time. There was also struggling grass, a red picnic table, a rotating pole clothesline, and a small patio with crabgrass between the cement squares. Cyclone fences separated our yard from the yards on each side.

The house next door, where my new best friend lived, was barn red. Paula and I were seven when I moved in. She was the middle child, very kind, and wicked-smart. Her body was rounder than mine—I was twiggy at that age. She had wispy blonde hair and blue eyes that were later masked by cat-eye glasses. In early adolescence, she'd wear braces. Her family was Catholic. We were, too, and so was another family in the court. On Sundays, we rolled out in a caravan on our way to Saint Anthony's.

Playing the accordion for Paula (left), Father Gurr, and Tim

Monica Hall

I attended Airport Heights Elementary, which was shouting distance from our court. It was named for Merrill Field, one of the country's busiest airports for private aircraft. Even today, I'm ten again when I hear a small prop plane. I feel the freedom of summer days after dark winter and taste the sweetness of the plump raspberries we'd ravage after raiding the neighbor's garden.

Paula's mom was like a second mother to me. Early on, I'd walk in the front door without knocking and jabber away. She'd tease me by saying, "Mary Monica, you could never be a nun that takes a vow of silence."

Paula and I spent the night with each other, played board games, and ice-skated at the school rink. We also ran through the sprinklers and built forts out of lawn chairs and blankets. We were inseparable for years, but at age ten, I briefly abandoned our friendship when a new girl to the court came to stay with her divorced father for the summer. I vaguely remember that she had round glasses. Fifty years later, Paula told me she'd confided in her grandmother about how hurt and lonely she was. Her grandmother, referring, to how I treated Paula, said, "Some people just dispose of people like an old newspaper." Once the girl left, Paula and I were besties again.

When we were in fifth grade, a girl at our school, Carol, wore a blonde wig that was too big for her head. She also had a shiny plastic leg that looked like it belonged on a store mannequin. She was taller and fatter than us and had missed two grades due to cancer treatments and surgeries. Her face was big and pale. She must have been on steroids. When she fell on the playground and cried, no one helped her up. I was afraid of her, and I wasn't the only one.

The following year, Paula and I attended her funeral. Later, Carol's sister told me she had been horribly sick to her stomach and died in excruciating pain. For me, the lesson was that cancer made you suffer and then you died anyway. I also learned that death wasn't just for old people.

As Paula and I got older, our interests shifted to playing Monkees records and hanging Bobby Sherman and Davy Jones posters on our walls. We also strung a makeshift telephone between our windows—juice cans on a string, which later graduated to a pulley system where we attached notes with clothespins. But the ruckus kept her father from his naps, so he nailed her window shut. This was way before the neighbors began gossiping about my midnight window escapades.

CRUSHED

In fifth grade, the nurse visited our class and shuffled the boys off with our teacher, Mr. Martin, while she remained to instruct us girls on sex education. I wondered, *Are the boys learning about periods, too?* She showed us films and abstract pictures of the male and female reproductive systems. It was so clinical that I had no idea how a baby was conceived.

A few months later, I heard about it in graphic detail when some kid told me what happens during intercourse while we walked home from the neighborhood baseball field. But he didn't stop there. I was sickened when he described blow jobs. I knew my parents hadn't done any of those disgusting things because Tim and I were adopted.

This was around the time I became more anxious to fit in and Mama's overprotectiveness became problematic. The cool latchkey kids occasionally let me hang out with them on the playground after school, and sometimes at recess, but I wasn't popular like them. Their popularity was rooted in the freedom I lacked.

One afternoon, while I was crossing the school lawn after the last bell, the cool kids approached. I was eager for the attention, and my crush was with them. It had been a long time since they invited me to hang out. My heart skipped a beat.

"Hey, Monica," Lynn said. "We're going to Carl's to play spin the bottle. Wanna come with?" My heart leapt at the thought of being at Carl's house, let alone kissing him. But if I asked for permission to go, Mama would call his mother to make sure there was parental supervision.

"Oh, that's right," Lynn said. "Forget it. Your mommy never lets you do anything. We don't want you around anyway!" With that, she pushed me. I tried to catch myself but landed on my bottom, spilling my books as I fell. I didn't look up but heard the cool kids laugh as they walked away. I hid my tears all the way home.

Not long after that, life started changing quickly. Though he'd been sober for twenty years, Daddy began drinking after work. His alcoholism had grown during his dry years; when he started again, the monster of addiction awakened. His cravings had him by the balls.

Being only eleven, I didn't realize what was happening. Daddy was in the land speculation business, and his drinking may have been spurred by the excitement of the impending $900 million in oil-rich land leases Alaska was about to receive. It was a potential gold mine for his business.

Before booze, Mama and Daddy rarely left us at night. But once they started drinking, it wasn't long before our stability crumbled. It started when they'd have a few nightcaps with Daddy's business partners and their wives. As it escalated, even Mama changed.

Tim's room shared a wall with the living room, where they entertained. He couldn't sleep with the cackling and booming voices. I became unhinged, too, but it scared my sensitive and devoted brother even more to hear Mama carrying on like a hyena.

23

He had a nervous stomach, and the change in our mother, combined with the chaos in the living room, made him moan over the toilet in the middle of the night. I couldn't sleep when my parents were drinking, worried Tim would cry and suffer.

Soon, Daddy began arriving home in the morning still drunk. In 1969, during the summer between fifth and sixth grade, I noted in my diary that *he didn't come home for a couple days.* I wrote, *Mama really scared us when she said she was worried that a bear might have gotten him.* The bear threat was real in Alaska. Years earlier, a family friend had his head knocked off with one swipe of a bear paw.

Daddy had left early one morning to look at property in Susitna, one hundred miles away. She called the state troopers to look for him while we drove the highway searching for his car and perusing bar parking lots. Finally, I spotted his forest-green Newport in the Outpost's gravel lot. Mama went in to get him. He'd been gone for five days.

His drinking was paired with a gambling addiction. Mama told me he'd sit at the card table for weeks at a time without sleep or food—only cigarettes and booze. I now realize he probably crashed in a flophouse or with some woman.

Thus ensued our family outings cruising parking lots at low-life bars and gambling halls in hopes of dragging him home. Life appeared normal between Daddy's binges, but impending doom surrounded us like a cloud of mountain ice fog.

Years later, Mama had a case of selective memory. She was quick as a whip well into her nineties, but when I mentioned things she wasn't comfortable with, she'd often say in a bewildered tone, "Oh, honey, I don't remember that." I think she played the I-don't-remember card due to shame. But the proof was in my diary.

DEBTS

Between drinking bouts, Daddy asked me to come along while he ran errands one day. I was about eleven. Mama always made Tim and me sit in the back seat, so I was elated when Daddy let me sit up front like a grownup.

It was a cool June day and my window was rolled down, letting in the clean scent of freshly mown grass. We cruised along Ninth Avenue parallel to the long Park Strip, which had been a dirt landing strip before Merrill Field opened in the '30s. Daddy held a lit cigarette, his constant companion, near the wing window.

A shiny blue sedan pulled up alongside us at a stop sign. Daddy pointed and said, "Look, sweetheart. That's a Mercedes-Benz. It's the finest car on the road. We will have one someday." He respected quality, and I wanted to be like him, someday riding around in a first-rate vehicle.

After paying utility bills, Daddy parked on Fourth Avenue in front of a bar. I was excited when he asked me to join him. It was dark and creepy inside and smelled sickly sweet. Little did I know that such places would feel like home one day.

"This is my daughter, Monica," he said proudly. There was a rush of compliments about how lovely I was. I loved how he showed me off. When we left, he leaned down and said, "Let's keep this as our little secret and not tell Mama." I nodded and beamed.

TOO PATHETIC

Because of all the kids who arrived during the oil boom, school was held in shifts when I was in junior high. I attended the early shift. I was always out the door before anyone else and walked the snowy mile to school. I was excited to be there—not because I wanted an education but because I wanted to socialize and crush on cute boys.

One frosty morning, I pushed the button to turn off my alarm clock as usual. I always woke to darkness and the familiar sound of the neighbor's car warming up. After my shower, I could still hear the motor and thought, *Mr. Webb should've left for work already*. I looked out the window and saw Daddy's Newport sitting in the driveway, exhaust escaping the tailpipe.

I woke Mama and we threw on our coats. Daddy's head rested on the driver's side window. The doors were locked. When he didn't respond to our banging and yelling, I thought he was dead.

Finally, he opened his eyes. He cowered, like Daisy when she peed in the house, while fumbling to unlock the door. With Mama on one side and me on the other, we helped him to bed. I'd never seen him drunk before—until then, he'd only arrived home drunk while I was sleeping or after I'd gone to school.

When Mama and I helped him out of the car, I spied a dangly earring on the floorboard. I pocketed it and later gave it to her. I don't know if she ever confronted him about it, but she did buy herself an expensive camel-hair coat.

Mama kept a quart of vodka in the cupboard for his hangovers. She grabbed the bottle and a glass, then closed the bedroom door. That afternoon, she sat Tim and me down to have the "Daddy is an alcoholic" talk. That was the first time anyone told me it's a disease. I learned many years later that he was a "periodic alcoholic."

Whenever he emerged from the bedroom after coming home drunk, he'd slump over the kitchen table with a Salem smoldering in the ashtray and mumble an unintelligible apology. I tried my best to avoid the kitchen on those days— he was too pathetic.

Money was tight and it upset me to see Mama so worried. More than once, I kept her company while she called around to the bars. When he came to the phone one night, she was so mad he wasn't lying dead in a ditch that she slammed the receiver and scared the crap out of me. We didn't see him for another week. Then, in March of 1970, he called Alcoholics Anonymous after two years of drinking. He began attending meetings, and within a few weeks, people who were rough around the edges began visiting our house and socializing with our parents.

I went along to a few meetings and recall the odd mix. It seemed like God had taken a dustpan and swept all walks of life into a heap, then dumped them in the AA meeting. Even though members had nothing in common, they hugged, laughed, and slapped backs like they were at a Titanic survivors' reunion.

MARBLE EYES

The summer when I was thirteen, about four months after Daddy quit drinking, I was walking home from the baseball field when I heard a couple of boys laughing and using the word "ball" like it meant something sexy. I'd also heard it at school but wasn't sure what it meant. To be cool, I laughed, too.

Around that same time, a new girl, Jill, moved to our neighborhood. I was at her house testing products from her mom's recent Avon delivery when Guy, my crush, cruised by my house. He was a tall strawberry blond with curly hair, zits, and braces. At the close of the school year, half the seventh-grade female student body had a crush on him. I doubted he knew who I was.

When Guy showed up in our cul-de-sac, he was with his cocky friend Benny, whose voice had changed. They stopped at the end of the court where my brother was playing and asked about me. "Tell Monica that Guy and Benny are looking for her and we want to *ball* her." Tim, of course, ran home with the exciting news.

When I came home from Jill's, Daddy began grilling me. At first, I was elated that Guy had been on my street, knew my name, and wanted to talk to *me*. He lived a mile away in a fancy neighborhood and had made a special trip! But my excitement was ruined by Daddy's interrogation, which seemed odd because Mama was the disciplinarian. He mostly nagged us about manners. Pointing to the door, he said in a metallic tone, "Get in the car. We're going for a ride."

Angry clouds sat low on the horizon and the air was strangely still. Even our active court was bereft of its usual sounds of laughter and kids playing. It was as if everyone sensed the coming storm.

As he backed down the driveway, Daddy looked like a stranger. We drove in silence out of the neighborhood. I felt queasy when I noticed he didn't light up, which he always did as soon as he got behind the wheel. A shiver crept up the back of my neck, but I kept my eyes on the road, wondering what he was thinking and where we were going. His knuckles were white from gripping the wheel as he turned toward the mountains.

His head whipped around and, like a rabid animal, he screamed, "You wanna be like those fucking whores on Third Avenue?"

My heart leapt into my throat. I'd never seen him look or talk like that.

"Those filthy broads will spread their legs for any scumbag who drops his drawers."

I couldn't believe the nasty things he was saying, nor could I understand why he screamed them at *me*. He would never talk like that in front of Mama. I inched closer to the door.

"Look at me when I'm talking to you!" His marble eyes were as dead as the stuffed animals mounted on my neighbor's wall.

I was trapped in a cage, and with every bellow, he grew while I shrank. All I could do was shake my head, but I wanted to throw myself out of the moving car. His tirade built momentum with every block.

"Those miserable *sluts* will suck off any greaseball who pulls on his pud! Is that what you want?"

This monster was not Daddy. White, foamy spit spewed as he yelled. I felt like I was in a tunnel. His mouth moved in slow motion as the world rushed by. I felt and smelled everything: my icy fingers tucked under my thighs, his nicotine breath, fresh air coming through the window. Grossest of all, the sting of his saliva as it landed on my lips. I willed the bile down.

He described what he saw as the filth of humanity, women whom he loathed, *like I was one of them.* We drove for what felt like hours. I shoved down tears because I sensed that he would like my vulnerability.

I didn't understand most of what he'd described or realize he was aroused—I just knew how disgusting I felt. Soon after, I began seeing bits of a blurred scene in my mind. As the years ticked by, it came into focus.

I couldn't see the woman's face, but there was a stained mattress beneath her naked body. Empty glasses and trash scattered on a nightstand. The floor was littered with garments and sheets. Beams of smoke filtered between blackout drapes and split her ghoulish form in half. Her legs hung off the bed and her arms were out to her sides, like she was on a cross. The man's effort rocked her. Other men leaned against a filthy wall, waiting to mount her like rutting hogs. She neither enjoyed it nor acknowledged them.

For many years, I thought Daddy must've described that scene, but decades later, when I discovered I had many repressed memories, I wondered if he had taken me to visit a whorehouse that day.

Either way, that car ride was the start of my rapid descent.

WRECKING BALL

None of the bad things that happened to me affected my future as much as that car ride. It was crushing to discover that Daddy, who had always made me feel special, thought I was like the whores he loathed.

Even if I could've articulated such humiliating things, I wouldn't have shared them with anyone, especially Mama. By then, I'd begun to sense she was jealous of me, although I'd yet to consciously realize it. I just thought she didn't like me that much.

When Tim and I were in grade school, Daddy would say in reverence, "Mama is a saint ... I couldn't even get her in the sack until we were married." We'd nod. *Yes, of course, Mama is a saint.*

Years later, I wondered if he had some twisted Madonna complex and worried his daughter might be like the sluts and whores he disdained but couldn't resist when he'd traveled the country as a young man, something Mama alluded to many years later. Perhaps he thought pure and beautiful Mama was his chance at redemption. In any case, Daddy put her on a pedestal and passed that on to us kids with his saintly talk.

Practically Still a Virgin

About ten years after Daddy's death, when I was in my thirties, I asked Mama why they adopted. I'd assumed she couldn't conceive. I'd put off asking because I intuited that this question would be on the do-not-ask list. I was right, but not for the reason I thought.

I took a gulp for courage. "Why couldn't you get pregnant?" I knew I'd gotten too personal when she huffed and turned from me in anger. My heart broke a little every time she did that. With her back to me, she spat, "There was nothing wrong with *me*." After a brief pause, still turned away, as if it were my fault for asking, she snapped, "Well, if you have to know ... Daddy had scar tissue from venereal disease."

"Oh," I said like it was nothing. Curiously, I wasn't surprised.

That car ride shifted my focus from gaining good attention from the popular kids at school to gaining bad attention from the kids with a propensity toward delinquency. I planned to carry my virginity as a badge of honor, gain Daddy's approval, and regain my dignity after being rejected by the cool kids in elementary school. I'd be the badass virgin, Monica Hall. Kids who grew up among dysfunction would look up to me, and I'd belong.

For years, I wondered why I became a wrecking ball at thirteen. I learned when one experiences trauma it's common to suppress feelings and develop survival strategies. Mine was to become so powerful no one could hurt me again, or so I thought.

LONE WOLF

The kids I hung around didn't always have hot water, but they did have junkie siblings who carried guns and knives. One's sister was a prostitute and in prison for dealing drugs. Another's living room was filled with gaming tables for the illegal after-hours gambling joint her father ran.

Shortly after the car ride, I became fast friends with Kelly, who was a year younger than me and trying to survive her chaotic family life. When I met her, I felt like I belonged. Eventually, she'd help me understand things we never talked about as kids.

When I'd started junior high the previous year, I assumed the new faces had attended different grade schools. I had no idea most kids had recently moved north because of the oil boom. They had fancy houses, and their fathers had important jobs at the new banks and oil companies. They were popular and cared about their grades. I wanted to be among them, but I didn't fit. Nor did I belong with the smart kids, like Paula and her friends, who were wholesome and cared little about status.

The pretty cheerleaders had their high school sisters' hand-me-downs, wearing cute miniskirt dresses and shiny patent leather baby doll shoes with silver chunk heels. Mama would never let me dress like that. I had no idea where to shop for cute clothes even if she would've let me wear them. We still shopped at the kiddie store and from catalogs.

Kelly lived a few blocks away. She was quiet and brooding, wore Levi's, smoked, and wasn't anxious to be noticed like me. Her dad said they had Nez Perce blood, which seemed evident in her looks. I envied that. We were both five feet tall and could pass for sisters, but her face was fuller, and her eyes were brown while mine were hazel.

Being adopted, I wasn't sure of my ethnicity, but I wanted to be American Indian too. With my olive skin and long, dark hair, I was often told I looked like Cher, who I thought was exotically beautiful. We both had crooked teeth, and I could see the resemblance, but I didn't *feel* beautiful. Maybe I was drawn to American Indian culture because of the songs and movies that made it cool. When Cher released her hit song "Half-Breed," I wondered if the title could apply to me, too. (I naively assumed at the time that the song was about her.)

What I found most attractive about Kelly was her freedom, although it came at a price. Her overwhelmed alcoholic mother had too many mouths to feed and could barely keep track of her three boys under the age of ten, let alone Kelly and her older siblings. Her creepy, often-drunk stepfather worked hard, but it wasn't enough and the cupboards were frequently bare. Kelly sometimes stayed for dinner. When we had pork chops, she'd strip them bare, nibbling every bit of meat, fat, and gristle. Then she'd stash the bones in her pocket. I found it shocking at the time, but now I realize she was just hungry. When I was in my thirties, Mama told me she'd wondered why I chose lower-class friends.

Years later, Kelly told me her favorite teacher had hung black construction paper along the bottom of the windows so she couldn't stare outside during class. Perhaps she was thinking about sliding down the icy gravel-pit hills beyond the schoolyard woods. Or maybe she was trying to forget the sleepless nights when her drunken stepfather climbed through her bedroom window. In any case, he introduced Kelly to her love of reading when he gave her *The Hobbit*.

In addition to her younger brothers, Kelly had an older sister, Leslie, who was married and lived down the street. She also had two cute older brothers, Tommy and Steven, who mostly ignored us but made sure we didn't get into trouble. They belonged to a crew of badass boys who were always together. They were a force to be reckoned with, armed with switchblades and guns. They fought, intimidated people, dealt pot and hash, committed petty crimes, and—unbeknownst to me—shot heroin. Tommy was the ringleader, and the crew flew in and out of Kelly's house like pigeons from a coop. Her mom treated them like they were her own.

Kelly's oldest brother was four years older than me. Tommy wore his dirty-blond hair parted down the middle, stringy and hanging in his eyes. What he lacked in height, he made up for in attitude. His handsome baby face wore a permanent scowl. Years later, Kelly told me her brothers practically raised her. I remembered that she'd always looked over her shoulder, hoping Tommy wouldn't "find out" lest he "kick her ass," though he never laid a hand on her.

Her other older brother was two years ahead of me with brown puppy-dog eyes and a baby face. The moment I saw Steven, I had a huge crush. He was cute, funny, and kind to me, but he'd never shown signs of seeing me as anything other than a kid sister, even though I swooned in his presence.

I wished I had an older brother who'd watch out for me. In contrast, my little brother had soft blond pageboy hair, blue-gray saucer eyes, and snow-white skin. He dressed his troll dolls and played the violin.

Practically Still a Virgin

Our family had dinner together almost every evening. Daddy watched us like a hawk and picked us apart for any infraction of table manners. Our house was a place to escape, not visit. On the outside, my family looked put together. In reality, we weren't. I've since read that low self-esteem can be caused by unsupportive parents, trauma, and poor performance at school—all of which I had.

I envied that, unlike me, Kelly wasn't a lone wolf. Her older brothers looked out for her. I had no one, so I was attracted to large families whose open-door policy made me feel accepted. It wasn't so much their class level I related to. Decades later, Kelly explained it best: "Broken kids recognize broken kids. They're easier to be friends with because they're less likely to judge and are just trying to survive."

HASH THIEF

With Kelly, I finally found my niche. I replaced my desire for good grades, cute dresses, and popularity with cutting class, waffle-stomper boots, and ratty clothes. I admired her older brothers and their tough friends for their freedom and the respect they received when they stomped around the neighborhood. I wanted that for myself and sought it with everything I had. It would soon become my downfall.

One Friday after school when I was fourteen, Kelly's mom left us to watch her little brothers while she ran errands. We were in the living room making plans for the evening. The house was chaotic as the kids chased their dog in and out of the bedrooms. Kelly sat in the chair by the front door, and I plopped myself at the end of the sofa. I didn't pay much attention to the shaggy-haired guy smoking at the other end. I hadn't seen him before and guessed he was waiting for Tommy and Steven.

Soon, the back door creaked. Kelly's eyes widened. I turned to see Tommy wearing a scowl. Billy and Steven followed. I'd seen Billy many times over the last couple years because he was one of the crew. Even though he was only

Billy (back middle) with Tommy (left), and Steven (right), 1973

eighteen, he looked much older than the others, with dark hair, swarthy good looks, sideburns, and a goatee.

Tommy passed me on the sofa to lean against the front door, arms crossed, legs shoulder-width apart. His face was stone, like a gargoyle. Even the kids sensed the temperature change and retreated to a bedroom.

All eyes turned to Billy, who stood against the wall across from the sofa. No one moved or even breathed. Billy was five-foot-ten but seemed much taller. His shoulders were back, his fists were clenched, and his chin was tilted upward as he glared at the guy on the sofa.

I shivered from the look in his icy green eyes. A few days earlier, I'd heard someone had stolen the crew's hash and they suspected it was one of their friends. I thought, *This must be the thief.*

By the shocked look on the guy's face, I could tell he hadn't expected this reception. I wished I wasn't sitting so close. The depth of Billy's stare, which was fixated on the thief, made him look like the northern lights embodiment of Charles Manson. Billy said nothing. He didn't have to. All exits were blocked.

When the guy stood to leave, Billy nodded toward the door. He growled, "Let's ... step ... out ... back."

A few long seconds elapsed before Billy stepped aside to let the thief pass and walk toward the back door. He and Kelly's brothers followed through the kitchen and out the back door. Loving the action, but also spooked, I felt like I'd had a front-row seat to the best show in town. I picked up my books and headed home.

I knew Billy was taking the thief into the woods through the trail that led from the backyard. I imagined Billy's cold eyes as he pressed a knife to the thief's throat.

Later that night, I asked Kelly what happened. She didn't know, but her brothers got their hash back. That guy didn't come around again.

DOWNWARD SPIRAL

At twelve, I took my first hit off a joint in seventh grade PE class when we were supposed to be cross-country skiing. My friend Lorna got it from her big brother. By then I'd already been smoking cigarettes for a while. Leaning against a birch tree, I only took a few tokes. I didn't feel anything, but it still became a regular activity—not because I liked it but because I thought it made me look cool.

When Daddy was gambling and drinking, he'd stagger in while everyone slept and empty wads of hundreds, fifties, and twenties from his slacks pockets onto the dresser. The next morning, I'd pick a large bill off the top, unnoticed. This attracted an abundance of friends since I could buy as much marijuana as I wanted.

Once he started going to AA, I didn't know what was worse: his previous disappearing act or the gushing over his new sobriety. He'd sit at the kitchen table in his wifebeater and boxers, reading spiritual books and telling me how grateful he was. I was pissed because he didn't leave cash on the dresser anymore.

My behavior worsened during the summer after eighth grade when I met Nick, my first boyfriend. He was my friend

Marla's brother. Nick's straight shoulder-length hair was parted on the side and hung over his eye, which made him look a bit like a pirate. With bulging black eyes, he wasn't conventionally cute, but I was attracted to his bad-boy attitude. He also had a soft side. We dated for nearly a year. Nick introduced me to sniffing glue, vandalism, and breaking into houses. I never broke into a house with Nick, but he showed me his pocket-sized pack of handmade tools he used to pick locks. I did, however, break into houses with Marla.

Due to the rash of break-ins, Daddy got a burglar alarm that hung over the peak of our front door. When temperatures dipped below zero, it sometimes malfunctioned and woke the whole neighborhood. On those nights, I'd shudder at how mad my parents would be if they discovered their daughter was the neighborhood burglar.

Marla and I once broke into a friend's house while the family was camping. We rummaged through their refrigerator, and I made myself a bologna sandwich. I also took half his sister's babysitting money, which was stashed inside a Band-Aid tin. A few weeks later, I saw her outside Pay-N-Pak, our neighborhood store, and asked with concern, "Didn't you have a break-in?"

She nodded. "Yeah, while we were camping."

"Oh, that's awful!" I looked her in the eye with the most sympathy I could muster. "Did they catch 'em?"

"No, but they think they know who did it. They just don't have enough evidence to take prints."

They know it's me! I tried to keep a straight face, but my heart pounded so hard I thought she might hear. I was so terrified I couldn't breathe. I knew I'd eventually get caught because I couldn't stop. It was my first addiction.

ESCAPE

On Alaska nights, I was never afraid to walk alone on empty streets and wooded trails. It didn't matter if there was a tar-black winter sky or never-ending summer twilight. I felt safe under the Chugach range, its jagged horizon looming overhead, verdant green in summer and protective white in winter. Eventually, I learned that not even the mountains could protect me from myself.

Mama sensed spending the night with Kelly and Marla wasn't a good idea, but she didn't know I was sneaking out my window and putting myself in real danger. The movie theater was the one place she felt safe leaving me unsupervised.

Seeing the Fireweed Theatre's bank of windows and its expansive red carpet quickened my pulse because it meant I'd soon be dropping acid and getting attention by beating up girls in the restroom. Like many of my friends, I was always high when my parents picked me up. I struggled to "maintain," not letting on that my vision was a kaleidoscope of psychedelic colors and I couldn't comprehend Mama because her voice sounded like a record playing backward.

Once home, I was desperate to avoid the paranoia I experienced in a confined space. On many of those nights, Kelly slept over. We'd sneak back to the theater for the midnight movies or trip at Harrel and Randy's house because their single mother worked graveyards.

Harrel had thick reddish hair and was my boyfriend's best friend. Randy was the same age as Kelly. We were all good friends.

When we were in junior high, Randy was shot in the hip while breaking into a house. In the hospital, I saw the bullet's small entry hole. His butt cheek was an explosion of Frankenstein stitches. Had my parents taken one look at these boys, I would never have been allowed to leave home. They were the epitome of hoodlums—*we* were.

Even when I wasn't high while climbing out my window, I craved freedom from my overprotective mother. I'd head to the shortcut through the woods along Chester Creek to hang out with whoever had something going on. Sometimes I'd sneak into Nick's window and we'd make out into the wee hours of the morning. But we never went all the way because I gripped my torch of virginity.

In junior high, none of the other badass girls were virgins. They mostly came from foster care or alcoholic homes and seemed proud to be called "slut." Those girls wouldn't just beat you up—they'd screw your boyfriend, too. I felt proud to be a virgin, an anomaly among badasses even at fourteen.

Many girls lost their virginity as early as eleven or twelve. One blonde girl's stepfather had been raping her for years. She screwed half the boys in junior high and, later, high school. I think the Last Frontier was different because we were so far north, isolated with long, dark winters. The influx of oil money also brought opportunists, perverts, and pedophiles who knew they could do shit in Alaska they couldn't get away with in the Lower 48. Even today, Alaska's sexual assault rate is three times the national average.

Practically Still a Virgin

Since "badass" and "virgin" weren't synonymous, I was unusual—special. I told myself I wanted to remain a virgin because of my Catholic upbringing or Daddy's repeated emphasis on virginity when bragging about Mama's sainthood. But really, it was because of the things Daddy said during that car ride.

Despite Nick's "bad" persona, he was sweet. I only had to turn him down for sex once. One morning, we'd been making out for hours when he climbed on top of me, searching my face for an answer. I looked him in the eye and said, "Niiiick," like I was sad to let him down and disappointed he would try, knowing how much virginity meant to me. Without protest, he got off. We broke up after nine months when he began seeing someone else. Six years later, he perished in a fire while strung out on downers. He left behind a two-year-old son and the girl who didn't have a virginity complex.

TOUGH SLUT

Shortly after Daddy took me on that raging car ride, I became feared by the weak and loathed by others who I foolishly thought liked and respected me. No one wanted to get on my bad side lest I follow them home from school or chase them from the movie theater. But when a new girl arrived midyear, her reputation preceded her. Stephanie had straight blonde hair, piercing blue eyes, and a cold, pretty face. She wasn't much taller than me, but her reputation as a hard, tough slut made her more intimidating. We'd even heard of her on our side of town. Until her arrival, I was the most feared girl around. I figured we were either going to be enemies or buds. I didn't want to upset my place in the badass social order, so I decided to make friends in case she could kick my ass.

I must have wanted to prove myself the day she arrived. We were at the Tastee Freez across from the junior high. To show Stephanie how tough I was, I pushed around a timid girl and demanded that she give me her ring. The girl sobbed and begged, but even though she was terrified, she refused. Stephanie stepped up. She yelled and pushed, insisting the girl hand over her grandmother's ring. The girl's body quaked, cheeks wet with tears. I couldn't bear it and said, "Let's go." To my surprise, Stephanie backed off.

My huge ego demanded, *Look at me, look at me!* This was fueled by a bottomless need: *Please, please look at me.* When I was feared and respected (or so I thought), I felt the power I lacked at home—and, in some sick way, I loved it. That power replaced the respect Daddy had once given me. I also think I was unconsciously trying to prove I was important even though my first mother hadn't thought I was worth keeping.

From ages thirteen to fifteen, I was on and off restriction for arriving home late, fighting at school, or cutting class. But because Mama was so wrought with denial, she was a push-over and believed most of my lies and excuses.

Decades later, I found a "pink slip" the school had sent home to be signed. Of course, my parents never saw any of those slips. I was mortified that my science teacher had torn a hole in the paper from pressing so hard with a red pen as he

Paula and I celebrate our Holy Confirmation, 1971

47

wrote, *Never in all my years of teaching have I had a student as disruptive and difficult as Monica.* Now, I wonder why I kept it.

Once I met Marla and Kelly, Paula and I rarely hung out. She was a studious goody-goody and I obviously was not, nor did I want to be. But we did take Holy Confirmation classes together, saw each other around the court, and she occasionally stopped by the house. I took our friendship for granted.

CASE CLOSED

After a night at the movies when I'd taken a feel-good dose of mescaline, I stopped by Mama's room on my way to bed. We were chatting about her art class when, with a curious expression, she said, "My goodness! Your pupils are so large."

I thought, *Shit! I don't feel very high, but they must be dilated.*

When she rose to grab a hand mirror, I gulped back a groan. I about had a heart attack when I saw my pupils were huge next to her pinholes. "Look how much smaller mine are," she said.

How was I going to get out of this?

Mama said, "It must be because my eyes are so light-sensitive. That's why I have to wear sunglasses when I go out."

I nodded. "Yes, that must be it." My parents had no idea I was smoking, let alone taking psychedelics.

The following weekend, I dropped a strong hit of LSD and tripped so hard that nothing made sense. Approaching our front door when I came home from the movies, all I could think of was avoiding eye contact with my parents and sneaking out as soon as they went to bed. Fluorescent swirling colors, sounds, and even my footsteps were in slow motion.

They were reading at their usual stations when I walked in the door. I hoped they'd be asleep soon. "Hiiiii," I said as I bent in slow motion to unlace my waffle stompers. Did my voice sound as weird to them as it did to me?

I felt Mama looking my way. "Hiiiii, hoonnneyyyy. Howwww waaaaas the mooovieeeee?"

Trying to maintain, I said, "Great," hoping I sounded normal. I kept my head down while I carried my boots through the living room to set them at the back door in anticipation of sneaking out.

Almost to my room, I realized they'd do me no good at the back door. I made a U-turn, paraded back through the living room, grabbed the boots, and walked past my parents to place them at the front door. Once again, it dawned on me that I'd need my boots in my bedroom to sneak out. I'd just bent over to grab them again when Daddy barked, "Monica, what have you been drinking?" Observing me must have been akin to watching a tennis match.

I answered with as much indignation as I could muster. "Nothing!"

"Then what have you been smoking?"

I needed to give him an answer to divert him from the obvious. "Cigarettes."

Daddy popped off the couch and ordered me to the kitchen, "Monica, come in the light. I want to see your eyes!"

Clutching my boots, I had no choice but to follow. He had me lean over the table under the hanging lamp as he prepared to study my eyes. I was so high, my pupils were no doubt black holes.

He hollered like the house was on fire. "Oh, my God! Honey, come here and look at her eyes!"

Mama walked over, took a quick glance, shrugged, and walked away. "They're normally like that." That was it. Even when the obvious was staring at her, Mama denied it.

DADDY DEAREST

I had Mama's permission to do homework at Lorna's after school. The days were short, and it was already dark when we arrived at her house. I was excited because her big brother was going to share his hash with us.

I'd never tried hash and watched with intense interest as he unwrapped a small square of tinfoil, revealing a pungent, earthy chunk of hash. He carefully broke off a piece and placed it in the bowl of a tiny brass pipe. Phil took the first hit, then handed it to me. It burned my throat and made me cough. But before long, we were belly-laughing so hard we couldn't catch our breath. The high reminded me of LSD, except everything was hilarious. I was still high when it was time to head home, so I waited. I didn't want to leave until I came down.

Punctuality was never my strong suit, but I was at least an hour late and Mama had to be worried her baby Forbes might be lost to her forever. Because Daddy was protective of Mama and I'd worried her by not phoning, my tardiness would no doubt warrant a stiff restriction. When I walked through the door, my stone-faced parents ushered me to their bedroom. This was a first, and I knew I was in huge trouble. Daddy closed the door.

He demanded, "Where have you been?"

"I stayed late at Lorna's."

"I know you stopped somewhere. Where was it?"

After smoking that killer hash, I wasn't at my sharpest and hadn't prepared a clever excuse. I couldn't tell him I'd been high out of my mind on one of the most wonderful trips of my life.

This interrogation was definitely a buzzkill.

Mama was oddly silent. In fact, I can barely recall her being in the room.

Daddy continued to yell. "Tell me where you stopped on the way home!"

I insisted I hadn't stopped anywhere. Still, he got it in his head that I'd been with Harrel and Randy, the brothers whose mother worked the graveyard shift. I wasn't aware he even knew about them. When he mentioned the boys, his tone shifted from accusatory to cold and flat. He turned and opened the closet door, then fumbled around inside. He produced a wire hanger and, like a street vendor crafting a balloon animal, began shaping it into a long oval.

I didn't comprehend what he was doing but knew in my gut something was wrong. It was like he was reenacting a ritual. Now, I realize he enjoyed having me watch.

I can't remember if he had me lie on the bed or if he beat me where I stood, but I recall the shock of the first strike on my thigh. The firebolt awakened every nerve, and I shrieked in disbelief and searing pain. I'd never felt anything so excruciating and couldn't believe Daddy would willingly hurt me like this.

"Tell me you're lying! Tell me you're lying!"

It didn't take long to break me. But he beat me with even more fury when I twisted and shrieked, "I'm lying! I'm lying!"

The room was a blur as his arm rose again and again. I bounced around, trying to escape the pain, but the strikes kept coming.

"Stop! Stop! Stop!"

I don't remember how or when it ended. I don't even recall walking to my room.

My next memory is of gym class the following day. When I got dressed in the locker room, I asked Lorna and a few others if they could help hide my welts from the teacher. As I stepped into my gym uniform, the girls circled. One covered her mouth and said, "Oh my God! Your dad did this to you?"

"No fucking way!" said another. I was normally a glutton for attention, but I shrank in shame that my parents could do this to me.

"You've gotta go to the nurse and show the principal," they said.

I pulled down the sides of my gym shorts and shook my head. "It's okay. I don't want trouble at home." We filed out to sit on the gymnasium floor while waiting for our teacher's instructions. I felt consoled as a few girls sat beside me so my thighs wouldn't be in the teacher's line of sight.

In the '60s and '70s, an occasional "whippin" was an acceptable means of punishment, but it would make a horrible mess for my parents if the authorities saw my legs—my beating went beyond the norm. Since I'd been programmed by the stories of the baby elephant, I knew it would kill Mama if I went into foster care and she lost her precious Forbes.

Fifteen years later, on a hot summer afternoon in 1987, I was living in California and driving on the freeway when I was hit with a devastating memory that knocked the wind out of me and sent me chest-first into the steering wheel in wracking sobs. I could barely see the off-ramp.

I flashed back to the night of the beating. I'd been weeping silently into my pillow when I heard a light tap on my door.

I cracked it, and relief flooded me when I saw Mama, who had witnessed the beating. She'd finally come to soothe me, croon, brush my hair from my forehead, wipe away my tears, and tell me she was sorry—she should've never let him hurt me and it would never happen again.

I turned to show her my thigh and, in a distraught whimper, said, "Mama ... look." She stared at my wound for a second, expressionless, then turned her back on me and shut the door.

When the memory surfaced, I felt rejection in every cell and wept uncontrollably by the side of the road. Later, still shaken, I called and asked about her reaction. In a dismissive tone, she said she didn't remember, was sorry "if" she did that, and had no idea why she would have turned away from me. I hung up and sobbed.

Years later, when I could see with more clarity, I thought back to her cold denial. I'd felt both hurt and blamed because instead of apologizing, she insinuated that I'd either imagined the flashback or lied about it. Then, five years after the memory resurfaced, she said, "I made him stop when I saw pleasure in his eyes. I told him, 'That's *enough*!'"

This was unsettling, but I was grateful Mama had finally stopped him.

SPIDER AND THE FLY

A few weeks after my fifteenth birthday, in the summer of 1972, Kelly found Tommy's stash of "reds," downers that make you feel drunk. She snagged two for the Rare Earth concert we'd be attending that night. I hadn't tried reds before, or even had my first drink, but we each took a capsule on our walk to the Sports Arena, a huge gray Quonset hut used for concerts, hockey games, and events.

The band was in full swing when we entered and were swallowed in a cloud of smoke. Among the hundreds of rocking bodies, I felt a thrill like I'd had while riding the Hammer at the state fair. We made our way through the crowded floor and climbed halfway up the bleachers.

As the reds kicked in, my head felt like a rotting cantaloupe left too long in the sun. I needed to get on even ground. Tugging at Kelly's sleeve, I attempted to make my way to the floor. But after the second step, I fell in slow motion, taking out rows of concertgoers like a snowplow.

"Stupid bitch!"

"Lightweight! Go home!"

All I wanted was to be cool, and this was the epitome of uncool.

Out of nowhere, Billy, who'd threatened the hash thief the previous year, helped me to the floor. He shouted over the band, "Stay put! I'll be right back." He soon reappeared with Kelly's brothers and a few of their friends.

Tommy, looking surprised, grabbed Kelly by the sleeve and led us into the lobby.

"You're not supposed to be here! What the fuck? Are you two drunk?"

He bent to look into her eyes. "Are you on reds?"

She nodded, then studied the floor.

"Where'd you get 'em?"

With the innocent eyes she reserved for her big brothers, Kelly answered in a sheepish, slurred voice. "Outta yer bag?"

Ordinarily, Tommy would've been pissed about having his drugs stolen, but he had a hard time hiding his amusement while we bumped into each other like a couple of drunken sailors on leave. The others snickered, too. Tommy said, "I'm taking you home!" No one voiced displeasure at leaving early. Tommy was boss.

Once out of the concert's stifling confines, the reds were magic and my doubts melted away. I was pretty, smart, and cool. Most of all, I didn't care what anyone thought of me, even these intimidating older boys who were good-looking and respected. Almost every badass on the East Side feared this crew. I felt "enough" for the first time in my life.

We meandered through sleepy neighborhood streets to a wooded path, then across Lake Otis Road toward the trail that led to Kelly's backyard. We'd taken these shortcuts countless times to avoid being detected by cops. Walking with these boys, I felt like a groupie with a backstage pass.

We stopped at the trail's edge to have a smoke. My body felt malleable, like a piece of soft clay. I fell backward like a rag doll—dizzy, laughing, and enjoying the lack of control.

Billy helped me up and let me lean on him to get my balance. I soaked up the special attention as he helped me over the rocks in Chester Creek, making sure I didn't fall in. I think that's when he became interested in me.

When we arrived at Kelly's, the boys didn't protest as we followed them into the basement, where we usually weren't allowed. I was hoping to talk with Kelly's cute brother Steven, but he was tired and climbed into one of the cubbyhole beds built into the wall. The brothers lived in a trailer a few miles away but often hung out and crashed in their mom's basement among the washer, dryer, and mismatched furniture.

With Steven passed out and Tommy outside, Billy slid across the couch and leaned in, too close. His voice was friendlier than usual. "Monica, how old are you now?"

The reds were wearing off. I tried to act mature. Sitting up taller, I wished I had more confidence, like the older girls.

I answered with as much maturity as I could muster. "I turned fifteen last month. I'm a year older than Kelly. I'm starting at East in a few weeks." I cringed, hating that I talked too much.

I felt uncomfortable, but Billy leaned in even closer. His breath smelled of warm bread and cigarettes. In almost a whisper, as if I were a beautiful woman and not a fifteen-year-old girl, he said, "You sure have grown up. I'd really like to take you out sometime." No one had ever talked to me like that. My heart pounded and I tried to keep my hands still, but my fingers flicked like they were attached to puppet strings.

I was unequipped to handle that kind of attention. Billy was older and more mature than the baby-faced boys I liked. The idea of being alone with him made me a little sick inside. "My parents don't let me go out with guys yet."

He leaned in again. "Come on, man. You could sneak out your window. I know you and Kelly do it all the time."

My heart raced and my voice wavered. "I don't know."

I'd never been on a real date. Despite the gnawing feeling in my stomach, I felt important because one of Tommy's friends wanted to take me out. It could mean another chance to hang out with Kelly's brothers and their friends. I envisioned sitting among the crew and their cool girlfriends, taking hits off a joint being passed around the circle. I'd laugh when the guys roughhoused and cut on each other. But as much as I wanted that, Billy made me feel weirdly exposed, like he could see my insides. I wasn't sure how to refuse.

"Don't worry," he said. "We'll have a great time."

I chewed my lip and looked into my lap, afraid he would see my nervousness.

"How 'bout I meet you tomorrow night at the school."

My mind raced. I didn't know what to say. I shifted, trying not to squirm. He lit a cigarette, drew deeply, and flicked the match onto the basement floor. When I looked up, his eyes were hot and bright. He grinned and ran a hand through his dark hair. In a soft, taunting voice, he said, "Monica, you're not afraid of me ... are you?"

I was confused, but wanting to be mature and fearless like Kelly's brothers, I sat up straighter and said, "No, I'm not afraid. Yeah ... okay."

"Right on," he said. "Tomorrow night, on the school lawn." He gave me a side smile. "See you at midnight."

Now, I realize Billy kept his interest in me quiet to shield it from Kelly's brothers. With Tommy outside and Steven passed out, they never saw the dance between the spider and the fly. It was common knowledge the fly was a virgin.

My agitated stomach warned me not to go as the date approached, but I was afraid Billy would tell Tommy and Steven if I didn't show. They'd think I was playing games like a stupid kid. I idolized them and wanted their approval more than anything, so I didn't question Billy's interest. I sensed it was odd for a nineteen-year-old to date a fifteen-year-old, but I didn't realize I could be in danger. For support, I asked Kelly to spend the night and accompany me on my date.

As usual, we stuffed my bed with pillows after my parents were asleep, then popped out the window and walked to the school. Like a couple of wannabe hippie chicks on the corner of Haight and Ashbury, we sat cross-legged puffing Marlboros. When a high-pitched whine broke the silence, I was afraid the motorcycle would wake the whole neighborhood. "That's him," I said, stubbing out my cigarette and standing to see Billy's dark hair whipping his angry face. He straddled a small white Honda and wore a T-shirt under an open jean jacket, which flapped in the wind.

He'd barely stopped the bike when he growled, "What's Kelly doing here? I thought it was just gonna be the two of us." I saw the same scary eyes he'd used on the hash thief. His anger surprised me.

"I don't know. She's spending the night."

He gestured to Kelly. "Get on. I'll take you to Tommy's. Monica, wait here. I'll be right back."

My heart pounded as they disappeared toward the crown of mountains bordering the city.

Confused and alone in the cool twilight, I lit another cigarette and wondered what to do as I stared at the mountains' peaks and crags. I couldn't go home without Kelly—Mama expected to see her in the morning and might call her mom to see why she went home early. Billy would be even more pissed if I ditched him. I was also afraid Kelly's brothers would think I was lame for making him go out of his way because I couldn't make up my mind. I'd expected Kelly to be with us as we hung out with Billy and her brother's friends. I was a doe sitting in a field, waiting for the lion to pick me off.

Fifteen minutes later, he rode up and nodded toward the back of the bike. "Get on! Let's go!" He didn't seem angry. If anything, he was indifferent, like he was on a mission and I was just along for the ride. I wondered where we were going but was afraid to ask.

The streets were empty. It was still light as he drove to an unfamiliar area on the edge of town. Normally, I jumped at the chance to ride on a motorcycle. I loved the wind in my face, but the engine's scream and the whistling wind did nothing to drown out my mounting concern. *Is he still mad that I brought Kelly? Why are we going so far?*

LOUSY LAY

I sat on the motorcycle behind Billy, heading to our date. I was uncomfortable being so close and having to put my arms around his waist to hang on. I trembled in my light jacket, more from trepidation than from the wind.

He pulled into the parking lot of a beige apartment complex and parked next to a dumpster. He said, "This is my brother's place. He's gone tonight and said we could use it." I followed him up the stairs, and he opened the door to a studio apartment that smelled of fried food, stale pot, and cigarettes. The curtains were closed, and it was dim inside. My feet rested on the matted rust-colored shag carpet. I'd hoped we'd hang out with a group of friends, but the place was empty.

"You want a beer?"

"No thanks."

The only place to sit was a burnt-orange sleeper sofa pulled out into an unmade bed with white sheets. I sat on the edge, in front of a coffee table doubling as a nightstand. The refrigerator door clicked and I heard a pop as Billy opened a beer. I sat on my hands so he wouldn't see them tremble.

I wondered what we were doing there. My eyes wandered around the room. The walls were blank except for a picture

61

of a sun with orange, brown, and rust-colored stripes. It was ugly, nothing like Mama's paintings.

Billy set a can of Bud on the table and arranged himself next to me on the bed. I was silent as he removed rolling papers and a baggie of pot from his jacket, then rolled a joint. We passed it a couple of times, but I was so nervous I could barely inhale. I didn't catch a buzz or feel the slightest bit high because my adrenaline was on overdrive. I wanted to go home but was afraid to ask, especially after coming all this way.

He moved fast—he was kissing me one second and my clothes were off the next. I was paralyzed by how quickly he undressed me. Nick had never been like this. Billy was no boy; he knew exactly what he was doing. He was determined and practiced, unhooking my bra with a one-handed snap. He pulled down my pants like he'd done it a hundred times. With one hand, he unbuckled his belt and kicked off his jeans.

He got on top of me and tried to open my legs with his knee. I was terrified. I didn't want it to happen, not this way. Not with him. I think I expected similar consideration from Billy like I'd received from Nick. But that wasn't happening here.

With as much courage as I could muster, I looked into his fierce, determined eyes. "What if I said no!" It was more of a firm statement than a question.

Billy's jaw was tight and his mean eyes bore into me. Between clenched teeth, and with the same menacing voice he'd used on the hash thief, he threatened me. "I don't know. I've never raped a fifteen-year-old girl."

The stabbing force of a red-hot poker knocked the wind out of me. He was inside me. I thought I was going to puke. The rage in his breath ripped at my insides. His eyes were wild and full of power.

I squeezed mine shut and pushed my pelvis away from him with each thrust, trying to escape the painful lunges that landed with such intensity that I couldn't breathe or even grunt. Finally, it stopped.

His dead weight was heavy. He smelled of sweat, his hot breath sticky on my ear. The sheets were cold and wet on my legs, and I could barely breathe. I was afraid to move and longed for home. Eventually, he got up and put on his jeans. I stood and searched for my clothes, trying not to appear desperate to cover myself. He turned to the bed and bellowed, "You weren't no damn virgin!"

He felt cheated because there was no bloodstain. He'd wanted to break a virgin. I said nothing for fear of provoking him and had no idea why there wasn't any blood. I kept my eyes down, not wanting to see him looking at me naked, never wanting to see his face again.

The last thing he said was spat in disgust. "Next time, fuck the headlights off me." My mind flashed to how I'd pushed backward into the bed every time he slammed into me. Yeah, I was a lousy lay.

I continued looking down as I silently dressed. I didn't want him to see the shame on my face. Shame at his disappointment, shame that I cared, shame that I'd come here with him, shame that I'd lost my virginity, shame that I hadn't said "no." Most of all, I was ashamed of my weakness.

My virginity had been my identity, my armor. I'd been a badass and virgin all in one. However misguided my perceptions were, that identity made me whole. Suddenly, it was gone.

As I followed Billy down the stairs and left that awful apartment, I had no idea how much confusion I'd later feel about what had happened. It would be years before I'd describe it as rape.

I got on the motorcycle and forced my arms around his body. His jacket was open, and I felt the warmth of his belly through his thin T-shirt. I thought I might be sick but talked myself through it. *It's okay. You can make it. You're almost there.* I perched my feet on the pegs so my legs barely touched his thighs.

My battered bottom straddled the seat and I winced with every bump. My mind flashed to the foldout bed and the humiliation I'd felt when he was done with me. My only solace was the wind on my face.

After less than ten minutes, a ride that felt much longer, Billy dumped me at the trailer where Kelly's brothers lived. I didn't look back. The drapes were closed except for a small window over the sink. Snores escaped from the bedrooms and Kelly slept peacefully on the couch. The whole world was asleep except for me. I felt very alone, but I didn't want to face Kelly's brothers with so much guilt and shame on my face. They'd realize what happened and decide I was a slut.

The place was a pigsty. I faced the foot-high heap of trash and dishes that filled every spare space on the stove, counter, and sink. I thought, *Tommy and Steven will be pleased with me if I clean up.* The feel of food scraps, trash, cigarette butts, and dirty dishes was somehow comforting. I found the soap and began scrubbing every plate, glass, cup, and utensil Kelly's brothers owned. I stared blankly out the window at the neighboring trailer, trying to wash away my shame.

It must have taken a couple of hours to wash all those dishes. As I did, Kelly's baby snores drifted from the couch. She sounded like a little pig, which made me smile. I watched her sleep for a minute, not wanting to wake her. The pillow was wet with drool, and I envied her peace. She growled when I nudged her shoulder, her usual grumpy morning self. It was 3:30, a safe hour to sneak into my bedroom window without being caught by Daddy, who was always up early.

Kelly padded to the back room to rouse Steven for a ride. He passed the spotless sink and counters without even noticing. I'd spent hours scrubbing scuffed pots and chipped coffee mugs to earn praise, but that didn't work out either.

We pulled into my cul-de-sac and walked to my window, still slightly open. A few minutes later, safe in bed, I lay awake with my cigarette glowing in the twilight, smoke threads winding together before vanishing above Kelly's sleeping head. She made more of her sweet piglet noises. I stubbed out my cigarette and rolled to my side, thinking I'd never sleep that peacefully again.

SECOND COMING

Luke came sniffing around not long after my "date" with Billy, just before I began attending East High as a sophomore. At five-foot-ten, seventeen-year-old Luke was handsome and of Scandinavian descent with thick side-parted blond hair that covered his ears and collar. He wore prescription aviator glasses and had a blond mustache.

Luke was the first guy to be interested in me who had his own car. It was a beautiful 1964 pearl-white Mercury with blue tuck-and-roll interior. His father was a professional and owned a nice split-level home; his family was more like mine than Kelly's.

Luke wasn't a goody-goody by any stretch, but he had proper grammar and opened my car door like a gentleman. Even though he was better looking than Nick, I was never into him. I just wanted to erase Billy. Mama had no idea I was riding around in Luke's pearl-white car or that we were spending time alone.

His bedroom was in the basement. There was one small window above his bed, high on the wall and level with the driveway. We were on his waterbed one afternoon, surrounded by pine paneling and black-light posters. His parents were at work and his brother wasn't home. No one could see us from outside unless they got down on their hands and knees in the driveway, but still, I knew someone could watch us if they really wanted to.

Our make-out session had gotten hot and heavy and my jeans were around my knees. Luke was desperate to go all the way, but I made it clear I was not having sex. I still reflexively protected my virginity, or maybe I was trying to reclaim it. I was in denial, evidence of how deeply I was affected by what happened with Billy and during that car ride with Daddy.

Even though Luke was a punk, he would never have threatened or forced me. Unlike Billy, his approach was to beg. Luke's once-confident voice pleaded, "Please, just let me put it right here. Please!" He wanted me to close my legs so he could stick it between my upper thighs, simulating inter-course. His whining contrasted with how cool I'd thought he was, when he rested one arm over the seat and flicked the turn signal without his hand leaving the wheel.

I wanted to pull up my pants and get a ride home, but that seemed cruel with how desperately horny he was. Instead, I pressed my thighs tightly together and crossed my ankles to ensure that horribly painful thing with Billy couldn't reoccur.

I turned and stared up at that tiny window, cringing, hoping his brother didn't come home and no one was watching while I endured him humping my thigh gap like a frenzied dog. It didn't take him nearly as long to finish as it had with Billy. When I reached down to pull up my pants, there was slime on my inner thighs. I was so grossed out and wanted to get the hell out of there.

The ride home was silent and awkward. I felt foolish, especially after he dropped me off like he was flicking a lit cig-arette out a car window. I was revolted because his affection had been disingenuous. All he'd wanted was a piece of ass.

That night, I was angry I'd felt sorry for him and let him do that disgusting thing on my leg. Once again, I hadn't said "no" and loathed myself for it.

Luke was supposed to be a distraction, but he only amplified what happened with Billy. I felt different inside after that—I no longer wanted to beat people up or break into houses. Instead, I identified with the people I'd hurt.

I wanted to be a different girl, meet new friends, and go out with nice boys who weren't like Billy or Luke. I looked forward to a fresh start at East High.

DESERT ISLE

Listening to my history teacher drone on about some break-in at an office building in Washington was as exciting as watching bread mold. I thought, *This is news, not history.* I tuned out, trying to find an excuse to leave class early. I wanted to take a quick cig in the school's designated smoking area before lunch and scheme on the cute boys as they exited the classrooms.

The bustling halls were a blur of shiny faces, tiled floors, and rows of lockers that extended like mirrors in a fun house. The hum of chattering voices, the stink of body odor, and the smell of stale cigarettes made a river of chaos. Packs of cute boys roamed in letter jackets, and pretty cheerleaders bounced through the halls with shapely legs in short pleated skirts. I was eager to be at its center, but I felt lost and invisible. I thought I'd been a big deal in junior high because of my reputation for beating people up behind the Tastee Freez, but now I realized I wasn't.

It was a good time to make a change. When I started at East and saw all the new faces that were unaware of who I'd been, I realized how much I wanted to be like the nice, cute, popular girls. Besides, Kelly had recently moved across town so I rarely saw her anymore. Although I missed her, I had bigger worries. I confided to Lorna that I'd missed a couple of periods. I asked, "Do you think I could be pregnant? It only happened one time, and I had my period after." Back then, girls I knew didn't talk to each other about the things we did with boys, so there was no pressure to give details.

"I don't think so, but maybe you should see the nurse just in case."

I thought, *It can't happen to me. I'm practically still a virgin.* It took a few days of encouragement from my friends before I had the nerve to visit the nurse.

While waiting in the hall, I watched a group of sophomore girls bounce past. They didn't notice I was sitting on my clammy hands. I envied their happy-go-lucky giggles. I wanted to be one of *those* girls.

Soon, the nurse called me into her office. She had kind doe eyes and a soft voice. "What can I do for you, Miss Monica?"

"My friends said I should talk to you. It's probably nothing, but I skipped two periods."

"Could you be pregnant?"

"I, uh ... I don't think so. It only happened once, and I had a period after." Talking about this made me feel sick. I fiddled with my zipper. "I thought I should check."

"How about we put your mind to rest and visit Planned Parenthood during lunch tomorrow?"

"Sure ... I guess so."

At the clinic, more pee got on my hand than in the cup. I handed it over like it was my last ounce of lemonade on a desert isle. While waiting in the lobby, I looked toward the icy windowpane and chewed my hangnail while the nurse thumbed through *Reader's Digest.*

Finally, we were summoned to the back. I sat with my hands folded in my lap like a good Catholic ex-virgin waiting for my penance. My heart pounded. The technician's face was expressionless when he said, "It's positive."

My stomach lurched, and my mouth went dry. I blurted, "No! That can't be right. I had a period after I had sex."

No doubt, the return to school was uncomfortable for the nurse. I wouldn't shut up. "I can't be pregnant. The test must be wrong."

Back at school, she called Planned Parenthood and requested a second test. The manager agreed the result was odd given that I'd had a period after intercourse. She would repeat the test herself the next day.

At Planned Parenthood, they let me watch the whole test, probably because they figured I might accept the positive results if I saw the proof. The clinic manager pulled from a drawer a two-inch cardboard square with a large brown circle in the middle. That's where she placed a drop of my urine, then swirled it around, mixing it with the mysterious brown substance. She stopped and studied the card but gave no explanation of what she was looking for. My pulse rushed in my ears as I watched her face for clues. She looked up with a smile. "It's negative."

I was elated as I returned to school and didn't give it further thought until I missed another period. I wasn't concerned about being pregnant anymore, although I knew skipping three periods wasn't normal. I told Mama in case there was something physically wrong with me.

She thought I might be low on iron because I was so thin and made an appointment with a female gynecologist. I peed in a cup and Dr. Sydnam did an internal check, which caused excruciating pain. I couldn't breathe and thought I was going to puke. It was the same way I'd felt with Billy. I later learned I had a tilted uterus.

As I dressed, a twinge of something "not right" briefly washed over me, but I brushed it aside. Mama dropped me back at school to finish my day.

That afternoon, I hopped off the bus and strolled up our snow-covered yard. Just as I touched the handle, the door swung open to fire-breathing Mama. "Monica, you're pregnant!" The rage on her face was terrifying. "I can't stand to look at you. Go to your room and wait until Daddy gets home."

I was so sick I couldn't breathe. Sitting on my bed, I thought, *I am the slutty filth of humanity Daddy despises.*

I never considered telling the truth.

MONKS

Trying to absorb the news, I didn't think further than *What will Daddy say? He'll think I've been sleeping around. How am I going to keep Billy a secret?* I knew pregnancy would mean leaving school and dissolving my dreams of dating cute lettermen—and, of course, a baby—but that was in the background. After what seemed like hours, I heard Daddy's car pull in and, eventually, his demanding voice.

"Monica!"

My heart thumped in my throat as I trudged toward the kitchen.

There was no aroma of dinner. Salem cigarette packs and an overflowing ashtray littered the table. The hanging lamp created a tractor beam of smoke.

Daddy said, "Let's go downstairs." I was probably ghastly white as he led me to the dungeon.

I followed my parents past the washer and dryer, back to the art studio where Mama created her masterpieces. I liked most of her work, but my least favorite piece was on the easel—*The Monks*, painted in muddy brown and gray. The haunting hooded figures faced me on judgment day. I was nauseous with dread and the smell of turpentine and linseed

73

oil. On the desk sat her artist palette, layered with blobs of oil paint, and a glass jar full of brushes. Our reflections were mirrored in the windows; outside, it was pitch-black.

I'd committed the unthinkable sin. I was no longer the Virgin Mary Monica—I'd forfeited the highest status possible in my Catholic family, and I'd pierced my parents' hearts with *my* act. I wanted to scream, *You can ask anyone! I planned to stay a virgin until marriage, like Mama!*

Enraged, Daddy demanded, "What's his name?"

I kept my nose down. No matter how many times he demanded the truth, I said nothing. Billy's name would never have been enough. Daddy would've pushed to learn how I knew him and where he lived. When he learned Billy was nineteen, he would've undoubtedly reported a statutory rape. My parents could never lay eyes on him. They would be aghast at his dark sideburns and how mature he was and revolted by the nasty stuff I'd done with him. They'd wonder what possessed me to go off with such a character.

In the past, I'd never defied my parents by refusing to answer or make eye contact. Mama would've considered it disrespectful and slapped my face. I'd always provided a plausible answer, often a well-crafted lie. Now silence was my only hope.

Mama hadn't helped me with my schoolwork or protected me from Daddy's beating. There was no way I could trust her with the important stuff I didn't understand, like feeling creepy around Daddy ever since he'd yelled at me about sluts and whores. Or how I felt at fault for what happened with Billy.

If Daddy found out, he'd make a huge stink, just like he had at my school when he thought our privacy was being invaded. Instead, I faced the firing squad, every word shouted with rage and disappointment.

Practically Still a Virgin

I couldn't bear the disgust in my parents' eyes. I kept my gaze on the floor and rolled my insides tighter with each demand. Daddy didn't hit me. If he had, I might have felt less shame.

What would Tommy and Steven think if they heard my parents were making a stink all over town? The crew would think I was just a stupid slut who got their friend in trouble.

Decades later, when I told Kelly what had happened with Billy, she said, "Monica, you should have told. If Tommy and Steven had known, they would've killed him."

Daddy gave up after about thirty minutes. I was banished to my room, where I shook with shame and tried to absorb what lay ahead. I'd just started my life over. I was meeting new kids and cute boys. Now I'd be hidden away. That's what "good" families did to knocked-up daughters, and preggo girls weren't allowed at school.

I'd be expected to give my baby up for adoption, just as my natural mother had. For our Catholic family, it seemed as simple as "break an arm, get a cast." "Have an illegitimate baby, give it away." It was too much to process.

As a distraction, I pulled my newest album, Black Sabbath's *Paranoid*, from its jacket. I was about to set it on the turntable when my door opened. It was Daddy. His eyebrows were shaped in a V and he held something in his hand.

"Read this." He threw a book at me: Adelle Davis's *Let's Have Healthy Children*. I never opened it.

STAY

Daddy barked, "Tim, sit up straight and put your napkin in your lap."

Mama scowled at him and glanced at me. "Can you please pass the salt?"

I handed her the shaker and pushed the disgusting corned beef around my plate.

Mama interrupted Daddy's relentless picking to say to me, "Honey, we're going to keep you home after Christmas break."

It had been over a month since the pregnancy discovery, and I'd been dreading this inevitable decision.

Mama said, "I found a couple of unwed-mother schools, one in Washington and another in Fairbanks."

I didn't look or feel pregnant and still imagined getting asked out for dates. I was in a state of suspended animation, somewhere between fantasy and nightmare. When I'd told my friends that pregnancy tests couldn't be trusted, there was fear in their eyes.

"They also have classes in town at the admin building."

It was too much to think about. I shrugged.

"You don't have to decide right away," Mama said.

Practically Still a Virgin

I'd never been away from home, other than St. Theresa's Camp, but I knew it would be hard to hide from the neighbors if I stayed. When I started showing, I wouldn't be able to go outside, not even in the backyard. From their high kitchen windows, the neighbors could see into our yard.

My parents wanted to protect our family's reputation, but all I cared about was preventing Paula's mother from finding out. Although she had been like an extremely religious second mother to me, she thought I was bad news—Paula had said so many times. This had always perplexed me. My delinquent behavior was never public knowledge, so why did she dislike me? Being knocked up would prove her right, and if the neighbors found out, so would she. I felt sure Paula would never tell her. Even though we didn't hang out much anymore, Paula remained my loyal friend.

Mama said, "We have an appointment at Catholic Charities next Tuesday with a nun who will facilitate the adoption."

"Okay," I said, trying to camouflage the stringy meat with my green beans. There was never any question that I would relinquish my baby. Maybe it was the times, or maybe adoption was just normalized in my family.

At school the next day, shivering in the smoking atrium, I watched Lorna take a long drag on her Kool. I'd quit smoking for my baby.

To get my friends' opinions, I repeated the options Mama had given for my removal from society. Lorna ground her cigarette into the dirty snow. Her green eyes were soft, and my heart warmed when she said, "Don't go away. You'll need your friends the most through this time." Everyone agreed, and their earnestness reassured me. "You gotta stay home," Lorna said. "Take classes at the admin building. Then we can come visit." She put her hand on my shoulder.

I had amazing friends, and I'd get through it with their support. I envisioned a stream of girls going in and out of my house over the coming months, bringing the latest gossip, feeling my baby kick, and watching my belly grow. I'd make one call when I went into labor and they'd rush to the hospital to wait for word on the birth.

THE RASH

I was four months along when my pants began getting snug. Around the same time, my friends returned to school after winter break. I stood at my window watching snow tumble like glitter under the streetlight.

In the living room, Johnny Carson delivered his monologue. The only sound from my parents was Daddy's laughing binge. It's interesting how few fond memories I have of Daddy. I can still hear his distinctive smoker's cough, the clip of his shoes when we went out in public, the swish of his suit pants when he walked, and the way he casually tipped his palm from the top of the steering wheel to see the speedometer. Most of all, I loved how his eyes gleamed when he smiled big and the way he laughed when he watched Johnny Carson. You could set your clock to it.

I couldn't fall asleep. I'd been itching for weeks and couldn't take it anymore. I wondered if something was biting me in bed. I turned on the light and threw back the covers. On my sheet were several dozen brown dots that looked like the beauty marks on my cheek. I thought, *Mama washes my sheets every week, so what are these blobs?*

I went to the bathroom to pee. While sitting on the pot, I wondered, *Could I have a weird pregnancy rash?* I bent to take a closer look. *Why would the rash only be on my privates?*

There were hundreds of itsy-bitsy brown spots in my pubic hair. *Maybe they're scabs.* I scratched at one and brought my index finger to the end of my nose for inspection. I almost screamed when I saw a bug-eyed crab flex its claws at me. I leapt off the toilet, pulled up my pajamas, and ran to tell Mama. She made an after-hours call to Dr. Sydnam and learned I had pubic lice. I'd heard about crabs but didn't know what they were, only that dirty people got them from sleeping around. My skin crawled at the image of that horrible little crab.

I knew what the doctor must think of me. First I got pregnant, and now I was infested, confirming my promiscuity. I figured Mama assumed I'd been sleeping all over City View—although decades later, she told me she thought I'd gotten them from a toilet seat. But I knew they came from that sleeper sofa.

By then, disgrace and humiliation felt normal. Dr. Sydnam thought I was like the girls I'd heard whispered about, the kind of girl that let a roomful of dirty guys pull a train on her. The kind of girl who caught crabs. The kind of girl Daddy had described on that car ride.

Mama dashed to the pharmacy to fetch some crab shampoo. Crouched in a whirlpool of indignity above the drain of our pink tub with the tiny-toothed comb, I saw images of Billy's angry face. I could taste his beer breath mixed with the tang of crab poison and feel the heart-stabbing humiliation of being splayed under him like a stuffed turkey. I purged my thoughts of Billy down the drain right along with those fucking crabs.

SISTER CLARE

After talking to Lorna and the girls, I told Mama that I wanted to stay home for the pregnancy. I looked forward to my visits with the nun at Catholic Charities. Sister Clare had an East Coast accent and called me darling. She looked older than Mama and greeted me on that first visit like we were lifelong friends. "Aren't you just darling!" I loved how she gushed over me. I craved the attention she showered and loved her instantly.

Sister wore a traditional navy-blue habit and there were brown curls around the white-trim edges of her blue veil. She had acne scars and wasn't particularly pretty, but her warmth and personality made her beautiful.

Our weekly meetings were my chance to have a friend and get out of the house. They were the outings I most looked forward to, even though I knew she meant to take my baby.

In the early days of my pregnancy, we rarely discussed adoption, but I knew Sister matched babies with couples who couldn't conceive and made friends with the natural mothers. Back then, mothers weren't allowed to meet their babies before relinquishing them, at least not at the Catholic hospital. Early on, I began prepping Sister so she'd let me see my baby. "Sister, I don't look anything like Mama. Do you think my baby will look like me?"

After my friends returned to school, the phone rarely rang and my calls went mostly unreturned. Nobody stopped by to gossip. I didn't see Kelly much, and Paula spent most of her time with her nice-girl friends.

As the cold Alaska winter of short days ebbed into nothingness, I turned my attention to Mama, my only *real* friend. She was so nice to me. We played cards and chatted like girlfriends. She also brought home crafts to keep me occupied. I assumed her changed attitude was because she felt sorry for how sad and lonely I was.

Between visits to sister Clare, I attended half-day classes twice a week at the school district administration building. We sat at long tables set up in a large storage room, surrounded by projectors and mimeograph machines. As usual, I zoned out.

There were approximately ten of us in various stages of gestation. I was the youngest next to Sherry, who was fourteen, sweet, soft-spoken, and blonde. Her thighs were enormous, and her hair always looked as if she'd just gotten out of bed. She lived with her parents and was planning to place her baby for adoption. As her due date approached, she became fearful. "I'm scared my baby will be breech! What if I can't handle the pain?" I tried to calm her, but her worries began weighing on me, too.

Caroline started a few months after me. She was seventeen, thin, and tall with short dark hair. She lived with her boyfriend. They were going to marry, and she wasn't yet showing. Van, who also sat at the front table, was almost sixteen—sweet but not very bright. She didn't know who the father was and planned for adoption. Both of them would deliver before I would.

The hard group sat at the back table, smelling of greasy food. They were like Stephanie, the mean girl from junior high, and reminded me of the runaways I'd come across when I escaped from my window. Even though I was anxious to get out of the house, I felt uncomfortable being associated with these girls, especially the rough ones.

One cold morning, Mama dropped me off as Anne arrived in a pickup. She was part of the hard clan, and I'd given her a wide berth. The previous day, she'd described both the size of her boyfriend's penis and the nasty things she did with it. She was sixteen, had coal-lined eyes and witchy black hair, and was swapping spit with the scary biker-looking guy dropping her off. He had long hair and a goatee. Walking in, I asked, "Is that your boyfriend?"

"My old man."

"Is he the father?"

"Yeah, I think so." The graphic description of her boyfriend's privates had shocked me, but after seeing him, I thought he seemed vaguely familiar. I was horrified that a girl my age would purposely do stuff with a guy like that. Years later, I realized he reminded me of Billy.

On the way to school, Mama always stopped at the Suds and Subs sandwich shop to get two footlongs, which lasted me through the morning. I stuffed my face so I could stomach my life. These girls were nothing like my friends at East who never spoke about sex, didn't smell like a diner, and didn't have biker boyfriends.

Eventually, I made friends with a new girl, Julie, who was seventeen but early in her pregnancy and not yet showing. Her parents lived near me, but she had an apartment with her husband and had previously given up a baby for adoption. I'd seen her around, but we ran in different crowds. It was a relief to have a friend who felt familiar.

Julie had a strong presence. I looked up to her because she was mature and had experienced what I was preparing to go through. Later, she helped with my breathing exercises and offered to coach me in the labor room. Julie also answered questions that Mama couldn't: how much weight did you gain, and why do I have leg cramps? She said her labor had lasted twenty-two hours. But she never said how she felt about the adoption.

One day, a visiting nurse spoke to our class about the joy of episiotomies and how the doctor cut a woman's privates so she wouldn't rip when the baby came out. This sounded horribly painful. More distressing was the information that the hospital wouldn't release us until we'd had a bowel movement.

This confirmed what Julie had told me: giving birth was like pooping out a huge turd. I couldn't imagine a baby coming out of that tiny hole, let alone a cut down there and possible tearing. The pain with Billy had been excruciating, but I couldn't fathom the agony of giving birth.

SNAKE FOOD

Tim watched as his science teacher demonstrated feeding a boa constrictor by dangling white rats and dropping them in the huge glass tank. Seeing the innocents huddle in the corner, noses twitching in fear, distressed my sensitive brother. At the end of class, he snatched one of the rats by its tail and zipped it into his jacket pocket.

Mama had allowed Tim to get pet gerbils but vehemently refused his requests for one of the pet shop's cute rats. She insisted that they were filthy, disease-ridden vermin that she would never allow inside her house.

Tim stashed the rescued rat in a cage in our basement rec room. I was around five months pregnant when I began creeping to the fridge every morning to steal some carrots or lettuce before going down to the dungeon to feed my new pink-eyed friend. I felt bad for him because he was alone and captive in the dark. But I justified it: at least he wasn't snake food.

I had been doing this for about a week when one morning, there was a raw, bloody stump where his tail should be. I searched the cage, digging among the pee-soaked newspaper shreds and hoping I wouldn't find it. I called Lorna, who had pet rats. She said, "They sometimes eat their tail when they're lonely." That made sense—rats needed friends, too. If I'd had a tail, I probably would have eaten it, just as I'd been eating everything else.

I snuck the cage up to my room, where I could give him some love. A few weeks later, Tim rescued a baby rat the size of my thumb. They became my best friends and slept in my dresser drawer. I let them run free during the day but was careful to keep my door shut.

Nine months pregnant in isolation with my pet rat, BB, on the dresser

We named the larger one BB, short for Big Balls, because as he grew, his testes dragged behind him like beanbags. We named the little one BM, Bowel Movement, because he pooped all the time. BM also stood for Big Muscles because even though he was a quarter of BB's size, BM was always tackling his larger friend.

Practically Still a Virgin

I wasn't concerned they'd be discovered. Our dog, Daisy, mostly lay under my parents' nightstand and had little interest in visiting Tim and me, unless we were throwing a ball. I didn't worry about Mama, either. She always knocked on my door and waited for me to answer, which allowed me to hide the rats when she visited my room.

I petted their white fur and tickled their tiny necks, just like I did Daisy. They even came when I called their names. But what I loved most was how they scampered up my arm to hide in the crook of my neck when they were frightened, like the time Tim knocked over my nail polish bottle. It was like I was their mama.

On lonely afternoons when everyone was gone, I'd lie on my bed delighted while they scampered over and around my bump. As they scurried, their tiny pink feet tickled me and made me giggle. They'd end with a full-on tackle, then snuggle in the crook of my neck. My babies made isolation bearable. I nurtured and cared for them like I would my own child, but in the back of my mind, I knew I'd eventually have to part with them—just as I'd part with my baby.

EEYORE

Three years before I got pregnant, Daddy found blood in his urine but ignored it for a year or more. He was eventually diagnosed with bladder cancer. The year before I got pregnant, my parents had flown to the Mayo Clinic in Rochester, Minnesota, so he could have surgery to remove it.

Catholic Charities sent some uncouth woman to stay with Tim and me. She laid around on the couch in a muscle tank, drank beer, and chain smoked. I thought she was swell. She let me stay out as late as I wanted and bought me a carton of Raleigh Filter Tip cigarettes. I frolicked in my freedom, clueless about the severity of Daddy's illness. I must have thought he was invincible.

He never seemed physically sick while I was pregnant—just pickier than usual. "All the doctors here are quacks," he'd say. He was supposed to have regular cystoscope procedures, where a tiny camera was inserted through the urethra to make sure the cancer hadn't come back. He confided that it was excruciating and repeatedly rescheduled with random excuses. We began to worry.

Daddy had become even more depressed and ridiculed my brother nonstop. We all dreaded weekends. Our only reprieve was during his long naps. One Saturday afternoon, Tim and I had been playing cards in the kitchen, laughing and shrieking in a race to slap cards on the deck. Tim was eating an orange when Daddy appeared.

"Why don't you slurp that orange a little louder? And get a plate, for God's sake!" Pick, pick, pick. The sight of Tim sent Daddy into a picking fest. "Ahhh, for Christ's sakes! Why don't you lean over your plate like a normal human being?"

The next day, Mama and I were playing cards when Daddy woke from a nap and stumbled into the kitchen, standing over the sink so we couldn't see what he was munching on. Mama said, "Honey, what are you eating?"

Mouth full, he mumbled, "An orange." As he headed back to the bedroom, he said, almost as an afterthought, "That sure was a dry orange."

Without thinking, I blurted, "It sure didn't sound like it!" Mama and I covered our mouths to hide our laughter.

When we pushed back on Daddy's cruelty toward Tim, he'd hang his head like Eeyore, the down-in-the-dumps donkey from *Winnie-the-Pooh*, and moan, "I can't do or say anything right in this family."

He was probably worried about money, too. Sales had been eluding him. Being self-employed, he didn't have health insurance, so all medical treatments were paid out of pocket. He began flying to Tijuana for his latest get-well scheme, the controversial anticancer compound laetrile. It was derived from apricot pits and mostly illegal in the United States.

At the time, I recognized how much Mama put up with being married to Eeyore, but I hadn't realized what I see now. Daddy had snatched her up for her beauty and purity, but he was also interested because she was ten years younger and compliant by nature.

Mama had a short fuse and would lose her temper on us kids. When we argued in the back seat, for instance, she'd turn around with one arm on the wheel and start blindly slapping. But I never heard her yell at or fight with Daddy. Maybe that's why she screamed at us; she was letting off steam that had been brewing because of her husband.

She had plenty of reasons to be upset. For example, he often traveled to the Lower 48 under the guise of sales seminars. On return, he'd hand her some crappy token he'd picked up at the airport but be sporting gold cuff links and an Omega watch. He also drove a new car with automatic transmission while she drove an oxidized heap with the shifter on the steering column.

She didn't complain but couldn't have felt safe driving her seven-months-pregnant daughter forty-three snowy miles to an out-of-town church where no one knew us in that green rattletrap. We went once a week for confession and mass, probably because she wanted to get me out of the house and offer me comfort.

The confessional stall smelled of wood polish. I confessed my sins through the screen and Father assigned penance—prayers based on the severity of my sins. I'd retreat to a pew and kneel in pretend reverence to rattle through the Hail Marys and Our Fathers. I always knelt longer than Mama did so she'd think I was sincere.

I was glad for the change of scenery, and under the influence of Saint Mama and Sister Clare, I'd become more reflective. Still, I never confessed the things I'd done when I was Monica Hall, the badass virgin.

Mama often prayed the Rosary. I knew the string of fifty-nine beads was used for reciting prayers, fifty-three of which were to the Virgin Mary. One evening, Mama told me that if I completed the Fifty-Four Day Novena (praying the Rosary fifty-four days in a row), all of my prayers would be answered.

Practically Still a Virgin

I did it twice, totaling 108 days, just to be sure. I recited over five thousand Hail Marys aloud, and prayed my baby would get good parents. Oddly, I didn't have any particular image in mind and didn't know what "good" meant in terms of parenting. I wanted to give my daughter what I had, two parents, but I didn't envision them being like *my* parents. I must have known something wasn't right.

JOURNALS

I'd made it through the long, dark winter. My baby was due on May 28, 1973, and I only had six weeks to go. That spring, I started to feel especially cooped up. During what Alaskans call breakup, the kids who lived on the court could never wait the week or two it would take for the sidewalks to melt enough for bike riding. This year was no different. While I sat in the house, they grabbed shovels to chip and scrape the remaining snow. I longed to be among them.

This was usually a happy season, but I grew more depressed. Isolation wasn't so bad when everyone was in winter lockdown, but now kids were outside. Their laughter felt like a slap across my face, and so did the screen door's constant bang as Tim freely went in and out.

It was late one sunny morning when I heaved myself out of bed and waddled to the kitchen. Mama was playing solitaire. As I rounded the corner, she said in a sweet voice, "Good morning, my dear. You sure slept late."

"I know. I didn't hear anybody leave this morning." I yawned and rubbed my huge belly. "I must have been really tired." I'd been sleeping more than usual, probably due to depression and being in the third trimester.

Practically Still a Virgin

"Why don't you get dressed? You can come along while I pick up groceries." We had a routine for these trips. We entered her green Valiant through the garage so no one would see my girth, and I sat in the car while she shopped. Instead of heading to Safeway, though, she pulled onto Fourth Avenue, parking in front of Woolworths. "I'll be right back," she said.

I watched with curiosity as she bypassed the dime store for Adam's Stationery. Twiddling my thumbs, I looked on with longing as Woolworths patrons shuffled through the doors. I wished I could sit at the lunch counter and munch on yummy French fries.

Mama was smiling when she slid behind the wheel and pulled out a green cloth-covered book. "Record" was written at an angle across its cover. With burgundy leather-like corners, it looked like something a spectacled banker might have used in the olden days.

"This is *your* journal, and there's one here for each of us."

"Thanks," I said as she dropped it in my hand.

We went to Safeway next. While Mama shopped, I cracked the cloth cover and wrote, *Monica Hall's Journal, April 20, 1973.*

Once Tim received his journal, the race was on. Most evenings, we'd scribble away. I'd say, "Hey, Tim, what page are you on?"

He'd scowl, look down, and make up a number far beyond where he really was.

"I'm way ahead. What's taking you so long?"

Mama knew we needed an outlet for our difficulties. She hoped Daddy would begin writing, too, but his journal remained untouched.

In the beginning, I wrote only as a game to impress Mama and annoy my brother, but the journal was my only outlet. It wasn't long before I had something to say.

HORNY DRUNK

The once-skinny girl who had bird legs and couldn't gain weight now wore tents. It was impossible to resist Mama's delicious toasted tomato-and-cheese sandwiches slathered with butter and Italian herb seasoning. Finding comfort in food would become a pattern throughout my life. The doctor suggested I start Weight Watchers. Mama attended the meetings and we followed the diet together.

After I got my driver's permit, she occasionally let me drive. One spring afternoon following my session with Sister, I was pulling out of the parking lot with my window down when a drunken man stumbled toward the car.

He was a few feet from my bumper. With brown leathered skin and between strings of greasy black hair, his blurred, vacant eyes stared into me like he could read my shame. Even though he slurred while he staggered toward me, I heard him loud and clear: "Heyou! Why doncha come o'er here and gimme somma that poosee?" The drunk man couldn't have known a pregnant fifteen-year-old was behind the wheel, but still, I could have died a thousand deaths because he said it in front of Mama.

Practically Still a Virgin

She didn't remember the incident when I asked her about it decades later, but the memory of his horny face is still vivid for me. It was as if the man had intuited how I felt about myself. I wonder if I would have ignored him like Mama did if I hadn't had a pervy father who put Mama on a pedestal, or that awful experience with Billy.

I was lying in bed that night, trying to remove the vision of that man's lined greasy face from my mind, when I felt ripples of movement. As I did every night, I nudged my baby back.

In my last few months of pregnancy, I sensed I was carrying a girl. I wondered, *Will she turn out to be smart, and will people like her?* I didn't think in worldly terms because I'd never once considered what or who I wanted to be when I grew up. I could see only as far as my own insecurities.

MESSAGE IN A BOTTLE

Toward the end of my eighth month, a lady from the state adoption agency visited school to tell us our options. I hung back after class. Supporting my heavy abdomen, I blurted, "I was adopted." She looked surprised.

"They got me from Canada but I don't have any information about my parents."

On my last few birthdays, I'd wondered if my mother was thinking of me. Because my parents had never mentioned any details about my natural family, learning her identity seemed as likely as finding the sender of a message in a bottle.

After school, I told Mama of my conversation with the adoption lady. When her green eyes pooled with tears, I knew I'd gone too far.

I reached for her hand. "It's okay, Mama. Don't cry." I wasn't sure why she was so sad, but I didn't think it had anything to do with my curiosity.

I put my hand on hers. She wiped her eyes and said, "Well, there *are* some documents in the safe-deposit box with information about your parents and your other name."

Holy shit! I tried to contain my excitement. I knew she would always be my mom and nothing could change that, but how I longed for those documents.

"Honey, if there's information about your parents, I wouldn't mind if you wanted to meet your natural mother one day." A bolt shot through me. I couldn't wait to see those papers. But I had to be careful not to push or let on how ecstatic I was in case it hurt her feelings or made her change her mind.

My desire to read those documents intersected with my growing obsession about finding my baby when she grew up. Since I was little, Mama had told me adoptive mothers fear the natural mother might change her mind and want to take the child back. Knowing this, I would never have interrupted my child's life no matter how much I suffered. But once she was eighteen, I wanted to know her.

I was careful not to share this with Sister; I planned to stay in touch with Sister Clare over the years so she'd give me updates and hopefully pictures. I feared she wouldn't be forthcoming with information if she knew my intent.

After returning from errands the next day, Mama pulled a long manila envelope from her purse. "Here, honey. This is what I have on your adoption."

My heart was beating as if I'd just run the fifty-yard dash. I said, "Thanks, Mama." Externally calm and collected, I took the envelope like it was as mundane as the church bulletin. I went straight to my room and opened the envelope. Inside were three folded papers. On top was my birth certificate. It contained Mama and Daddy's full names and the name they gave me, Mary Monica Hall, but nothing about my natural mother or father. I later learned that an altered birth certificate was the only one I would ever get.

Next, I unfolded the adoption order. It listed my original name as *Gloria Debra Reed*. My gaze lingered. *Gloria is the name she thought of with her very own mind ...*

Then I gobbled up the document containing non-identifying information about my parents. I wondered if my mother had named me after herself. I decided to search for a Gloria Reed when I looked for her.

I read that she was Irish Catholic. My father was French and worked as a railroad flagman. Because Reed was an Irish surname and my original last name didn't match my natural father's French ancestry, I assumed she couldn't keep me because they weren't married.

I read the documents over and over, looking for clues about who I really was. I tried to imagine what my mother was like. *Is she pretty? Wow, she has blue eyes? Mine are hazel–probably a mixture because his eyes are brown. She's three inches taller than me and likes to sew, but I can't follow a pattern to save my life. Wow! I have six real uncles. I hope I have a sister.* This was as close as I'd ever been to my real identity.

I knew relinquishing mothers weren't allowed to see their newborns at the Catholic hospital in Anchorage. No doubt, this was to ensure they'd be less likely to change their minds. I wondered if the same rules had applied to my mother.

The next day, I told Sister about my adoption papers. In previous conversations, I'd shared my curiosity about my real identity. Finally, I asked, "Do you think I can see my baby?" My heart was wreaking havoc on my rib cage as I searched her face for an answer.

Sister studied her folded hands, then looked me in the eye. Her wheels were turning. She said, "I'll send a note to the hospital and see what they say."

Playing the adoptee card was the only way I might get to see and hold my child, but I had to be careful so she didn't think I was wavering in my decision.

Practically Still a Virgin

When we were younger, Tim and I got a kick out of telling kids we were adopted. They'd say, "Really? You are? Wow, that's so cool! I wish I were adopted." But adoption was not a parlor trick, and I was beginning to panic that my baby and I wouldn't be able to find each other one day. To cope, I thought about how to ensure that we would, when she turned eighteen. I had no doubt that, like me, my child would want to know who she was and what happened to her mother.

THE GARDEN

On May 4, I officially began month nine. When I arrived for my meeting with Sister that day, I was surprised but happy to see her waiting for me in the lobby. I waddled down the hall, following her to her office and holding my belly in the wake of her navy-blue habit.

"I have wonderful news," she said as she gave me a big hug.

My heart raced. Had the hospital agreed to let me see my baby?

"Darling, I've found the perfect adopting couple!"

She presented this news with such excitement that responding with anything other than delight would have been sacrilege. I wasn't prepared for the announcement but must have known it was coming. Until then, Sister had never mentioned adoption or the parents.

I looked at the wooden crucifix above her desk. Previously, I hadn't noticed how much I related to the man on her wall—not because he was crucified but because of his destiny. He knew his fate but wouldn't stop it. As Sister gushed about the wonderful parents, I didn't voice any objections. Doing so would have made me a killjoy.

I craved her approval and didn't want to disappoint her by sharing my real feelings. My heart raced, my skin grew clammy, and my mouth pooled with saliva. I can't remember what I said, but because I was a chameleon, I probably mirrored her excitement.

Like me, the adoptive father had dark hair, olive skin, and French heritage. Even though Daddy could have been described similarly, I subconsciously assumed the adoptive father wouldn't be like him in any way. Sister also told me the mother had light hair. Like me, she was a big talker.

Even though I felt like the information was coming from the end of a dark tunnel, I didn't miss a word as Sister described the parents. Reality sank in. I was scared and horribly sad, but I didn't share those feelings with anyone. I couldn't—I didn't *have* anyone.

"You should start thinking about names," she said. "You'll receive a photo of your baby and a copy of the birth certificate."

My mother named me Gloria Debra, I thought. *But my baby won't get to keep her real name, either.*

That night, I realized it was the Catholic devotion day for my patron saint, St. Monica. I wanted my baby to have my name so she would be a part of me, even though she wouldn't see me or get to keep it. I decided to name her Mary Monica.

I never let myself picture her childhood—I just imagined examining her in the hospital and holding her in my arms. I never imagined her first steps or birthdays. Instead, I tried to envision what it would be like to meet her when she turned eighteen.

As a small child, I'd believed Mama when she shared my bedtime origin story. She repeated how much my other mother loved me, but those were just words compared to the maternal love I felt for my unborn child. Because of that love,

101

I knew my natural mother *really did* love me and would also want to meet me.

Sister suggested I read *Why Am I Afraid to Tell You Who I Am?*—a book about hiding one's real self and being afraid to open up to people. I couldn't get past the first few pages. I didn't tell her who I was because I had no clue. Gaining acceptance and approval were my life's work. I was whomever I thought you wanted me to be. I wasn't aware that my lack of self-awareness caused internal struggles, insecurity, and low self-worth. I didn't realize that this might be a consequence of being given away for adoption.

Clearly, Sister sensed I kept things from her. I hid behind talk of doctor visits, religion, and the Novena. I couldn't tell her what was really bothering me because it was a tangled bundle of shame that I couldn't articulate. If I had, perhaps she could have helped me understand what had happened with Billy.

I blamed myself for not being forceful with him. If I had been, I might still have the virginity I so deeply valued. I wouldn't be an isolated, grotesque knocked-up teen who was keenly aware she was producing yet another bastard, all while preparing to lose her baby. That was what I was, too--a person born of unmarried parents, illegitimate.

I was conflicted. Sister seemed to love me, but her job was to take my baby. I couldn't trust that she cared about me as much as she seemed to. She was both my friend and my adversary. Her job was to keep me healthy and ensure I remained committed to adoption. It was also her job to give the parents reports on my pregnancy and estimated delivery date. I was the host, and she had to keep the host healthy and compliant.

Weeks earlier, Sister had suggested I write a letter that the parents would keep for my baby. I asked her how to start the letter. I didn't know if I should say "my dear one." I thought it might offend the parents because she would be theirs, not mine. Sister said that was ridiculous because the baby would always be mine and the adoptive parents would love me because she's a part of me.

When I got in the car, I told Mama and she started to cry.

To get me started, Mama later wrote an example on notebook paper. But anything I could write would sound trite, like "I love you, but I can't keep you because you need two parents." I wanted her to have more than the cheap platitudes I'd heard growing up, and I knew my words would lack depth. I was humiliated by the thought of my child or her new parents reading my hollow juvenile scribble—confirmation that her mother was not only a slut, but a stupid one. In my eyes, the parents were superior to me in every way.

As a child, I'd wished my mother had written me a note in her own hand. It would have fulfilled an immense longing—I wanted it more than anything in the world. Had I received even the simplest of words, it would have given me peace. Still, I didn't have what it took to articulate the feelings bottled in my heart. Even now, words fall short, but this is closer to what I wish I could've written:

My Dear One,

When I feel you moving, and you do that a lot, I touch your little elbow or knee and cherish our short time together with all my heart. Even though I can't keep you, I love you deeper and sweeter than I could ever describe in words. I leave you, my darling, with two wonderful parents handpicked by Sister Clare, whom I love and trust. I'll miss you so much, but I have faith you will grow up in a loving home where you will be protected, cared for, and cherished. Knowing this gives me peace. I love you from the bottom of my heart, to eternity and back again.

Your Natural Mother

103

Monica Hall

It wouldn't have been appropriate to add what I clung to:

Like you, I was adopted. When I am old enough, I will look for and meet my natural mother because I need to know her, discover the circumstances behind why she couldn't keep me, and see if I look like her. In eighteen years, I will also search for you because I know you'll want to meet me and know me, like I do my own mother. It's a long time to wait, but in the meantime, live your life. One day, you'll look into my eyes and see your face smiling back at you. Hang tight. I'm coming and I love you.

Had I been mature enough to write that sweet letter or had the guts to write the addendum, I would've been able to tell the adults who pushed me toward relinquishment, "I want to bring my baby home. I want to keep her."

In 1973, the bias was toward adoption, and there was little to no understanding that being separated from one's mother creates a cavernous hole that can never be filled. Because of my self-centered fear and shame, I couldn't write the letter. I still live with that regret.

When I visited Sister a week or so before my due date, I brought a metal statue of the Virgin Mary that I'd picked out at the Catholic gift shop. It was five inches tall, painted gold, mounted on a wooden base. I wanted Sister to pass it on to the parents so my baby would have something from her natural mother.

MASQUERADE

In the last months of my pregnancy, I thought about my "real mother" more than ever. Before becoming pregnant, I'd thought of her as my "natural mother," the commonly used phrase at that time. But that had changed. Even though I'd never met her, I knew she was real. Just like my baby was cradled inside my body, I'd once lived inside hers.

Late in my pregnancy, I also started thinking about my family in a new way. The Halls were puzzle pieces that didn't fit. I wrote in my journal, *As husband and wife, Mama and Daddy aren't blood-related and because Tim and I were adopted, we aren't really brother and sister and we aren't related to our parents either. We are strangers pretending we're a family.*

I felt like an alien. My family members didn't have my blunt personality or motor mouth. They weren't show-offs or dare-takers. Nor did they have my free spirit, my exaggerated facial expressions, complexion, or skyscraping forehead. Plus, unlike Mama and Tim, I had zilch artistic ability, and unlike my parents, I sucked big time at math.

I once read that being adopted was like living in a house with no mirrors. Without family members to reflect my genetic traits, I was always searching for a place to belong.

Without footprints to follow, I was confused, lost, and lonely. I needed more than anything to meet my *real* mother.

I also thought my existence would be affirmed if I could hold and examine my baby. Somehow, I knew my child would look like me. Seeing a face in my own image would prove I belonged somewhere. Maybe then I would know who I really was.

As my due date approached, I became more anxious about the adoption and began wondering what my natural mother had thought and felt close to her delivery. I hoped to one day ask why she had given me up, but I never doubted she loved me. I longed to look into her eyes and bask in the beauty of my *real flesh-and-blood* mother. I wrote in my journal, *Now I understand what my natural mother went through. She must have had a lot of courage and I must have the same.* In a way, she *was* with me just by virtue of what she'd done.

Although I yearned for her, it never lessened my love for Mama. Even before my isolation, when she wasn't as nice, I loved her wholeheartedly. But when my friends abandoned me during my pregnancy, I realized how lucky I was to have her by my side. She'd become my lifeline.

When I arrived for my next visit with Sister, she popped up as always to give me a hug. "Darling, how are you feeling?"

I rubbed the small of my back. "Just a little tired."

As I adjusted in the tweed armchair and rested my hands on my almost full-term belly, she said, "Did the doctor say anything about how you're coming along?"

"No. She just wanted to make sure I was staying on my diet."

All my OB-GYN appointments were followed by a phone call or visit with Sister so she could be apprised of how her prize goose was cooking. No doubt the adoptive parents could hardly stand the wait. It wasn't uncommon for first babies to be overdue, but I knew I could go into labor at any time.

I was hungry, tired, and depressed with swollen ankles and puffy fingers. I said, "Have you heard back from the hospital about letting me see my baby?"

Her face brightened. "Oh, yes, dear. They're going to make a special concession so I can bring you your baby."

I wanted to throw my bulk across the desk and hug her, but I didn't want to alert her to my desperation, lest she change her mind.

Many years later, Mama said she thought my counseling sessions with Sister might help me face the adoption. Although I needed help with so much more, I shared only as much as I thought would please Sister. She was a clinical social worker, but I didn't know the weight of a thousand pounds would have been lifted if I'd just been honest and told her about what happened with Billy and how tainted I felt.

I also didn't tell her that I wanted to keep my baby or that I worried no *nice* boys would ever date me. I couldn't articulate my icky feelings about Daddy or reveal the horrible girl I'd been when I took drugs, broke into houses, fought, and vandalized. I thought she wouldn't like me anymore if I did. Beyond that, I didn't want the adoptive parents to know their child's mother was a permissive idiot. I masked these fears with my motor mouth.

I didn't talk to Mama about my feelings, either, because she cried so easily. The controlling, overprotective woman who'd ruined all my fun had become my angel. When someone mentioned an emotional movie scene and her lips began to quiver, she'd laugh and fan her tears, embarrassed at her sensitivity: "I can cry at the silliest things."

When I laughed, she laughed. If she teared up, so did I. I loved her more than anyone else and knew she was sad.

Not only was she worried about Daddy's health and the way he treated my brother, but she also dreaded the impending birth and the heartache she'd have to witness when I relinquished my daughter.

RATS, RATS, RATS

Tim got caught forging Mama's checks. The school called after finding one on the floor in the hall. He'd been cashing them at Pay-N-Pak. I was happy, both that Mama finally saw her pet wasn't the angel she thought he was, and that I'd have company other than my rats while he was on restriction.

I'd started leaving them in my closet when I was away. I didn't realize they were probably peeing everywhere. I just knew they needed their exercise and couldn't be cooped up all day. Somehow, I didn't see the parallels.

I called them "my babies" and sometimes "my brats." They became an endless source of entertainment. I'd slowly open their drawer and they'd race to the front, perching their tiny pink feet on the edge, whiskers moving at Mach 10, waiting in anticipation. I'd blow on them in a big shot of air. They'd pretend it was a gale-force wind and tumble backward, then race back to the edge for another go.

My nesting instincts kicked in as I made a home for them. I was giving my pet rats the mothering I longed to give my baby.

Monica Hall

When I returned from Sister's one day, I couldn't find BB anywhere. After tearing my room apart, I found him just in time. He was in my closet, lying motionless in a bucket and tangled in my white crocheted shawl. The yarn was cinched around his neck and his feet were tied up. When I finally freed him, he scampered up my arm, cuddled my neck, and nudged my ear.

Later that afternoon, I was lying on my bed watching my stomach roll like ocean waves. It was hard to ignore the sound of kids calling to each other in the glorious spring weather. That's when I heard an ear-piercing scream.

I hurled myself off my bed as fast as my girth would allow and panicked when I saw my bedroom door ajar. My babies were on their hind legs at the end of the hall, surveying the living room. Mama stood on the coffee table screaming. "Get those filthy rats out of my house now! Right now! Rats, rats, rats! I can't believe I have rats in my house!" She was livid, and we had no time to find them a proper home. I was heart-sick.

Tim stuffed BB and BM into a cage and started roaming the neighborhood. He was still on restriction, but Mama made an exception and let him out of the house to get rid of my babies. He saw a kid walking with a rat in a box, and the kid agreed to add my brats to his collection.

The previous year, Tim had peered through that boy's garage window. The space had been converted into a rodent and reptile room with guinea pigs, lizards, snakes, mice, and rat friends for my babies. That was good enough for Tim, and he handed off the cage.

Lorna or Jill would surely have taken them had I been allowed to make a few phone calls, but Mama wanted the dirty rats gone that very second. I was sick with worry as I waited for Tim to get off restriction so he could find the kid's house and give my babies to my friends so they wouldn't be lost to me forever.

Losing my rat babies gave me more practice in repressing pain—a skill I would soon master.

LIAR LIAR

Luke had been calling incessantly. Each time he was told I was out. He had also knocked on the front door, and Daddy told him I wasn't home. He came back that night and tapped on my window. I ignored him, but he didn't go away. Finally, I pushed the curtain back. He anxiously motioned for me to open the window. In a desperate voice, he said, "Monica, I have to talk to you."

"No, go away! My parents will hear you."

"Please, just listen to me. I know you're pregnant, and I really care about you and the baby."

"Get outta here!" I shut the window and locked it.

I can't stand him, I thought. *He is so damn phony. He makes me sick.*

Before that, he hadn't contacted me since humping my leg. It was creepy for him to be calling on a pregnant girl. We'd never had sex, so why would he care about the baby?

I was deeply ashamed about what had happened with both Luke and Billy. To make myself feel better, I decided to tell Sister what "really" happened—in other words, I planned to lie. I wanted Sister to know I wasn't promiscuous and hoped she'd pass it on to my baby's new parents. Then I'd find a way to tell Mama.

I can see now that my perspective had been screwed up by Daddy's obsession with purity and religion. Decades later, I learned he'd dated a girl for three years before he met Mama but wouldn't marry her because she wasn't a virgin. I assumed everyone thought unmarried pregnant girls slept around with no idea of the father's identity.

On May 31, three days overdue per my vague calculations, I visited with Sister. After I told her about my leg cramps, I began the release. "Sister, I have something to tell you."

She looked up from her calendar.

"I haven't told anyone this, but something happened." I looked at my hands as they rested on my bump. "Like Mama, I planned to save it for my husband."

She looked at me intently. I'd never opened up to her and counseling hadn't worked as she'd hoped.

"Staying pure meant so much to me." I paused and she nodded for me to go on. "Well ... I was a virgin when I went out with this guy. He really wanted to have sex ... but I didn't want to."

She leaned in, wearing her social worker face.

"He insisted, though." I took a deep breath and relaxed my shoulders. "He wouldn't take no for an answer, and I felt really bad." She craned her neck. Sister knew I'd been holding back for months. The breeze blew her curtains and the fresh air spurred me on. I took another deep breath.

"Well, Sister, because he was so determined, I let him put his penis between my upper thighs, but it never went in." I gestured with my hand to show what I meant, but the gesture fell flat because my lap was hidden by my abdomen.

Without taking a breath, I said, "Sperm can swim and stay alive for a while, and if they get near the opening of the vagina, they can swim their way in and get you pregnant. That's what happened to me. So, I'm really still a virgin. I know that sounds hard to believe, but it really happened." My face was bright and hopeful. "I know what I did isn't right, and I will save myself until I'm married."

This made me feel better—I couldn't fathom my parents thinking of me like the women Daddy described. Luke was the perfect solution to my problem, but I never would have come up with such a crazy idea if he hadn't knocked on my window.

I was naïve enough to think Sister believed me. A few days later, I told Mama. I knew she'd share with Daddy and felt gross knowing he'd envision me with my pants down.

Then, to complete the story, I wrote it in my journal: *I am not a slut and I have never had intercourse. That may sound funny but it's the truth. So therefore, I am really still a virgin. It's sort of hard to believe that a pregnant girl is a virgin. At least I know inside that I'm not a whore but it's too bad other people don't think the same.*

Claiming the blond-haired, blue-eyed Scandinavian boy was the father solved both of my problems. I could keep the secret of what happened with Billy and I could also be the Virgin Mary Monica, redeeming that part of my parents' opinion of me, or so I thought. But as important as it had been for me to know my own identity, I gave the wrong genetic information to my child.

Forty years later, Mama recalled that when I got in the car after my visit with Sister, my head spun toward her like Linda Blair in *The Exorcist*. In an ominous tone, I said, "I told her everything ... and I mean everything." She reminded me of that warning and said, "I was never quite sure what you told Sister that day."

"Oh, Mama, I was probably referring to the 'sperm can swim' story."

Practically Still a Virgin

Mama claimed to have forgotten so many things from those years, but not that. Maybe it stuck in her mind because she worried I'd shared that she let Daddy beat me with the hanger.

During those long, dark winter months, I didn't dwell on my predicament or think about Billy, other than during the crab infestation. I should have been horrified that my baby, who I cherished with the depth of a mother's love, had been fathered by a man I'd looked up to but now despised. But no father existed in my mind. She belonged only to me.

Mama told me many years later that when Daddy heard the virgin-mess-on-my-leg story, he didn't buy it. He knew it was someone else, someone older and more experienced.

I never mentioned Billy in my journal.

WILLARD

Shortly after Mama made me get rid of the rats, Lorna offered to take them. Tim went to get them as soon as he was off restriction for cashing Mama's checks. As he left the court to search for the boy he'd given them to, I watched out the window. Forty minutes later, he rounded the corner empty-handed. As he approached, I could see his sad face. My heart sank. I'd felt all week something bad had happened.

"Where are my babies?"

Teary-eyed, he said, "They're gone."

"What do you mean, they're gone?" He pointed toward the mountains and said, "I had a horrible feeling when I saw a house with a burned-up garage."

I felt like I was going to be sick.

"There were tables and melted cages in the driveway. It smelled really bad. I knew before I knocked on the door. The kid's father said all the animals burned up. They think the fire started from the heat lamps."

I sobbed in my room for days, careful to hide my tears from Mama because she was the one who made me give them away. They were vermin to her, and loving vermin was disgusting.

Practically Still a Virgin

I read Mama's journal decades later. She noted how sad she was for me when my brother told her I'd been crying for weeks, but she never once acknowledged my pain, mentioned her sadness, or expressed her regret to me. I wish she had.

I didn't just lose my sweet companions in that fire. Mama, my angel, betrayed me by sending them away, causing them to be burned alive.

Before Tim had rescued the rats from the boa constrictor, we'd watched *Willard*, a movie about a lonely boy who befriended a rat he named Ben. We also saw the sequel where Ben's rat friends were torched by a flamethrower. Ben made his way back to the boy, who tended his wounds. But unlike Ben, my brats didn't escape the fire and they weren't coming home.

YOU'RE SO LUCKY

The sun was shining and puddles replaced the winter slush. Lawns were mushy brown. The trees were still bare. Kids were playing outside in the warmer weather and making all kinds of racket. It wouldn't be long before Mrs. Webb across the street would be on her knees planting pansies. While I was still grieving my rats, Tim ran in and out of the house just to torment me. "Monica, I love the feeling of the cool wind blowing on my face while I ride my bike down the street. Don't you wish you could ride your bike too? Don't you, don't you?"

The smell of ozone on Tim's windbreaker made me yearn to hold him down and suck the air from his lungs. Instead, I wrote horrible things about him in my journal, paced the house, opened and closed the refrigerator, and cried. When my family went to the mall or grocery store, I sat in the car. When they attended mass, I stayed home. I was tired of being the outcast.

A few weeks earlier, Sherry, the obese fourteen-year-old who'd been afraid of giving birth, called to tell me about her labor and baby. Her breathless voice trembled as she blurted too many details. "Oh, Monica, it was horrible! So much worse than I expected!"

I presumed it was difficult because she was so heavy. I wasn't surprised she couldn't handle the pain; she was so meek and delicate. I was nothing like her and assured myself I would have a much easier time.

"Oh, Monica, when we saw her, we couldn't bear to part with her. I named her *Anna Rebecca*. She's so beautiful!" Sherry's love reached through the phone and stabbed my heart. Her baby was born at Community Hospital, where they didn't have the strict "you can't see your baby" rules for relinquishing mothers. I told her how much I loved the name and noted it in my journal. With heaviness in my heart, I said, "You're so lucky to have parents that stand behind you." Then I hung up the phone.

A couple of days past my due date, I got a call from Julie— the tall blonde from school who'd offered to be my labor coach. I'd since learned that wouldn't be possible; when visiting the nursery, I saw a sign on the labor room door: Only Mothers and Fathers Allowed.

Julie wanted to visit me that afternoon. All the nosy neighbors were at work, the kids were still in school, and Mama was running errands. I looked longingly out the window at the spring weather. *Screw it*, I thought. "Hey," I said when I called her back. "I'm coming over. See you in a few." Then I walked out the door.

It felt foreign to be free again, with fresh air blowing on my face. Earthy scents awakened my cells as I crossed the street. I couldn't believe how wonderful this simple act felt. I vowed to never again take it for granted. When I arrived at Julie's, we discovered there were no goodies in the cupboards, so we returned to my house for snack money. Then I remembered the two ten-speeds sitting in the garage. I said, "Let's take the bikes." To my delight, my coat hid my pregnancy when I bent over the handlebars.

Once I discovered my pregnancy couldn't be detected, I felt safe to ride around the court with the kids.

One afternoon, Paula's mom pulled up and called to me in her phony voice: "Oh, Mary Monica, I haven't seen you in such a long time! I was wondering what happened to you." Paula had told me her mom thought I was on a permanent restriction.

I knew she didn't like me and was just prying. I said, "Maybe I should come by and see you sometime."

When I read Mama's journal years later, one particular entry made my heart soften: *Tim went for a ride in Paula's car this afternoon. Somehow to me, this feels disloyal. They wouldn't let Monica ride in the car with Paula. They think she takes drugs! They are really ignorant people. [Paula's mother] is getting a master's degree in psychology this month. She's an educated idiot!*

But really, Mama was the ostrich who stuck her head in the sand.

I asked Paula if her parents had said anything more about me, and they had. When a neighbor was washing his car, he told Paula's father I was pregnant.

Her parents were active in our church and provided religious instruction to engaged couples in their home, which I thought was a hypocritical crock of shit. Weren't Catholics, especially those who taught religious classes, supposed to set examples of Christian principles like kindness and forgiveness? They certainly shouldn't be judgmental gossips. I recorded my anger in my journal: *I'm so mad I could spit! Paula told me tonight when she was walking out of the house her father said in front of the priest and their company, "When is Monica going to have her baby?" She looked at her mother, smiled and said, "Any day." And walked out.*

Practically Still a Virgin

I'd been hiding—not even going in the backyard—for fear Paula's mom would see me, affirming her poor opinion. What a waste of isolation.

Although the whole neighborhood knew and there was no reason to hide anymore, I wasn't about to strut around the cul-de-sac bloated with child just to see Paula's mom's smirk of confirmation. I imagined her thinking, *I knew she was good for nothing. I'm not surprised she got knocked up.*

Mama didn't let me ride my bike every day, but when she was at art class and Daddy was working, I rode downtown to snack on french fries at Woolworths. Riding with the wind in my face was my medicine. It felt surreal walking into stores again.

I spied a fake white-gold wedding ring set in a glass case at Woolworths for $3.18, so I snatched it up using the change in my pocket and unceremoniously slid the bands onto my left hand.

BLOATED BLOB

*T*hings I will give Mama for her birthday:
flowers
hand sewing machine
nightgown
charm
a grandchild

I was almost three weeks overdue when I rode my bike to Joan's house. She was a wholesome girl who lived down the street and who'd recently started visiting me. She was helping me sew a nightgown for Mama's birthday.

I felt free as I rode down the middle of the empty street past the elementary school, sitting up and spreading my arms like I was flying. The refreshing scents left by the earlier rain were exhilarating.

When I arrived at Joan's, I was disappointed to see one of her pretty friends who wore dresses, used hot rollers, and lived in a nice house. Apparently, Joan forgot she'd promised to help me finish the nightgown—especially disappointing since Mama's birthday was tomorrow.

Shortly after I arrived, the phone rang. It was Tony and George calling Joan and her friend for a double date. While

Practically Still a Virgin

I sat on the bed, they buzzed around applying makeup and fixing their hair, giddy with excitement as they tried on cute skinny clothes and threw the discards next to me as if I weren't there.

I was an invisible, bloated blob. Nice boys would never want to take out a girl who had a baby. I'd gained fifty pounds and had silver spiderweb stretch marks on my breasts, butt, and thighs—even on the inside of my chubby knees. I'd never be able to wear slim clothes or swimsuits again. The world was whirling and I was sinking.

"Monica," Joan said, "Tony will be here soon. You better go."

She wasn't being mean—she was just trying to protect my feelings. Earlier, she'd said Tony didn't like me due to rumors that I was a slut. I excused myself before the tears spilled from my eyes.

I leaned over the handlebars as low as my tummy would allow and peddled as fast as I could. The cool air bit at my wet cheeks as the months of isolation, shame, and hopelessness nearly choked me. I dumped my bike on the lawn, went to my room, closed my door, and buried my face in my pillow.

Daddy opened the door. "What have you been doing, and where have you been?" His interrogation reminded me of the night he beat me, when he demanded to know where I'd stopped on the way home from Lorna's. Crying in front of Daddy was worse than being naked in the middle of the street.

"Did you have Mama's permission to be out? Why is your door closed? Look at me when I'm talking to you!" He was enraged. He'd probably been waiting for my brother to get home so he'd have his whipping boy.

When I refused to answer, he turned and closed the door.

Later in life, when I identified his verbal abuse as a "valve release" necessary so he wouldn't explode with self-loathing, I realized we were more alike than I cared to admit. Like him, I also abused people because of my self-hatred but it only made me feel worse.

Even though he never apologized for the beating—or even mentioned it—I knew he wouldn't harm me again. I'd realized it a few months after it happened when I was wearing a ripped nylon jacket that was cool to me and my grungy friends. Daddy hated it.

When I arrived home that day, he lunged at me from the couch and attempted to tear it off me. "Get that lousy rag off!"

I sensed his feelings were similar to those he'd felt when he took pleasure in his handiwork with the hanger. Flashing back to the beating, I flailed and wrenched away, hysterical. I screamed, "Don't touch me! Don't touch me!" I laid it on a bit thick because I wanted him to think he had really trauma-tized me. That would show him.

He retreated. After that, I wasn't afraid of him anymore. I didn't respect him, either.

Joan and I finished the nightgown on Mama's birthday. The next day, the doctor sent me to the hospital for an abdom-inal X-ray. Per my shoddy calculations, I was overdue, but the X-ray showed the baby's head to be about thirty-eight weeks. "You're not quite ready. It'll still be a couple more weeks," the doctor said.

A few days earlier, my brother had purposely sneezed in my face. After the X-ray, I started sneezing too. That night, Sister Clare called and said Mother Superior was sending her Outside (a term Alaskans use for the Lower 48) for two weeks. She would be leaving the next day. I hoped she'd be back before the birth. I didn't know what I'd do without her—she'd promised to bring me my baby.

ELEPHANT LADY

In my dream, my lower back ached. I was lounging in bed, adding yellow trim to the white baby blanket I was knitting. I heard someone moan and wondered where the sound was coming from. Emerging from the dream fog, I opened my eyes. Not quite awake, I had a vague feeling I was supposed to do something important.

It was 5:00 a.m. on Saturday, June 23, 1973, just two days after the X-ray and two weeks before the doctor said I was due. I heard Daddy stirring in the kitchen. I lay still while feeling the familiar bump of a hand or foot, the ripple of movement across my belly, the ache in my lower back, and the rhythmic tightening of my abdomen. Labor had begun.

Fully awake now and working on the blanket for real, I timed the contractions. They were five minutes apart and uncomfortable. I was excited until I remembered what Sherry had said about how bad the pain got. But she was a scaredy cat. I wasn't like her and knew I could handle it.

The doctor said first babies took hours to come, but still, I was dying to tell someone. When I finished packing my bag, it was 6:00 and Daddy was reading at the table. Holding my belly, I said, "I'm in labor."

It was almost comical how terrified he looked. "Please let Mama sleep," I said. "The doctor says it'll be a long labor, and she'll need her rest." He nodded, his face ashen. Within minutes, he began pacing the house. Ten minutes later, he woke her. Still pacing, he said, "You better get her to the hospital!"

I was wheeled up to a labor room where I received an enema and was embarrassed that the nurse saw my privates while shaving me.

My labor was still mild, so I wrote in my journal: *I talked to my brother on the phone and told him not to tell anyone I'm in labor but he is a blabbermouth and told everyone, even Katie the lady who works the register at Pay-N-Pak knows.*

I didn't call Kelly, Paula, or any of my other friends. When Lorna had said, "you'll need your friends the most through this time," I'd envisioned them racing to the hospital. Now, I kept my labor hidden—maybe because it was the only power I had left when it came to my pregnancy, or maybe I just felt forgotten. If they didn't know, they couldn't hurt me by not coming.

At 1:00 p.m., a resident came for an internal check and laughed when she saw Mama and me playing gin rummy. She said my labor would probably last another fifteen hours.

I arrived at the hospital with courage, but it eroded as the day progressed. The two women who'd been admitted after me were now moaning and wailing in a chorus of agony, the volume of which increased by the hour. One of them howled, "Howie, Howie! Ohhhh-ooh, it hurts! Look what you've done to me, Howwiiiieeee!" The other roared like an elephant at slaughter.

I was reminded of Sherry. She'd rubbed her back raw and left welts. She'd also squeezed her mom's hand so hard she left bruises. Her graphic descriptions had scared me, and I wished she'd kept them to herself. But that didn't frighten

me half as much as hearing the torment firsthand. It was terrifying that I couldn't chicken out.

As my pain increased, Mama massaged my stomach
and lower back. The nurse came in and out, doing internal
checks. During one of these checks, there was a huge gush.
"Your water just broke! This should speed things up." After
that, the pain quickly increased.

Hearing Howie's wife through the walls did me a huge
favor. At the height of hard labor, I kept expecting the pains
to get worse, making me thrash and shriek like the banshee
down the hall. I guess I just handled it better, or maybe I
wasn't the screaming type.

During my three or four hours of hard labor, I used the
breathing Julie taught me. However, I'd caught Tim's cold;
the congestion made the huffing and puffing of my pat-
terned breathing very difficult. After a couple of hours, I was
exhausted and parched. There was not one bit of saliva in my
mouth and my tongue stuck to my lips. But they wouldn't give
me water for fear I'd vomit.

The bearing-down pains were a relief from the hard-
labor contractions, but when the nurse did her internal check,
she said I wasn't dilated enough. She said to resist pushing
because tearing my cervix would extend the labor. But no
matter how much I resisted, my body still needed to do what
it had to do: push that baby out. I was in the fight of my life.
To help me resist, the nurse instructed me to focus on a spot
on the ceiling.

I thrashed about for two excruciating hours, trying to
focus on that tiny dot, emitting primitive sounds so guttural
I can't describe them. I had become like the elephant lady
down the hall. Mama later said she'd never heard anything
like it and couldn't believe the sounds came from a human, let
alone her daughter.

Finally, sometime after 2:00 a.m., the doctor arrived, examined me, and told the nurses to let me push. That was the first time I'd seen her since my labor began almost twenty-four hours earlier.

I sat up, closed my eyes, tucked my chin, and pushed with everything I had. Between contractions, I couldn't keep my eyes open and flopped like a rag doll onto the raised bed. But when the pushing pains came, I grabbed those bars and bore down with the strength of a wild woman. This went on for thirty minutes before I was wheeled into the delivery room. I wanted Mama in there with me, so she trotted off to suit up in hospital garb and booties.

I was exhausted. I'd been up for twenty-four hours without food, sleep, or water, other than a wet rag to suck on. I'd also been in hard labor for many hours. When Mama entered, I was already in the stirrups and ready to roll. They draped a white sheet over my legs and strapped my arms to the steel bars I was supposed to grip. It took only a few more pushes before I felt a huge gush of what seemed like water. After that, I felt empty.

"Did I have my baby?"

The doctor confirmed but said nothing else. When I heard the dainty cry, all my fear and pain evaporated. I tried to sit, but the doctor was in the way so I couldn't see. "Is it healthy? Are all the parts working?"

Mama answered, "Monica, you have a little girl."

Her cry was beautiful. When I saw her lying there, I thought, *This is such a wonderful feeling.* Her hair looked red from the warming lights. I was relieved the pain was over, but I had no idea what I had yet to bear.

I'd ripped like tissue paper, both inside and out. As soon as they whisked my baby away, the doctor hunkered down to stitch me. After that, I remained in the recovery room for two hours, wide awake, and could think of nothing but holding my daughter. I'd later write in my journal, *I am looking forward to having more children after I get married. It would be so much nicer with a husband to share the joy with. It would be nice to keep all my children.*

Mama and Daddy came to see me in recovery. Daddy's face turned white when I jabbered about the delivery. "I have to get out of here before I pass out," he said as he rushed from the room.

"What's wrong with him?" I asked.

"Men are funny and can't handle such things," Mama said. I thought, *What a puss.*

Julie had told me delivery was like pushing out a huge turd. I thought it was more like pushing a watermelon through a straw. If men had to do what I'd just done, humans would have been extinct eons ago.

MORNING AFTER

The morning after the birth, I awoke to crushing dread. As the sterile white hospital room came into focus, I remembered: *I have to give my baby away.*

The nurse handed me a foldout menu and said, "You must be very hungry, dear." The cover displayed an image of a pink tray with scalloped edges, a bouquet of fruit in a clear parfait glass, plated bacon and eggs, and a virginal white teapot. The image was muted, a soft pastel in the most wonderful dream, the dream of a new mother. I wondered what it would feel like to be Howie's wife and the elephant lady, who I knew were holding and feeding their babies.

As usual, I ordered a huge breakfast, but the first bite tasted like cardboard and I couldn't swallow. There have been only two times in my life when food has lost its magic; this was the first.

Sister Clare's replacement, a nun in her thirties, was my first visitor that morning. Sister Louise had a kind, round face. She was smaller and more feminine than Sister Clare and brought me a lily of the valley bouquet. She said it represented purity. I figured this was wishful thinking since my pregnancy proved otherwise. But now I realize she meant my baby was without sin. She'd picked the flowers from the hospital garden.

The nun was sweet, but Sister Clare had held me together during my pregnancy and promised to bring me my baby. As Sister Louise set the white vase on my bedside table, I said, "Thank you. When can I see my baby?" To my relief, she said, "Let's go right now."

I yearned to examine Mary Monica's little face, touch her fingers and toes, press my lips to her cheeks, smell her, and imprint her to memory. Since my bottom was too sore to sit in a wheelchair, Sister walked me to the nursery down the long white corridor, past patient rooms and around corners, beyond the nurses' station. I wanted to run, but my torn insides could only bear scooting along inch by inch. It felt like my flesh was ripping open with each shuffle, but I'd have gone a hundred miles to get to my baby. It didn't occur to me then, but I've since realized it took so long to get to her because I was at the other end of the ward, far from the nursery and the mothers who were able to hold their babies, feed them, and take them home.

Arriving at the glass, I scanned rows of clear plastic bassinets with bundles swaddled like butterfly cocoons. My eyes stopped on a hint of brown hair. Even though I couldn't see her face, I knew she was mine. The nurse stood over the bassinet cradling the most beautiful sight I'd ever seen. She pointed to a small room adjacent to the nursery. My heart pounded so hard I could hear the blood rushing in my ears.

When the nurse placed my baby in my arms, nothing compared to the warmth of thousands of butterflies fluttering through me. I kept repeating, "Oh, she is so beautiful. She is so cute! Oh, she is just so beautiful." She was proof that I mattered in the world.

I kissed her nose and smelled the soft folds of her neck. Nothing existed but us. She smiled and knew I was her mama.

We shared long second toes and heart-shaped lips. Her perfectly shaped head had just a shadow of brown hair, and her skin was velvety smooth—no wrinkles. Unlike mine, her right ear had an extra ridge inside. I felt like I'd known her for eons. The visit lasted maybe five minutes. Then, even though I had yet to sign the adoption papers, the nurse took her from my arms like I was an inmate and my visiting time had expired.

How dare they? I thought. *She's still mine!*

Before my parents visited me, they met with Sister Louise and saw their new granddaughter. During the three days when I was hospitalized, Sister took me to see my baby a couple of times with my parents and again with just Mama and me, but she never brought her to my room as Sister Clare had promised. My brother stood at the nursery window for hours, providing commentary about each baby.

By the third day, I could sit in the wheelchair and either Paula, Kelly, or my brother would wheel me to the nursery to admire her through the glass.

Sister Solange, the elderly French nun who wore a white habit and was about the size of a ten-year-old child, visited often. She brought pamphlets, cards, little gifts, and a holy book. She was the same nun I'd impressed at age five when I told her I wanted to do good for God and wished to be a nun when I grew up. Thankfully, she didn't remember I was that same girl.

Father Hornick visited, too. He was the friendly young priest who used to be at our parish but had moved to St. Benedict's in Oceanview, a coveted neighborhood with fancy houses, some of which had views of the inlet. We snickered when he told me Sister Solange went from room to room in the hospital, lifting patients' arms to read their wristbands. If the band didn't say "Baptized Catholic," she would drop it like a rock and move to the next.

Practically Still a Virgin

With my bottom being so sore, coughing and sneezing—which I did often, thanks to my cold—were excruciating. I couldn't imagine what mess I had "down there" and vowed never to look. I shuddered when I remembered what the nurse at preggo school had said: "They won't release you until you have a bowel movement." But the physical pain was only a shadow of what my heart was pushing down.

I couldn't share my fears with anyone. The nun was there to deliver my daughter to her new parents, who had waited a few extra weeks due to the confusion surrounding my due date. Mama, Daddy, and Sister Clare all expected me to do "the right thing," a phrase I heard over and over.

SIGNING

She was born on the Sabbath day. She's named Mary Monica, just like me ... I got to see her with Mama only a couple times before they started bugging me about signing the blasted papers.

I wrote this journal entry shortly after returning home from the hospital. I'd done what was expected of me leading up to the birth, but it's clear I was suppressing rage. Decades later, Mama reminded me that Sister said the adoptive parents could pay my medical bills. Mama was surprised when I sneered, "Oh ... they're going to pay."

On the second day following the birth, Sister Louise delivered the adoption documents for me to read. I hadn't seen Mama all day, which was odd because she'd been by my side nearly every second the day before. I was worried and scared. I knew I should digest every word, but I was in the midst of an emotional shutdown and couldn't comprehend what I read. I needed Mama.

An hour before I was scheduled to sign, Sister returned.

"Where's my mom?"

Sister pulled up a chair. "Your mother asked me to deliver a message."

I froze. Something really bad must have happened.

Practically Still a Virgin

"She couldn't tell you herself because she feared she would get too emotional and didn't think she'd be able to get the words out. She said she couldn't live with herself if she was to separate a mother from her child. She wants you to know that if you find it in your heart to do so and you decide you want to keep your baby, you can bring her home." With no further discussion, she gathered the papers and left.

All along, I'd been pushed up the gallows steps. Then, at the last minute, the noose was placed in *my* hand. One would think a girl in my shoes might ask herself a lot of questions: Would Mama rush out to purchase a crib and diapers? Would she care for my daughter while I finished high school? Would I have Mama's support to help raise her, like Sherry's mom, who couldn't stand to part with her grandchild? How would this work? But I was overwhelmed, alone, and frozen with confusion and thought none of these things.

Since it hadn't been an option, I'd never allowed myself to imagine what it might be like to raise my baby. Instead, I'd internalized my origin story, which inadvertently groomed me to relinquish my own child: *Your other mother loved you so much that she wanted you to have a mommy and a daddy.* How could I selfishly keep my baby when my own selfless mother hadn't? My daughter deserved two parents, like I had. But doesn't one hold tight to those they cherish? I think that unconsciously, no matter what I was told, when my mother gave me away, I felt unlovable.

I now wonder if it was cowardly for Mama to have Sister Louise break this news. Did she do it to absolve herself of guilt?

By doing the "right thing" and relinquishing my child, I would be salvaging the worthiness that had been taken from me through my own adoption.

I didn't know any of this then, at least not consciously, and I'd never voiced my wishes even though it felt wrong to give away my baby. She was my only flesh and blood tie, a life I'd carried and sustained in my womb for almost a year. Relinquishing her went against every grain of nature and violated my inherent maternal instinct. But because adoption was presented as the only option, I never once said, "I want to keep my baby" or even, "Can I keep my baby?"

When the opportunity arose, I was touched by what I thought was Mama's compassionate offer. But as it had with so many other bad experiences, my brain was just protecting me from being blindsided by the only person who had been there for me during those long, dark months. I wouldn't be able to acknowledge her betrayal for over forty years.

I had no time to think or process, and I now wonder if Sister was doing damage control by leaving the room rather than initiating a dialogue. After all, it was her job to deliver my baby to the adoptive parents, and this couldn't have been her first rodeo with a family's misgivings. Decades later, I learned from Mama's journal that Sister Louise had offered to deliver the message. Sister may have been concerned there would be a course correction if Mama started the discussion.

Until that day, my parents had made all my decisions. I wasn't even allowed to decide where to buy my own clothes, yet minutes before I was to sign my baby's life away, Mama put the onus on me. I signed.

The memory is a blur. I remember being in an office, but according to my journal, I signed in my hospital room. Sister Louise and my parents felt like shadows to my right, but I can't see them in my mind's eye. All I see is a black-capped pen and Sister Clare's absence.

In my head, I heard Sister's enthusiasm for the parents she'd handpicked. The "wonderful" parents would be devastated if I backed out. They'd been waiting so long, especially since I was overdue, and I'd grown to love them through Sister Clare. She'd told me of their excitement every week, including the expectant adoptive mother's suggestion that Mama drive me over a bumpy road so I would hurry and go into labor. I hated to let them down, and I hated to let my parents down. I would've never been able to face Sister Clare if I kept my baby. Always a people pleaser, I surrendered my child to avoid disappointing everyone who might withdraw their love and approval if I didn't.

I intentionally looked away from my parents and signed without shedding a tear. I had to be strong; if I let the floodgates open, I'd make Mama cry and might not be able to go through with it. Decades later, I read my journal entry from that day: *I wanted to keep her so badly but I knew that it wouldn't have been right. I followed my head instead of my heart.*

For decades, I was plagued by Mama's words that I could keep my baby "if I found it in my heart to do so." Because I decided not to keep her, did that make me heartless?

Fifty years post-relinquishment, I understand that my parents were trying to protect my future by leading me toward adoption. They didn't want me to grow up so fast, saddled with the responsibilities single motherhood would bring, losing the freedom of youth. And who would want to marry a girl with a child? Mama and Daddy believed adoption was the best way to give me a good life.

I later learned that my brother wanted me to bring her home; he was inconsolable, Mama said, and promised to babysit.

I kept everything from those few days—the pen, the Catholic items from Sister Solange, the meal menu, my wristband, greeting cards—all stored for safekeeping in an old photo album box that I labeled "Mary Monica" in black felt pen.

I signed the papers on the second of my three days in the hospital. On the last day, after the dreaded bowel movement, Mama and I saw Mary Monica one last time. We held her, kissed her, and basked in her beauty. I kept repeating, "She is just so beautiful, she is just so beautiful." She cooed, smiled, and turned her face toward my voice. There was no doubt she knew I was her mother.

I don't know why I wouldn't let myself cry. Maybe I knew I'd never stop. I thought I had to be strong. Maybe it was my nature to show strength even when I felt weak. I knew it would take everything I had to walk out that door and leave her behind for at least eighteen years—longer than I'd been alive.

It was June 26, 1973, when I admired her in the bassinet for the last time. When I looked at Mama and saw the tears in her eyes, I was already shutting down. I thought, *The other mothers get to leave with their babies.*

From the front seat of Mama's car, I looked back as we pulled away from Providence Hospital's ocean-blue walls and wailed inside with an anguish so deep, I feared I wouldn't survive. In silent desperation, I repeated, *I just won't think about it right now, I just won't think about it right now, I just won't think about it right now.*

When I left part of myself at the hospital, it was like a shade had been pulled down and my world went dark. My worst anguish was denying my own maternal instincts to build a family for two strangers.

SWEET SIXTEEN

My memories of the days after the birth are vague. But a few things stick out in my mind, like the disaster at the movie theater. A couple days after I was discharged from the hospital, my parents took me to the movies. Although there was no mention of my loss, I assume they were attempting to get my mind off it. I wore the white muslin smock top with embroidered yoke that Mama had bought for my return home.

When we spilled into the lobby after the show, the next crowd of moviegoers waited at the velvet ropes. As my eyes adjusted to the light, I wondered, *Why are they gawking?* I looked down in horror to see the peak of my breasts circled by donut-sized rings: milk. We called the doctor, and she told Mama to bind me with a white sheet, like a mummy. It hurt like hell, as did my stitches. But the emotional struggle was worse. My memory of holding Mary Monica was always interrupted by the view of the hospital as we drove away.

I longed for her heart-shaped lips, the weight of her in my arms, and her warmth as I buried my nose in her neck. Whenever I felt I would drown, that I'd never surface, I repeated my mantra: *I just won't think about it right now. I just won't think about it right now.* My earlier escape, bike riding with the wind in my face, wasn't possible while I healed.

When Mary Monica was thirty-three days old, I wrote, *Today is my birthday! I am sweet 16 and never been kissed, ha!* It was sarcastic; everyone knows a teen mother is far from her first kiss. I received a clock radio and a lime-green beanbag chair to complement my new purple walls, freshly painted as if we were trying to wipe clean the last ten months. The whole family was down, and it didn't help that it was drizzly and gray outside.

Cutting my cake, miserable, on my sixteenth birthday

My journal entry continued: *I wonder if my other mother is thinking about me. I think about my baby all the time. [My other mother] must be wondering what I am like at 16. It's sort of a weird feeling hoping that someone I don't even know and someone that doesn't really know me is thinking and wondering about me.*

Mama made a cake, but I blew out my candles with the enthusiasm of the terminally ill. Daddy never wished me a happy birthday.

Practically Still a Virgin

The following week, I had my postpartum exam with Dr. Sydnam. Most new mothers brought their babies and talked about breastfeeding, the feelings of being a new parent, and when it was okay to resume sex. But not me. The doctor made sure everything was back in place, my stitches had healed, and my breasts had dried up. You'd think she'd have asked how I was feeling after surrendering my baby for adoption, but she didn't. Instead, she handed me a beige compact, opened it to rows of little birth control pills, and explained how to take them.

It would be years before I recalled the moment when, in my eyes, the doctor diagnosed me as a slut. The evidence pointed to a sexually active teen: pregnant at fifteen and crawling with crabs. I stuffed them in my purse and left, feeling defeated.

I'd been honest when I told Sister I planned to save it for my husband. But after Dr. Sydnam put me on the pill, I knew I'd never regain respect. I poured my feelings into my journal: *I'm going to have a hard time getting decent guys because they probably won't have me because I've been pregnant. Then all the creepy guys will want to take me out for a piece and nothing else. I've got to find out where my head's at. I seem to be all screwed up.*

Shortly after my birthday, I got a job serving caramel corn and scooping ice cream at the mall. That's where I met Brent, a cute blond-haired, blue-eyed surfer-looking boy. He seemed to really like me, and I was infatuated. He'd come by the house a few times to pick me up for work, and Mama approved of him.

One day, we went to his house to hang out. Brent put on an album, and I tried to disappear as his hand fondled my webbed breasts and moved over my wrinkly tummy. This was the first boy I'd made out with since having Mary Monica. When he wanted to go all the way, I thought, *He really likes me, and I'm on the pill. Even Dr. Sydnam thinks I sleep around, so it doesn't matter anymore.*

As Brent rocked above me, I floated somewhere between the shadows of Carly Simon's melody and the image of Daddy's Salem glowing in the dark. The song about closing wounds and hiding scars hit home that night as I tried to fall asleep. I never heard from Brent again.

EXIT

I returned to East for my junior year at the end of August, two months after Mary Monica's birth. Reflecting on that first semester, I don't remember getting back to the things I'd missed while pregnant. Instead, I worried what others thought of me because I'd given up my baby.

Sitting at my desk, I was acutely aware of the stretched-out skin bulging over the top of my pants. I tried to cover the proof that I'd had a baby by holding my arms across my midsection, and I was painfully aware that other girls didn't worry about fluorescent stretch marks. It never occurred to me that I might not be the only girl suffering from self-doubt and body image insecurities.

By Christmas, I was finally in the groove of things. I'd dropped from 140 to 114 pounds and nice boys liked me. But Daddy had other ideas. He'd say, "When the depression hits, money will be as worthless as the paper it's printed on. Gold and silver will be the only currency with value." He decided we should move to California, where we could grow our own food and be close to the Mexican border for his anti-cancer drug.

He liquidated our properties and assets into $100,000 of gold bullion and silver coins, with an additional $100,000 in cash. He purchased a Ford Galaxie 500 and outfitted it with heavy-duty shocks for the army ammunition boxes we'd use to transport the loot.

The car was ferried to Seattle, and until we could send for them, we boarded Daisy and our white mouser, Thomas, who we got at the pound after Mary Monica's birth.

The day Patty Hearst was kidnapped, February 4, 1974, we boarded a Western Airlines flight. Mary Monica was eight months old. Once we left Alaska, I knew I'd never spy her in a stroller or in the arms of a light-haired woman at the mall or in the grocery store. I hated leaving, but I'd dreamed of living in California. We were headed to the land of freeways, palm trees, and movie stars. It was a new beginning.

LOWER 48

Seattle was chilly, gray, and wet, not unlike many summer days in Anchorage. We caught a cab to the ferry station, picked up the blue Ford, and headed south on Interstate 5. I didn't know yet that we were embarking on a four-month tour of the Pacific Coast, during which we'd smuggle laetrile vials over the Mexican border and then hit the road again, while Daddy changed his mind about California and tried to decide where we'd call home.

When I should've been finishing my junior year, we rented houses and stayed in countless motels. In balmy San Diego, Tim and I briefly attended school and made a few friends. Mama even sent for the animals. But when Daddy told us to pack up because we were heading to Seattle, we didn't even have time to empty our school lockers. Daisy hopped on Tim's lap while Thomas settled into the rear window, and we hit the road.

Like a rock band on tour, we spent our nights under a blur of flashing vacancy signs. But not so for our stop in the town of Everett, Washington, where the air was pungent with a never-ending fart smell. Daddy said it was sulfur from the pulp mill. I couldn't fathom how anyone could stand to live there.

That evening, I was waiting in a sketchy motel parking lot watching Daddy struggle to carry the last ammo box to our room when a man approached him and said, "Here, let me give you a hand with that!" What could Daddy do but let the man take the handle? The man's arm dropped almost to the ground. "Wow! What do you have in here, gold?" Daddy sat up all night with the Smith & Wesson.

We finally bought a beautiful house in Edmonds, Washington. It had a two-car garage and Betty Crocker kitchen with saloon doors. Most impressive were the expansive windows with a view of Puget Sound's shimmering blue waters. At sunset, the wall became a theater of color. I was reminded of Sleeping Lady at midnight, which made me homesick. But after a month, Daddy sold the house for a loss because he noticed a small crack in the basement foundation. He feared the ground could be unstable like the ground in the swanky neighborhood that had liquefied in the earthquake. He worried we'd roll into Puget Sound.

After nearly four months of being cooped up in the car with her family and pets, Mama put her foot down and told Daddy we had to settle. Being nomads went against her grain because her family had moved so often during the Depression and she hated it.

The Golden Key Motel was our last stop. It sat off the freeway in the Sierra Foothills of Auburn, California. It was a place where 4-H Club was the primary social activity and country teens passed the time by learning canning and grooming livestock. This sounded like a fate worse than death. Luckily, my parents just used it as a base camp while looking for a home close to Sacramento.

PIE FACE

Our parents told us the new house was located on Maui
Way, almost twenty miles outside Sacramento in the
bedroom community of Fair Oaks. Making friends was my
only focus, but if I'd tried to imagine the neighborhood, I
probably would have envisioned tropical breezes, pineapples,
and a beautiful lanai overlooking palm trees.

We headed west on the interstate. After half an hour, we
took an off-ramp onto a busy thoroughfare lined with banks,
strip malls, and unceremonious office complexes. After about
six miles, we turned onto a small road dotted with pastures,
cows, and a sign that read "Tomatoes 35 Cents a Pound." I
choked back a moan. Our home was in a housing tract with
rows of nearly identical shoeboxes that had swamp coolers
atop lava-rock rooftops.

Any visions of grandeur the Hawaiian street name might
have conjured were erased by a 900-square-foot three-bedroom, one-bath tar paper shack with a freshly planted palm.
The cherry Ethan Allen dining table we bought in Washington would've filled the living room. Untacked shag carpet
and red-and-white flocked wallpaper rendered me speechless.
As we stepped from the car, Daddy said, "Don't worry, it's

temporary. We'll find something better once we get settled."
We never did.

The house was borderline hideous, but it was on a third
of an acre with a beautiful backyard. Fruit trees rimmed
the fence, and there was a diamond-shaped river rock rose
garden near the covered patio. The mulberry tree was the
focal point, surrounded by a quaint blue octagonal bench that
became Thomas's perch.

It was early June and school had just ended. The Sacramento Valley heat climbed into the hundreds, leaving the
swamp-cooled air inside muggy. Sometimes the streets got so
hot they could fry an egg.

Our neighborhood lacked streetlights. On lonely summer
evenings, I sat on the warm sidewalk searching the sky for the
Big Dipper and North Star—both of which appear on Alaska's state flag—imagining Mary Monica in her crib, hugging
a teddy like I had hugged Forbes. She was almost one.

Tim wasn't as lonely; he had a new friend who taught us
California teen culture. Skateboarding hadn't been a thing in
Anchorage, and up north we didn't listen to soft rock like The
Beach Boys. We soon adapted to the California lingo: trick,
bitchin, boss, cherry.

We'd only had three channels in Anchorage and were
overwhelmed by cable TV—there were so many options, we
couldn't ever decide what to watch. There were also swim-
ming pools, suntans, convertibles, Hawaiian shirts, and puka-
shell necklaces. Best of all, there were no more scrub pines or
drizzly summer days.

Mary Monica's first birthday was on a Monday. I imagined her neighbors, church friends, and, of course, Sister
Clare carrying brightly wrapped boxes trimmed in pink
ribbon, climbing the steps to a fancy house. A dark-haired
father and light-haired mother laughed while their daughter
slapped her cake and smeared frosting in her wispy brown

hair. I yearned to press my lips to her frosting-dressed cheek and taste the bittersweetness of her first birthday without me. When I saw mommies instinctively kiss their babies, I'd scowl and think, *You have no clue how lucky you are*. Some days, I felt the longing would kill me.

After a few weeks in Fair Oaks, I made a friend, a doe-eyed cutie with bangs and straight blonde hair who could pass for Barbie's little sister, Skipper. I told her I'd given a baby girl up for adoption and shared how much I missed her. It felt good to have a friend to confide in—if I mentioned it to Mama, she'd cry.

That summer, Skipper and I spent most days slathered in Hawaiian Tropic suntan oil. She, in her baby-blue gingham bikini, turned golden brown. I wore a one-piece to hide my wrinkly tummy and was surprised that my pale white skin browned right up like many of the people we saw in Tijuana.

Unfortunately, Skipper broadcast the juice about the new girl. By the first day of school, rumors swirled. I'd supposedly had three abortions and given up two kids. The boys wanted to kiss my ass and the girls wanted to kick it. After Skipper's betrayal, I kept my grief to myself.

During the first week of school, a group of girls invited me to join them for lunch. They told me some cute blond water polo jock liked me. I was excited to make friends and was curious about the boy. A day later, while I was perusing the dessert aisle, the girls I'd had lunch with the day before passed me and sat with girls who threw hateful looks my way.

I chose a seat at the far end of the cafeteria to avoid being a reject in the crowded courtyard and pushed my tater tots around. I was the last to dump my tray and went outside to wait for the bell to ring. Soon, I noticed a group of at least six girls heading my way. A couple of them were my former lunch friends, but they didn't look friendly.

A tough-looking girl I'd never seen before stepped forward and shoved me. "Monica, you know you're nothing but a fucking slut!" With another shove, she yelled even louder. "You're nothing but a fucking whore!" I felt the open mouths and silent stares of half the student body.

After almost being a virgin and spending six months with Saint Mama, I yearned to be a classy girl, but this bitch wouldn't stop. With each push, I wanted more than anything to shut her up. I held my clenched fists tightly to my sides.

How many times could I stand to hear her call me a slut and a whore? How many times had those words already rung in my ears? I couldn't take it anymore and she wasn't going to relent, so I did something I'd never done before: I turned to walk away. A second later, something sweet and mushy went up my nose and into my eyes. Although I couldn't see, I heard them laughing. "Look at the whore now!"

It took a second to register that someone had smashed me in the face with the piece of banana cream pie I'd eyed in the lunch line. I never turned back. Somehow, I found my way to the small washroom behind the cafeteria.

I'd just wanted to make friends. Instead, I was hiding in the bathroom, sobbing as I rinsed my face and sticky hair. When I stood and looked in the mirror, I saw the upside-down faces of all the girls I'd hurt back in Anchorage. I'd just gotten some of what I deserved.

I soon learned the tough girl and her crew had been put up to it by a monster cookie named Beatrice. Apparently, Beatrice had a crush on the boy who liked me. She had at least six inches and twenty pounds on me, but she wasn't tubby—just a big girl. She had black hair with twin white strips in the front. She swore like a truck driver, lived in a rich neighborhood, and pushed her weight around like a bull.

Practically Still a Virgin

Beatrice and her friends threatened to jump me after school, blocked my way in the halls, and harassed me at every turn. Meanwhile, I dated the cute boy of her dreams.

Midway through the year, I was in the bathroom when she banged the door open. Enraged, she yelled, "Get out of my way, you fucking whore!" Then she pushed me so hard that I slammed into the wall. The next thing I remember is someone yelling, "Stop her! She's gonna kill her!" I came to on top of Beatrice, her lovely long hair wrapped in my fingers as I bashed her nasty head into the tile floor. We were both suspended, but no one bothered me after that.

I eventually found my place and rode the line between jock chick and head chick. I enjoyed the best of dating athletes and hanging out on the front lawn between classes, smoking cigarettes and selling joints. School was working out just fine.

COUGAR

After graduation, I began saving for a car by working on commission in a hip clothing boutique within walking distance of our house, inside the nearby mall. One afternoon, Daddy walked into the store just as I hung a pair of cuffed flares on a dressing room door. He'd never visited me at work before and my heart softened to see him. He was excited like he used to get back in Anchorage when he was in the middle of a big business deal. I hadn't seen him like that for a long time. "Sweetheart, I found the perfect car for you."

I knew he was talking about the used car lot where he'd bought an ugly brown Plymouth Valiant a few months earlier. I groaned internally, knowing it would be some dorky-ass car, but I didn't want to let him down.

"I'll pick you up after work," he said.

When we arrived, the lot owner pointed to a vehicle sitting next to the building. I thought there must be some mistake. He opened the door of a forest-green two-door, four-on-the-floor 1967 Cougar with fat tires, high-rise manifold, Holley four-barrel carburetor, and a glasspack muffler. My heart raced when I envisioned how cool I'd be in that muscle car.

Practically Still a Virgin

The three of us got in for a test drive. When I put it in gear and tapped the gas, the car leapt and scared the crap out of me. I had no idea how to drive a vehicle with such power, but there was no way I was going to let on that I didn't.

I spun it through the hilly, narrow, and winding village neighborhood. I scared the shit out of both myself and the lot owner as I tried to keep it on the road. He later said he never went on another test drive. My driving didn't bother Daddy, though.

I forked out the $700 and headed home in my new hot rod. My arrival was announced long before I pulled up to the house. Mama about croaked when she realized the sound was her daughter in her new car. That car spoke volumes about what Daddy thought of me.

I was relieved to have a job and wheels. When I'd needed to borrow money, ask Mama for a ride, or use the car, I always paced, wringing my hands and rehearsing my words to avoid her condemnation, which always hurt. She'd look down her nose at me and scoff. "Oh, you would, would you?" However, Tim was granted whatever he asked for while I was left feeling unworthy. She didn't always reject my requests, but I often went without to avoid risking feeling bad.

During this time, Daddy made many trips to Mexico for laetrile. He'd become fond of the doctor and believed he was curing his cancer. On his last trip, Dr. Ernesto Contreras recommended a cystoscope and celebrated that the cancer was almost gone. When Daddy asked why he still had blood in his urine, the doctor assured him the cancer was just sloughing off—not to worry.

Mama finally convinced him to consult a local doctor, who discovered the tumor now filled his bladder and had metastasized throughout his body. Daddy became despondent, not only from the prognosis but because he'd been betrayed by a man he'd trusted. I felt sorry for him and wanted to snap that doctor's neck.

Daddy tried herbs and a natural doctor, but in the end, he began chemo infusions that made him severely ill. He said he was going to beat it, but I dreaded what was coming. I remembered Carol, the girl in Anchorage with the prosthetic leg and blonde wig. She never got better.

WEIGHT OF DREAD

Daddy's suffering came to an end in January of 1977. He was only sixty-one but looked ancient. I was nineteen and hardly ever home because I couldn't bear to see or hear him in pain. The song "You Should Be Dancing" by the Bee Gees had just come out and I stayed away by using my fake ID to go disco dancing with my friends at local nightclubs. Later, I felt all-consuming guilt because I'd abandoned him due to my selfish weakness.

When I arrived home one night, Mama was playing solitaire at the kitchen table. I came home early—before midnight—because we had to pick Daddy up from the hospital the next day, which was always exhausting. I was standing over her when the phone rang.

Earlier that day, my parents were on the freeway, heading home after looking at property. Daddy never let go of the delusion that he would soon be back in the moneymaking business. Suddenly, he was struck with excruciating pain. He screamed and thrashed around the front seat, opened the window, and hung out up to his waist. Mama tried desperately to keep the car on the road while she pulled at his coat. He even tried to climb over the back seat to escape the pain.

He suffered for almost two hours before he was admitted to the hospital and given narcotics. Daddy had been sleeping comfortably when Mama left him. I was relieved that I hadn't been with them—it was torturous enough just hearing about his suffering. At the same time, I was ashamed that I'd rather Mama live with that memory than me.

I froze as she answered the phone. "Hello?" There was a pause. "Oh no."

It was the tone people use when somebody dies. My heart dropped.

Then, in a relieved voice, she said, "Oh ... gooooood."

My heart quickened. Maybe he hadn't died after all.

But he had. The nurse said he didn't suffer and passed away in his sleep. I was relieved he wouldn't be in pain anymore but numb with shock that he was gone. It had been only three years since we pulled into the driveway.

The following morning, I wasn't fully awake yet when I was overcome with the crushing weight of dread. I didn't know why at first, but when I opened my eyes, I remembered. Daddy died. It was the same feeling I'd had when I woke up in the hospital the morning after giving birth to Mary Monica. Both times, I couldn't eat for days.

I was inconsolable at Daddy's funeral. None of my friends attended, so I was surprised when Skipper, the gossip, showed up at my door holding an apple pie. Later, one of my friends said she didn't think I cared because it seemed like I hated him.

I had recurring nightmares where he was alive and healthy. I was so happy. It was all a mistake and he wasn't dead—but then he was diagnosed with cancer and had to go through it all over again.

Between losing Daddy and relinquishing Mary Monica, I had plenty of pain to numb. In the two years following his death, I looked for him in nightclubs and drank too much Scotch whiskey. It's a miracle I didn't kill myself or someone else on the twenty-mile drive home from the clubs. I remember coming to once on the Marconi Curve—a narrow stretch of freeway where fatalities were common—while covering an eye to block the double vision.

During that time, I had one crappy sales job and one abusive, cheating boyfriend after another. In the mornings, I'd regain consciousness and shower. I'd be so hungover I'd lie on the floor to blow-dry my hair. To quell the dizziness, hand tremors, and nausea, I'd drink Johnnie Walker Black Label from a coffee mug on my drive to work. Mama began to worry about my drinking and complained that I was never home.

ALMA

At twenty-one, I moved in with Danny. Looking back, I can see that I cared about him but wasn't in love. He filled the void that Daddy left—that is until he got sloshed, which he often did. He embarrassed me when he became a braggart and flirted with women. Having one lush in a relationship was enough, so I quit drinking.

A year into our relationship, I read an article about the Adoptees Liberty Movement Association, a group that helped adoptees search for their parents. Danny was supportive and attended ALMA meetings with me. There, I met an older couple, Charles and Millie, who'd helped their adopted daughter find her first family. I hoped ALMA would still be around when Mary Monica turned eighteen.

Under Charles and Millie's tutelage, and with Mama's encouragement, I strategized a plan and set up a notebook to organize my research in. Then, I began searching. I still have the navy-blue three-ring binder bulging with tabs and correspondence.

The year 1980 was a time before the Internet, open adoption records, and open minds. My original birth certificate was sealed, and I was incensed to be denied the most basic of human rights: the truth of my origin. Still, I knew I'd been adopted from a foster home in Edmonton when I was almost four months old. That was something. And I still had access to my adoption order, which listed my original name—the name my mother gave me. The name she spoke with her lips, the name she wrote with her own hand. I was Gloria Debra Reed.

It had been seven years since I was pregnant with Mary Monica and first saw the document containing non-identifying information about my parents. I filed it in my search binder under the tab "facts." It was the only thing tethering me to my origin. I knew my mother came from a large Catholic family, the Reeds, and had six brothers but no sisters. I also knew I was French and Irish. I assumed she gave me up because she wasn't married, the same reason I'd given up Mary Monica. I also thought she might share my name, Gloria.

After sending copious letters with countless dead ends, I contacted the Edmonton library to obtain phone book listings. I hoped one of my uncles might remain in Edmonton. I called each Reed with a made-up story because I didn't want to cause problems for the family if my birth and adoption were a secret. I also worried family members would provide misinformation and block me from finding my mother if they knew the truth.

"Hello, I'm Monica Hall calling from California. I'm doing genealogy research. My grandfather told me I have distant relatives in Edmonton with the last name of Reed. Do you mind if I ask a few questions?" All the responses were friendly, so I continued. "My grandfather told me the Reeds are Catholic and there were six boys and one girl in the family. They would be somewhere in their fifties now. Are you from that family? Or do you know that family?" Without exception, each person I spoke to was welcoming and helpful—but none were related to my mother.

I called all the Reeds in Edmonton one morning, approximately sixty in all, but some didn't answer. In the evening, I went back to the list. I was at my desk with the phone pressed to my ear when, in a Canadian accent, a man said, "Yah ... there were six boys and one girl in our family." I stood to take a breath. I was talking to my *flesh-and-blood* uncle.

He was friendly but asked if I could call back in a few days because he had company. I wanted to ask if it was okay to call the very next day, but I was afraid he might become suspicious.

I didn't know what to do next and immediately called Charles and Millie for advice. Charles suggested I get my uncle to agree to as many facts as I knew during our next call. If he denied my birth, I could come back with, "But you agreed that the women in your family have brown hair and blue eyes and are about five-foot-five. You also said your family was Catholic, and there are six boys and one girl in your family."

I lay awake that night as every possible scenario crop-dusted my mind. Would my uncle deny my birth? Would I soon hear my mother's voice? What did she look like? Did she think about me? Would she cry when she found out I'd contacted her brother? Did her family know about me? I also imagined Mary Monica searching for me. I knew she'd have similar questions and feel the same anticipation.

I called back the next evening. After some brief chitchat, I said, "Pat, I haven't been completely honest. Does the name Gloria Debra Reed mean anything to you?"

He paused a moment. "No?"

"Well, I'm Gloria Debra Reed, and with all the information you've given me, I believe your sister is my natural mother. I was given up for adoption."

Practically Still a Virgin

My heart was in my throat. He was silent for a moment before saying, "Hold on." I later learned he'd set the phone down to ask his wife if she knew anything about my birth. As I waited, my mind raced. Where did he go? What was he doing? Was he running away? Was he thinking up a lie? My mother was so close. She couldn't slip away from me now.

After what seemed like an eternity, he returned to the phone. In a matter-of-fact way, and with a playful rhyming cadence, he said, "Evidently ... I'm your uncle." I'd never felt so elated in my life. Nothing compared to the feeling of knowing my mother was in sight.

For years, I'd dreamed of meeting her and asking questions—most importantly, *why?* But my uncle told me it wouldn't be possible. My mother, Ida, had passed away from a brain aneurysm when she was thirty, leaving behind my three young siblings. She hadn't given me her name after all.

My heart jumped into my throat. The excitement and anticipation I'd felt moments before turned to disbelief. How could that be? I'd read the adoption papers countless times, looking for clues about what she'd been thinking when she signed them, imagining what she looked like and what she'd say when we finally met. I'd felt she was within reach when I was pregnant, preparing to give her granddaughter up, and needed her to show me the way. I also thought I'd felt her imagining me blowing out my candles on my sixteenth birthday, like I had with Mary Monica for the past seven years. I was in shock. All that I'd hoped, dreamed of, and yearned for was impossible. She'd already been gone eight years when I gave birth to her granddaughter.

During that same call to my uncle, I described my features and told him my adoption papers said my father was French, a flagman on the railroad.

"That's not your father. Your father is Joe Connelly," he said.

161

"Who's Joe Connelly?"

"The man she was dating. He has to be your father."

"What about the Frenchman she put on the paper, the one who worked for the railroad?"

"Oh, no. That man can't be your father. He's dark ... he's ... *dark* dark. He's black."

I learned that "black" was commonly used for very dark-skinned indigenous people.

Since my early teens, I'd wanted to be American Indian, like Kelly. Through Uncle Pat, I discovered both my parents had Cree heritage. Europeans gave us the name Cree, but we call ourselves *nêhiyaw*.

I learned my maternal grandmother (Granny) was also Cree, but my maternal grandfather (Grandad) was a white man with English and Irish heritage. I'm told he was a jolly drunk and rotten husband who could "sell ice to Eskimos." It seemed my drinking, high forehead, light skin, sense of humor, and gift of gab came from him.

Ida had listed my real father on the papers but omitted his indigenous heritage. Back then, dark-skinned, indigenous people, like my father, had the lowest social status. That might explain Uncle Pat's reluctance to accept a dark-skinned man as my father. Or perhaps he didn't know she'd been dating my father and only knew of her relationship with Joe, who was Irish, fair-skinned, and better matched the physical description I gave of myself when Pat and I first made contact.

Uncle Pat knew my father. He called him Chaps, a nickname he'd picked up on the railroad because he constantly used ChapStick. Pat didn't tell me at the time, but his given name was Harvey Gilbert Letendre. Once Pat realized Chaps was my father rather than Joe, he said, "Yah, leave it up to me. I see him at the bar and I'll talk to him." I was puzzled by his reluctance to give me Chaps's full name so I could call him myself. Pat beat around the bush, hinting something about my father's wife and having to tread lightly.

Over the next few months, Uncle Pat visited the bar a few times, trying to catch my father alone or at least out of his wife's earshot, but she was always by his side. I tried not to bug him, but as weeks passed, Pat either felt sorry for me or got tired of having nothing to report. One evening, he scooted onto the barstool next to Chaps and tried to be sly without alerting his wife. But she knew something was up and told him, "Anything you have to say to Chaps you can say to me."

After that, Uncle Pat finally gave me my father's number. During our first conversation, Chaps stumbled over his words and his voice was unsteady. I later learned he was very shy. He told me that Granny, Ida's mother, had called him when I was born to inform him he had a daughter. When he and his wife visited a café or saw a young woman around town, he'd say, "I wonder if she could be my daughter?"

CHAPS

Chaps was extraordinarily handsome, worked for the railroad, and was of Cree and French ancestry, as was his wife, Helen. So was my mother, but Ida had her father's fair skin, light hair, and blue eyes.

As a teen, I'd been envious of Kelly's American Indian ancestry, but with the invention of home DNA kits, Kelly found she only had European ancestry. It turned out I was the one with indigenous heritage.

In the 1950s, it was common for agencies to alter an indigenous child's ethnicity for closed adoptions because of racism. When I was adopted, I presented as Caucasian because my dark hair had fallen out. I was also light-skinned like my mother and my Irish grandad. In childhood photos of Ida with her brothers and cousins, she was the blonde white kid in a sea of dark heads.

I sometimes wonder if my Cree ancestry fuels my deep need to know and understand my roots. Prior to European contact and colonization, the Cree were nomadic people who followed seasonal migration of the buffalo and had a rooted bond with their extended families. Even today, my birth family keeps close contact, though they live hours apart, with frequent visits and family reunions—unlike my adopted family. We were isolated in Alaska, far away from California, the birthplace of my adoptive parents and their limited smattering of relations.

Of Ida's four living brothers, Uncle Pat was the only one who hadn't moved to Vancouver. If I'd waited a year to search, his name would have also disappeared from the white pages.

Mama was highly annoyed when my boyfriend, Danny, said, "Now that Monica knows who she really is, we can get married." She took this to mean I had previously been a non-person, not realizing that's exactly how I felt. Danny understood what Mama didn't: adoption meant I lacked identity because I didn't know where and to whom I belonged. Danny promised he'd take me to Canada to meet my family on our honeymoon. I couldn't wait to hightail it up north.

I began exchanging letters with my relatives and immediately connected with Susan, the child Ida had seventeen months after my relinquishment. Her full lips and mouth make her look like our mother. When I show her photo, people often say, "You can tell you're sisters." Every time I hear it, I glow. We began calling each other "Sis" early on; forty years later, it still gives me joy. All my life I'd wished for a sister to trade clothes and share secrets with. Now, I had one. Actually, between Ida and Chaps, I had three sisters. I also had four brothers.

All I could think of was getting to Canada—letters and phone calls weren't cutting it. I needed to bask in my family members' mannerisms, identify similarities, and touch my flesh-and-blood relatives.

I was more excited about the promised honeymoon in Canada than I was about marrying Danny. I set the wedding date, sent invitations, and bought an old-fashioned lace gown and veil at a secondhand store. This surprises me now because such places smell of hard times and make me queasy, yet that's where I chose to buy a dress—a subconscious choice, for sure. Had I been marrying a man I adored, I doubt I would've chosen a Goodwill gown.

A week before the wedding, Danny came home insanely drunk—again. I told him I was calling it off, but he promised to quit drinking for good. I knew he was full of shit, but I was looking forward to meeting my family on our honeymoon and was too embarrassed to tell guests I was backing out.

I should've been more embarrassed marrying a drunken fool. My wedding day was an omen. For one thing, my hairdo was hideous. Between that and the dress, I resembled a pilgrim. Before walking down the aisle, I lay in a pew with my feet propped up on the backrest above my head to stop myself from vomiting and passing out. After the wedding, Danny never again mentioned taking me to Canada.

CAMERA CREW

Shortly after I married Danny, Chaps stepped off the plane in Sacramento to meet me. A news station had contacted the local ALMA chapter for a series on adoption, and ALMA put them in touch with me to film our reunion. They would later interview us at my home.

Chaps didn't know a camera crew waited at the gate. His wife, Helen, told him the secret just as he stood to depart the plane. He was nervous even before that. Unlike me, he was shy, soft-spoken, and humble. It was hard to get a read on him because he was so quiet and seemed to feel unworthy of me. Did he feel guilty for not being in my life?

In pictures from his youth, he looked like Elvis. Women swooned, and some asked to take his photo, which always embarrassed him. Even thirty years later, when he was in his eighties, he looked youthful; I witnessed women in their fifties hitting on him. He was exactly how Ida described him in the paperwork: *very* polite and good-looking.

From the beginning, his wife was usually the one who answered the phone, called, wrote, and signed cards. When I called, Chaps was often gone on a "run" with the Canadian National Railway So, most of what I learned about my new family was relayed through Helen. In years to come, she always kept communication open and made sure to ask about Mama and Tim. Even so, going through old files decades later, I saw Chaps's signature on the money orders that arrived for Christmas and birthdays.

During our first meeting, at the airport with the camera crew, I wore my royal-blue linen jacket with matching skirt and tasteful floral silk blouse. In the scratchy VHS recording,

Chaps & Helen taken shortly after my birth. She is pregnant with my half brother Kane

Practically Still a Virgin

I'm jabbering with the reporter, tapping my foot, and twisting back and forth toward the gate. I remember my thoughts. *Will we hug? Will we look more alike when I see him in person? Will I feel the connection I've been searching for? Will he like me? Will he be proud?*

As the plane approached, my heart was pinged with tiny arrows. After all these years of wondering about my origin, I was going to meet my *real* father. I stood at the gate and peered down the tunnel for his dark head. When I saw him turn the corner, I waved. We made eye contact, but my excitement deflated when he hung his head and hunched his shoulders. It would be years before I realized he did this because he saw the cameraman and not because I disappointed him.

He looked terrified and shrank behind Helen as they walked up the ramp. He grabbed the back of her shoulder like a child playing choo-choo train.

I was nervous. After a brief and awkward hug, more like a shoulder-butt, I said, "How are you?" I later searched him for common features, like I had with Mary Monica, but all I found were my long second toe and his lips with a cupid bow, two peaks on the top lip. I'd noticed these same features when I examined my baby in the hospital seven years earlier. Still, I wasn't disappointed. I adored the sweet, bashful, and kind man. He was everything I wasn't, and I admired his humility. Chaps left most of the talking to Helen, the family's driving force. Although it wasn't her nature to be warm, she was thoughtful and friendly.

I didn't feel the immediate connection I'd hoped for. Instead, I felt bad that he was terrified by the camera crew and the attention. Had I been waiting to meet my birth mother instead, I know I would have felt differently. Although I loved and adored him, he seemed like a consolation prize.

I took Chaps and Helen to meet Mama and Tim. Mama was happy for me, but having them all in the same room was awkward. Chaps felt insecure and struggled to make conversation, so we didn't stay long.

Prior to their visit, Helen had sent a large manila envelope of family pictures. Photos of my sister Jenny caught my eye. She was exotically beautiful with dark eyes, velvety brown skin, and my exact crooked teeth. We also shared our father's lips with a defined cupid bow. She was even more beautiful than Cher, who had fascinated me in the '70s, long before I knew I was a "half-breed." I wondered if I'd ever get a similar envelope filled with my daughter's childhood photos to fill in the years I'd missed.

A few days after our meeting at the airport, the camera crew arrived at my house to complete the adoption series. They set up lights in my living room and wired us for our interview. Chaps sat next to me on my sofa, his mouth so parched from fear that the recording captures the sound of his tongue sticking to his lips. On the other hand, I was poised like I was about to be interviewed by Johnny Carson.

Chaps and Helen said Ida's family looked down on Chaps and his extended family. The Reeds felt they were superior to a man who lived on the wrong side of the lake, whose relations were darker, and who had my father's last name.

My first parents' story reminded me of *The Hatfields and the McCoys*, rooted in a real Civil War–era family feud with a Romeo-and-Juliet narrative at its middle. I liked to fancy myself part of that romantic story rather than believe my mother gave me away because she didn't want me.

Decades later, I asked elders why the Letendre name had a bad reputation. They shared the legend of a relative who, generations back, was associated with a murder he *didn't* commit. The bad feeling stuck for over a hundred years; even today, the name remains somewhat tarnished. Maybe some of the relations fought and caused trouble because they were living up to their name. Perhaps that's where I got my scrapping spirit.

When I met Chaps, he worked for the railroad, as did his oldest son, Kane—the baby Helen carried while Ida was pregnant with me. She married Chaps about a year after my brother was born. Kane was only six months my junior. It seemed strange to have a sibling so close in age, a brother with whom I shared time in utero, yet in a different womb.

Ten days after Chaps and Helen went home to Canada, Danny began staying out all night and cheating. We'd been married a month. Years later, I cut him out of my wedding photos and regretted that we divorced instead of getting an annulment, and I had to count him as one of my husbands.

ELEPHANT-SIZED TEARS

A few years before Mama died, she gave me her journals even though she knew I was writing my memoir. I couldn't bring myself to read them until two years after she passed and when I did, I wondered why she gave them to me. Maybe she'd forgotten the things she'd written. Or was there a part of her that wanted me to know how much I'd hurt her?

I was reading about her experiences in 1980—shortly before Chaps visited Sacramento. I was shocked by the depth of her internal struggle. I guess I hadn't noticed because I'd been in the honeymoon phase, a term that's often used to describe adoptees in early reunion.

I was at Mama's one afternoon while her friend Mrs. Burney was visiting. I was talking about my birth family discovery and said, "Chaps, my father," so Mrs. Burney would know who I was referring to. The next day, Mama was angry. When she repeated what Mrs. Burney had said after I left, Mama matched her indignant tone: "Well! I was under the impression that Howard was her father." For years I hated that woman for trying to come between me and Mama. Decades later, Tim also relayed how Mrs. Burney would drop by uninvited and intoxicated, saying things like, "How well do you really know that daughter of yours? Get their address and send them the bill since they're her family now."

At the time I thought Mama's anger was irrational. Had I been more mature and less self-centered, I would've realized how sensitive she was. I imagine I said something like "You and Daddy are my only parents. I love you more than anyone in the whole world, and nothing and no one could ever change that!" I'd assumed she knew this and would be happy for me because she was my mom and had encouraged my search.

I've read about adult adoptees who feel pain and guilt when their adoptive parents elevate their own insecurity above their children's wholeness and peace of mind. I was blessed I didn't have a parent like that. Mama mostly purged her feelings into her journal: *Monica received pictures of her father. His birthday is June 13th and he is 49. She is sending him a Father's Day and birthday card. For Howard's sake, I deeply resented that and I told her so .... I guess I'm just petty and jealous sometimes, and possessive too, and I didn't like her calling that man "father."* Her conflict went on for thirteen pages.

She wrote: *Would I have wanted to take her as a daughter knowing she would turn-coat when she was grown?*

Would having her in her growing-up years, with all the problems and heartaches involved, have been enough reward for me?

Ah, yes! Give her to us. That will be fulfillment enough! When she is grown, she will be lovely, well-mannered and bright. You will be proud of her now and you may take her to yourselves to enjoy the results of our efforts.

The answer is no. I would not have taken her on those terms. Not as my daughter.

A large part of the fulfillment in raising children is seeing them grown in happy rewarding lives of their own. If that part is to be chopped out of a parent's life, it isn't worth the effort. The only com-

pensation would be the parent's own growth and all the joys and sorrows of raising a child.

Reading her words, my mouth dropped open and I froze with disbelief. She would not have adopted me? She was my mom! She'd erase me just like that? No first steps, no bedtime stories, singing at the piano, praying the Rosary? Did she ever love me unconditionally? Her words were clear. She said that if she had to do it again, she wouldn't have adopted me.

It's incredible that she could admit this, even to herself. Mama must have been really overwhelmed with feelings that were impossible to ignore. Feelings that were fueled by Mrs. Burney and her own fears and insecurities. But Mama's words stabbed my heart. Her love suddenly felt conditional—a transaction dependent on my continued loyalty. But my loyalty wasn't the real issue. I *was* loyal, I just wasn't from her womb. And I couldn't solve that problem for her, no matter what I did.

Mama had been gone nearly three years when I read her words. Her voice was so clear and her conflict so loud that I cried elephant-sized tears.

EDMONTON

After I left Danny, I began drinking again. At my apartment, the party often began and ended with cocaine, Scotch, and jugs of Almaden wine. I kept the door revolving with a variety of crappy sales jobs and party-loving roommates. Nightclubs went by the wayside for a neighborhood hole-in-the-wall with a pool table. Mostly, I was killing time until I could meet Chaps's kids and then head to Vancouver to meet Ida's family.

When my high school friends were beginning careers, buying homes, and starting families, I was focusing on the next party. My boyfriends were controlling, and when we were drunk, we were both jealous and abusive. One broke my arm and another my cheekbone after I clocked him for coming home from the bar late. They were also about as reliable as my vehicle and employment attendance.

My dented Toyota Corolla had no carpet, floor mats, or air conditioning, and the insurance was in Mama's name. I drove around in that hotbox schlepping coffee and Honor Snacks in blazing hundred-degree heat. I'd park and walk door to door, cold-calling on shadeless warehouses and industrial parks, trying to get businesses to sign up for our coffee delivery service and take my Honor Snack tray.

Selling the coffee service wasn't so bad, but getting rid of the boxes of melting candy bars was something else. I'd approach the roll-up warehouse doors in my fetching skirt, wilting hair, nylons, and heels carrying that damn tray. As I approached, I saw the workers' wary looks: *she's hot, but she's carrying that fucking tray.* I'd say something like, "How you guys doing today? How do you handle this heat? I'm melting, and so are these snacks. How 'bout you take them off my hands?"

They'd indulge me while I tried to talk them into taking the cardboard tray. Everyone knew the drill. The box contained a slot for change but always came up short when the snack truck arrived to refill and collect the money. The honor system didn't work.

Finally, at the end of August, Chaps sent me a plane ticket and I quit my job. A few weeks later, he picked me up from the airport. His hair looked different than it had when he'd visited California. When he'd gotten off the plane to meet me, it had looked almost like a pompadour. He still combed it back, but it was no longer puffy. On their visit to California when Helen announced he'd gotten a perm, he hunched his shoulders in an embarrassed, bashful laugh straight out of *Snow White and the Seven Dwarfs.* I now wonder if he got it special for our reunion.

As we drove north from the airport, the sky was the largest I'd ever seen. Puffy, mammoth-sized clouds white as ribbon pushed against limitless blue. I felt so tiny. Then I noticed there were no mountains. Prairie stretched as far as I could see. It felt foreign. In Anchorage, the Chugach Mountains were always watching, and Fair Oaks had rolling hills within canopies of trees, the Sierra Nevada on the horizon. Yet the prairie landscape felt familiar at the same time. It was, after all, where my ancestors had hunted buffalo.

Practically Still a Virgin

After we'd been driving for almost thirty minutes, the capital city of Edmonton, on the North Saskatchewan River, burst from the vast flatland like an origami popup. As we approached, Chaps took a detour to show me the sights along the river. I tried to show interest because he was so proud being my tour guide, but all I could think of was meeting my siblings.

We drove for another twenty minutes. It was getting dark when we pulled in front of a simple mid-century house. It sat along the frontage road of a main thoroughfare and had lava-rock siding. There were no trees in the small, grassy front yard.

Chaps carried my bags. I followed him up the steps and thought, *I hope they like me.* I gulped as he opened the door. A beige velvet sofa with a rust-colored print faced me, and to my right was a large china cabinet filled with shiny black-and-teal pottery. The living room was immaculate.

Helen emerged from the kitchen and greeted me with a hug. A second later, I heard footsteps on the stairs: my siblings. Jenny was even more beautiful than in her pictures. Kane had the same black hair and eyes as Jenny and Chaps but his nose was crooked, like a prizefighter. We stood in awkward silence. I wouldn't meet my younger brothers until the next morning.

Chaps stepped in and said, "This is your sister, Monica. Why don't you guys go to the bar?" Helen agreed and shooed us out the door before I'd even been shown around. It seemed odd for parents to encourage introductions by drinking.

We sat at a round pub table while listening to a hard rock band. Kane wore a black corduroy button-down shirt. The top three buttons were undone, with just a glimpse of his hairless chest showing. His light jeans were pressed down the center, and he wore an engraved silver belt buckle. I learned the boxer's nose came from his Golden Gloves days.

Jenny was a twenty-year-old single mother who had her own house-cleaning business, a crew of women working for her, and an apartment where she lived with her three-year-old son. I thought, if I'd had the chance, maybe I could've supported myself and my child, too.

There was very little conversation and they seemed to communicate without talking, which was unnerving and made me feel separate from them. They seemed content to hold their beers and listen to the band, but I wanted to get to know them. I wondered if they even liked me. Soon I realized being reserved was their nature. Discos were sacrilege in these parts, but I embraced the pub culture. It was all about AC/DC, pool halls, and partying in the basement. We certainly had that in common.

The next day, I met my brothers Royce (fourteen) and Darcy (seventeen). They, too, were reserved and had the same silent communication style as Kane and Jenny, but still, my heart grew two sizes being among my four siblings. I loved passing them on the stairs as we ran back and forth from the TV room to the kitchen for snacks.

At the bottom of the stairs was a laundry room with a huge chest freezer where Helen stored meat. We never had anything like that in my family. Nor did we have a place in the basement where we could hang out with our friends, watch hockey games, smoke cigarettes, drink beer, or sneak the occasional joint. At the far end of the room sat a bar with a red Naugahyde rail. Smoked mirror squares covered a wall decorated with Edmonton Oilers banners and Budweiser signs, like in a real tavern.

There was always a pot simmering on the stove. The kitchen counters were worn with use, and so were the cabinets. It was a small two-bedroom, one-bath house but they made it work with rooms in the basement. I loved that none of the plates, flatware, or glasses matched, and instead of Tupperware, they used plates to cover leftovers—if there were any.

At Chaps's house, there were no 6:00 p.m. sit-down dinners with "mind your manners" and "put your napkin in your lap." It was every man for himself, and you had to get to the food before it was gone. I was mesmerized by the after-dinner choreography where one sibling grabbed a broom and another hovered over the sink while someone else wiped up and put the food away, then moved on to dry dishes and stack them in the cupboard.

This was unlike my upbringing where Mama made dinner, I set the table and washed dishes, and Tim did whatever he wanted. I also marveled at the skill with which my siblings whirled a paring knife around a potato. I couldn't manage the knife, so I bought a peeler. I can still feel the warmth of inclusion that came from standing over the sink and peeling potatoes with my siblings. All I'd ever wanted was to be part of the stew.

On the second night, Chaps and Helen took me uptown to show me the city. Although I'd never get to meet my mother, these people had known her. As Chaps drove, I leaned forward with my arms on the back of his seat and asked, "What was Ida like?" I leaned in close so I wouldn't miss a word. Helen, unable to mask her disdain, said, "She was one of those party girls who slept around town."

She didn't mean to hurt me, but the letdown was severe. As Ida's daughter, I felt the familiar pang of criticism. Had she thrown me from the moving car, I couldn't have felt more injured. I don't think Chaps was seeing them at the same time, but Helen was three months along with Kane when I was born, so that probably caused resentment.

I wanted to crawl under the seat and cover my head, but instead, I shamelessly matched her judgmental tone and said something like, "Oh, she did?" For years, I felt guilty for betraying Ida so Helen would include me in her family.

Chaps said, "Your grandmother called when you were born and wanted me to come to the hospital, but I didn't go." He said this like it was unreasonable to be asked to see his daughter. Helen nodded and added, her voice heavy with resentment, "They didn't want anything to do with Chaps. Your grandmother only wanted him to pay the hospital bill." She said this as if refusing to take responsibility for his daughter justified his absence.

My throat swelled in a wave of rejection. I wanted to ask, *Wasn't I important enough to pay the bill for? Didn't you want to see me?* Had I possessed more courage, I would have asked these questions. Instead, I sat back and pushed down tears.

I think Chaps's refusal to claim me was a result of his laid-back personality, Granny's disapproval, and Helen's pregnancy and strong opinions. But I still couldn't understand his actions when I was born. At least he acted differently later on. Because he knew how important it was to me, he went through the red tape of requesting Ida's death certificate and giving his permission as my father to release my original birth certificate and sealed adoption records, the ones with Ida's signature. He also told me I was conceived on Halloween.

While I was staying with Chaps, Uncle Pat and I also spent many evenings belly to the bar drinking good Scotch. He was my mudhook, more than I'd imagined an uncle could be. For the first time in my life, I felt adored, safe, and accepted without judgment.

When I asked Uncle Pat about his sister, he said she was kind, generous, fun-loving, and liked to play jokes. But he didn't tell me any stories.

THE DUPLEX

When I returned from Canada in 1981, my crappy coffee and Honor Snack job took me back—on the days when I'd actually showed up, I'd made lots of sales. But I rarely had gas in my car and I often asked for a pay advance.

I moved out of the apartment and into a duplex where there were nightly parties. Anyone who could provide cocaine and make a booze run was invited, mostly guys eager to contribute in hopes of getting laid.

Sex was the last thing I wanted when I was partying. All I wanted was more cocaine. We'd stay up late playing cards or dice around my dining room game table. We often tap-tap-tapped on the mirror well past dawn. Not coincidentally, my roommate had a small business selling cocaine out of her bedroom.

Many of my belongings went missing, mostly jewelry that I foolishly kept on my dresser in a porcelain dish that had been a gift from Chaps and Helen. I was either too lazy or too trusting to find better hiding places for my treasures, problematic since some of the people at our parties had gotten into a cheaper drug, crank. When snorted, it sent fire shooting up your nostrils with a wasabi burn to the back of the brain. It caused an intense need for more and kept you up for days. Those people would steal from their own mothers.

I stuck with cocaine and loved it so much, a whole stash wouldn't have lasted me a day. I knew where my roommate hid her inventory, and I sometimes snuck into her room, replacing most of it with baby laxative. Soon, rumor got around that her coke was bunk, which puzzled "us." I've since heard it said that the difference between an alkie and an addict is that they'll both steal your wallet, but the addict will help you look for it.

Burnt out but awake from a night of cocaine and booze, we'd hang blankets over the windows to shut out the morning light. Coked-out partiers littered the hazy living room, chain-smoking and taking hits off a bong, trying desperately to come down.

I hated the feeling of grinding teeth and physical exhaustion, my mind spinning a hundred miles an hour, being awake with the sun coming up for yet another day. The only thing on TV at 4:00 a.m. was the "horse of course" and that curly-haired guy with the paintbrush. I'd loved watching *Mister Ed* as a kid, but in the end, he was my nemesis.

My drinking and drug use had escalated by the winter of 1983, when I was twenty-six, three years after Chaps came to visit me in Sacramento. Mary Monica was ten years old and in fifth grade, the age I was when Daddy's drinking went off the rails. I didn't worry that she'd have a drunk, creepy father like mine—I trusted Sister Clare and was certain she had good parents—but I did worry that I'd never know or be called to her side if something happened to her.

I couldn't imagine what my life would have been like if I'd kept her. Would I be a better woman because I'd have someone to give my love to, someone to live for? Would I spend my nights at PTA meetings instead of partying? Would

I make breakfast in the morning instead of getting queasy at the sight of eggs?

I thought I was hiding my drinking from my family. I was living on my own, and to my knowledge, Mama had never seen me drunk. But decades later, I realized I was wrong. She wrote, *I must admit I am concerned for Monica. She is drinking a lot these days. There is not much I can do for her.*

SAN JUAN CLUB

Some mornings I was so hungover that my coworker, Kevin, with whom I occasionally made sales calls, would take me to some dingy bar so I could get a couple of drinks down.

My rough hangovers were precipitated by nightly visits to the San Juan Club. Cigarette smoke, the crack of pool balls, and the waft of spilled beer composed its charm. Behind the bar hung a backlit mirror in which reflections grew ghostly as the evening progressed. To the left was a short hall with a phone booth at its end. That's where I called for cocaine when I had a good drunk on. The goal was achieving the perfect blend of anesthesia and buzz so I could drink longer. I spent so much time in that bar that I became good enough to play in the women's pool league, and I often played for money.

Rich, the bartender, was middle-aged and weathered from a life of heavy drinking. When I walked in, he'd set a Black Label on the bar before I had a chance to order one. When I was broke, he'd front me until next time. He'd eighty-sixed me for fighting more than once, but I'd just go to a different hole-in-the-wall for a few weeks. When I thought enough time had passed, I'd show up again promising to be a good girl. He'd always let me return but kept a close eye on me.

The women's restroom was tucked in back, by the phone booth, not visible from the bar. Having the bathroom hidden from view was convenient because Rich didn't always know when I was in there kicking some bitch's ass. I'd reverted to my pre–Mary Monica behavior—I'd forgotten my intention to change my fighting ways and be a lady.

Early on, I judged the old men with bulbous noses and bloodshot eyes who bragged about the old days and became more antisocial and belligerent as the evening progressed. But as my drinking accelerated, I sometimes found myself lined up with those old-timers at 6:00 a.m., waiting for the doors to open.

When I wasn't at the San Juan Club, I was partying at home. One night, my roommate's boyfriend brought some crankster friends, one of whom was an Amazonian with straw-bleached hair, tarantula lashes, and bulging cleavage. She was much bigger than Beatrice, who'd attacked me in high school. The Amazonian sneered when we were introduced, then looked through me like I didn't exist. She had six inches on me and outweighed me by at least forty pounds.

The banter was flowing, the ice cubes in the wine glasses were tinkling, and the dice cups were slamming. She'd been giving me the evil eye and throwing sarcastic comments my way for the better part of an hour. I ignored her until my patience waned.

Finally, I'd had enough. I pointed to the door and said, "Get out."

"Fuck you, bitch. Why don't you make me?"

I stood and pushed back my chair. Suddenly, people were moving breakables and lifting my beautiful lamps out of the way as the Amazonian and I careened around the dining room, the living room, and finally the kitchen. This bitch was big and strong. I began to panic that I might get my ass kicked, weakening as the fight went on and on. In the background were shouts and cheers from my roommates and boxer-nosed half-brother, Kane, who was visiting from Canada.

I stood over the Amazonian. I'd knocked her down in a corner of the kitchen and hoped she wouldn't get up. I was exhausted and could hardly lift my arm. Kane yelled, "Monica, hit her again! Kick her!" I could barely draw my foot back but kept going because of the encouragement. Beaten and humiliated, she finally threw in the towel, slunk out of the duplex, and took her lowlife friends with her. Today, I can't think of a scenario where I would have someone like that in my home, let alone be violent with them.

The next day, I arrived at work with scabby knuckles. I could hardly walk or sit, and every muscle hurt from overexertion. My tightwad coworker, Kevin, invited me to lunch, which seemed suspect. Over pizza, he told me I didn't have to live like that anymore. If I stopped drinking, I could have gas in my car and money in the bank. I was hurting from the fight, so my ears were open. He told me how bad his life had been before he sobered up, and he offered to introduce me to women who could help with my drinking problem.

After hearing his pathetic story, I pitied him and understood why *he* stopped drinking, but *I* wasn't that bad. I just needed to get in shape—after all, I'd almost had my ass kicked. I'd go to the gym instead of the bar and all would be well. I'd get dolled up in my *Flashdance* attire to get some male attention, lift weights, and twist with a broomstick over my shoulders to thin my thick aboriginal waist.

The gym was a great replacement for the San Juan Club. I had somewhere to go to fill my loneliness, and I made it home early enough to prepare my clothes and lunch for my kick-ass coffee and Honor Snack job. I always needed a goal or plan—to be going somewhere or doing something. If

Practically Still a Virgin

I wasn't, I felt restless and feared my feelings would bubble up. I couldn't risk letting the darkness out of that box. I'd sit in front of the TV and dine on broiled fish, baked potatoes, and broccoli. I was content and wondered why I hadn't been living this way all along.

One afternoon, a few months after my last visit to the San Juan Club, I got a call from Moe, a bubbly blonde who was new to the bar. She'd heard of my routine and also wanted to get in shape. I was anxious to share my newfound healthy lifestyle and offered to pick her up the next evening at the bar.

As I pulled into the parking lot, I recognized the familiar vehicles, many of which had been intimately acquainted with my fender. The wooden front door with its diamond-shaped window banged when I entered. While my vision adjusted, the syrupy smell was both nauseating and comforting. It reminded me of the relief I felt when I had a cold glass cupped between my palms.

As I pulled a stool next to Moe, I asked, "You ready?"

She nodded. "Yeah, let me finish my glass."

While I grabbed the dice cups, I noticed my reflection in the mirror and admired my slim face, which I attributed to weight loss. Really, the bloat from my overtaxed liver had receded. I winced when I saw my outfit. I'd thought I looked cute when I left the house, but my bare shoulder screamed, *You're a fraud!* A regular called out, "Hey, Rich, can you get Monica a wine?" I wasn't interested in drinking but didn't protest. I was more concerned with my ridiculous getup.

Rich set the glass down. I usually drank Black Label Scotch—it took a lot more wine to get a buzz. I sensed it wasn't smart to drink but thought, *Wine is harmless.* I quickly finished my glass and was ready to go, but Moe wasn't done with hers. I thought, *While I'm waiting, I'll have another. It can't hurt. Two glasses aren't that fattening, and I'll work it off anyway.*

We never made it to the gym.

VANCOUVER

Two years before that fight in my living room, when I was twenty-four, I'd flown to Vancouver to meet Ida's family. My sister Susan and I were already acquainted because she'd visited me in Sacramento after I left Danny. During my trip to Vancouver, she was twenty-two, pregnant, and ready to pop. A wooden cradle filled with folded receiving blankets was sandwiched between her waterbed and wall, and her dresser was filled with baby clothes, some new but many used. She pulled a tiny onesie from a drawer and held it up to show me. I could see she'd done this many times, and I envied her.

For a brief moment, I flashed on what could have been. I pictured a white wicker bassinet skirted in yellow gingham beside my twin bed in Anchorage. Had I brought Mary Monica home, Mama would have bought everything brand new. She hated used things, probably because of her impoverished childhood. As much longing as this vision caused, I still thought I'd "done the right thing" by giving Mary Monica two parents like I'd heard all my life.

On the first night of my visit, Susan took me to meet my brother Casey and my four surviving uncles. (The others had passed, one from a heart attack and the other from a car accident.) Uncle Pat, my anchor, Ida's oldest living brother, had even flown in from Edmonton to attend the reunion party at my youngest uncle's home.

Pat was first to the door and greeted me with a huge hug. Hearing the crack of pool balls and laughter from the other room, I knew I'd found home. Even though I loved Chaps and my siblings, we were so different. I wished I felt the innate connection they had without uttering a word. I could already tell I was more in sync with Ida's family.

From around the corner, someone shouted, "She's here!" In seconds, the entry was full of relatives giving hugs like I'd never known and saying, "Welcome to the family!" I can't remember my family ever hugging, but if we did, it would have been the timid kind that looked like burping a baby. I was embraced like I'd been lost for more than twenty years—which I had been. It was the warmest greeting I'd ever had, and I knew without a doubt I'd be giving Mary Monica a similar welcome one day.

Throughout the party, my uncles hung on my every word. I wondered if it was because my appearance brought a little bit of their sister back to life. I could almost see Ida there among them, laughing, holding a pool cue, and cutting up with the boys. Watching them play pool, laugh, and joke felt so familiar. My identity was flooding in, filling every nook and cranny with warmth, relief, and joy. For the first time in my life, I really belonged.

I was like them, so I was like my mother. The lock of reunion clicked into place. The faces I'd been searching for filled me with laughter, jokes, beers, drinks, and sarcasm that came as easily as honey on toast.

It was my uncles who brought Ida to life—not my siblings or Chaps and Helen. Uncle Donny, who was slim, quiet, and sweet, said my parents got together when they joined him on a double date. Drop-ins at his house were a family tradition, and a pot of coffee was always on the burner. I loved that.

The next day, Susan took me to meet her dad, Ida's husband. As we drove to his girlfriend's home, she warned, "Dad doesn't like many people." I'd heard the same thing from my uncles but thought, *He can't be that bad. I'll win him over.*

Since her father, Tom, was the key to my mother more than anybody else, I could hardly wait. They'd met right after I was born, so he'd know why she gave me up. But as we approached our destination, I sensed my sister's apprehension and began to feel like I was about to have an audience with Don Vito Corleone.

Susan's baby was due any day. I followed behind while she waddled up the walkway and entered the house. Looking back, I can see a freeze-frame of the inhabitants, but the room isn't in focus. Maybe it was a family room or a converted garage. It felt very large, and I felt small.

Tom sat on the sofa. To his left sat my brother Casey, whom I'd met the night before. He was tall, ruggedly handsome, and shy. Thirty years later, he would unexpectedly pull his Harley into my driveway for a week and build a potting bench, grape arbor, and fence while I was at work. He also cleaned my gutters and had dinner ready when I got home.

Tom had dark hair, a receding hairline, and a stern face. At the far end of the room stood two hard-looking men wearing black leather vests—I later learned they were Hells Angels. To their right was their mother: Tom's girlfriend, Evi. She was a marginally attractive, tough-looking middle-aged woman with a hard-set jaw.

I immediately felt like an intruder. Introductions hadn't even been made when one of the biker-looking men said, "It looks like the slut hasn't popped yet."

Stunned, I waited for the retort from either Susan's father or our brother, but it didn't come. All the muscles in my body tensed like they had that day in the school courtyard when that bitch called me a slut. It took the same self-control to not spew the room with expletives.

Fuck you! was on the tip of my tongue for that smug son of a bitch. For Tom and Casey, *What the hell is wrong with you to let him speak like that to your daughter and sister?* But pissing off Tom would have locked the door on Ida, so I kept my mouth shut. Such treatment didn't ruffle Susan, though; it was as if she expected it, which made me sad. I wondered how I would have fared in that family. We didn't stay long.

A day or so later, we visited again. That's when I learned Tom was a wealthy drywall contractor and the loudest, most opinionated, overbearing, bigoted asshole I'd ever met. But I played along, hoping he'd find me deserving of his stories about Ida.

That evening, a few of us sat outside at Evi's house. My disdain for Tom swelled while he accosted the whole neighborhood with his political rants, which included insults like "fucking Yanks." Tom made Archie Bunker look like the Fairy Fucking Godmother, but I nodded in agreement and pretended to hang on his every insult and swear word. I apparently passed the are-you-worthy test because Tom opened up about my mother.

He told me Ida was the middle child, sandwiched between six boys, and was treated like a workhorse. Tom said my mother gave me away so I wouldn't live that same life. As distressing as this was, I clung to it because I wasn't unwanted. She loved me! She was saving me and was so strong in her belief that she was willing to suffer my loss. Tom added, "She would've had to leave you at home with your grandmother and uncles while she went to work."

He also spoke disparagingly about my uncles and Irish grandad, which didn't ruffle me because he didn't have a good opinion about anyone.

The workhorse comment was corroborated a few days later. Granny's sister, Auntie Emily, said, "I felt so sorry for her. She was a lovely person and treated so poorly. I'd sometimes have her stay with me so she could have a break."

When I met Granny, it was hard to believe—she was gentle and loving. Decades later, I understood the disconnect when my own children said about Mama, "Grandma is soooo sweet." I'd quickly retort, "Yeah, but that is *not* the woman who raised me!" If Tom and Auntie Emily were right, Granny had softened with age. She must have been overwhelmed with the responsibility of seven children—especially with a husband who, like Daddy, drank and disappeared for weeks.

Like most teens, she must have resented how the workload interrupted her social life. I certainly resented my brother and Mama when I had to do the dishes, iron and starch Daddy's shirts and handkerchiefs, set the table, wash and dry the dishes, clean the bathroom, and dust while Tim had little to no chores. I felt especially resentful when I remembered all the siblings pitching in to clean up after a meal at Chaps's, even though Jenny was the only girl. With their nonverbal communication, they interchanged duties like silent film stars.

When I visited Granny, I never mentioned what Tom and Auntie Emily had told me about how poorly she treated Ida. But Granny did have a few stories of her own hard life. During one of my grandad's disappearances, she and her children became homeless. She spoke like she was reliving the horrible experience and was still bitter at what she'd endured being married to a drunk. To Grandad's credit, I heard he was a happy drunk who never physically or verbally abused anyone. I missed the parallels to my own drinking, which was about to get much worse.

BOTTOM

On that fateful night at the San Juan Club, Rich served me my second wine as I waited for Moe to finish her drink so we could hit the gym. While sitting at the bar, my shoulder bare in my *Flashdance* attire, I cringed realizing how stupid I looked. I also noticed Dave. He was a regular, a few years older than me, kind of square, had a good job, and owned a home. I'd observed his routine for a while. Dave would have exactly two beers, play one game of pool, and play a few hands of liar dice.

I marveled that he always went home before nine. I couldn't understand how he did it. On weeknights, I wanted to be like Dave, but somewhere after the second or third drink, I'd forget my intention to have just a few.

What I didn't know was that, like Daddy and my grandad in Canada, I had what I later heard described as "the phenomenon of craving." Somewhere between drink one and drink three, once ease and comfort kicked in, I'd forget my promise to cut the night short and get ready for a solid sales day.

My second glass of I'll-burn-it-off-at-the-gym wine led to a blackout and more than a week of binge drinking, searching for cocaine, partying with strangers, and hangovers where I told myself I wouldn't drink ever again but then did that very night. The cycle ended with me on my bedroom floor sobbing, in and out of a blackout, curled in the fetal position at 2:00 a.m. and wanting to die.

I was like Daddy. He quit drinking for twenty years, but when he picked up again, it was like he'd never stopped. I'd only been dry a few months, but the progression accelerated at an alarming rate when I started again.

On that last night, I'd gone to the San Juan Club on a weeknight, lonely and thirsty. There was no cocaine to sober me up, so I drove home in and out of a blackout—luckily, I lived close by. I was seeing double and must have been swerving something terrible. I vaguely recall trying to get my key in the slot when I got home. I woke my roommate and her boyfriend by hammering on the door. She yanked it open. "What the hell are you doing? Where's your fucking key?"

That pissed me off and I chased her to her room. She shut the door just before I caught her. I body-slammed it, but she let go so I careened headfirst into the dresser. Enraged, I picked up her boyfriend's belt and went after her. Allegedly, I dropped it after he intervened and before anyone got hurt.

I remember it like the end of an old black-and-white movie just before the film runs out. Flashes of the scene flicker as I lie curled in the fetal position on my bedroom floor, convulsing in sobs. The booze wasn't working anymore. My medicine had turned on me. Instead of numbing my pain, it amplified it. I hated my life. I hated myself. I hated everything. There was no relief and I wanted to die.

My roommate said my guttural sobbing went on for hours. The next morning, I called my sober coworker, Kevin, and asked for help. I was twenty-six, and that was March 21, 1984.

UNDERSTAFFED

When I talked with Ida's husband, Tom, he told me something that has haunted me ever since: "Your mother said her father tried to give her away for drinks at the bar." I caught my breath and wondered if he noticed my unblinking stare as the movie screen in my mind ran a scene.

The background is blurred, but a pretty girl of about fourteen stands in the frame. Her shoulder-length hair is wavy, dishwater blonde, and pulled back from her high forehead in a cloth headband. She wears a beige cotton dress. The hem brushes her knee and her blue eyes gaze down on the soft leather of her saddle shoes. A man with wheat-colored hair slumps before her on a stool. She had been sent to fetch him. His arm is stretched across the bar as he slurs, "Aye ... you can have my gurl . . . for a jigger of that rye." Her shoulders flinch. She steps back and my screen goes dark.

I don't know if what Tom said about my grandad is true, but I haven't been able to shake it. For a moment, I saw Daddy sitting at that bar and wanted to reach out and shove that drunken sot off the barstool.

I felt Tom's pain when he lowered his booming voice. His speech slowed, his jaw softened, and his tone expressed regret.

"She cried herself to sleep every night for you until she died." I repressed the crushing urge to put my face in my hands and weep, not only because I identified with the heartache of losing a baby but because my mother had still grieved my loss seven years after my birth. Just like I was still grieving Mary Monica.

Tom said, "We met right after you were born and tried to get you back, but it was too late." I buckled inside. It sounded like this had happened only a few weeks after my birth. Mama and Daddy had waited almost four months to get me because the Alberta government was understaffed that summer. I doubt anyone told Ida I was languishing in a foster home. Had she held on, she would have had a father for me. She wouldn't have cried herself to sleep, and I would have known my kin.

I saw sorrow and compassion under Tom's thick exterior. He'd been willing to take on her infant daughter as his own, so he wasn't as much of an asshole as he appeared.

I also sensed Tom was plagued with guilt under all the ranting and judgment. Like me, he hid his tender underbelly. I felt sad for him and held back tears—not just to make him more comfortable, but also as a matter of strategy. I sensed he would stop talking if I showed emotion.

Ida had made it clear that if anything happened to her, she didn't want her children to be brought up like she was. When she died, Tom sent my siblings to live with his mother on a farm in rural Wales. Over the next four years, he built his drywall empire back in Canada. He brought the kids back when he married my namesake, Ida's cousin Gloria. I wonder, if my mother hadn't given me up for adoption, would I also have been sent to Britain?

My conversation with Tom made me realize Ida and I may have shared pain caused by mothers who favored their sons, fathers who didn't deserve us but whom we loved anyway, and not being able to keep our babies.

My sister Gwen once wrote in a letter, *Dad believed giving praise or affection was a sign of weakness and to push one to excellence he used a loud angry voice to get his point across.* I thought about how difficult a husband like that would've been for me. I could see why Ida's cousin Betty Lou later told me that my mother was unhappy in her marriage. I wondered if Tom was part of the reason she cried herself to sleep at night.

She must have seen the softness Tom rarely showed the world, but I also wonder if she saw him as a means to get me back, like how I'd married Danny for the nonexistent honeymoon in Canada.

Decades after my talk with Tom, Betty Lou wrote, *Helen was mistaken that Ida slept around. Not so. I know a few of her boyfriends who ditched her because she wouldn't "come across" as was the term then. Also, she was not a party girl, she just liked people and having fun, but as to drinking parties, not so much.*

Betty Lou and Ida, circa 1955

I was grateful for Betty Lou's letter. It had bothered me for years that Helen had called Ida a party girl who slept around. Perhaps Helen had assumed that since I had a loving mother and never knew Ida, I wouldn't be hurt or mourn for someone I'd never met. But having Betty Lou redeem Ida's virtue further confirmed what I always felt. My birth mother was good and kind, and she always loved me.

MOTHERLESS

Betty Lou sent a manila envelope with pictures of herself and my mother wearing floral print dresses and posing with girlfriends. In all of them, Ida wore a big smile.

Decades later, Betty Lou wrote to me, *Ida had a sparky temper, a short fuse but rarely did I see her angry, and she was very quick to forget and forgive.* When I was younger, when a friend hurt my feelings, or we got in an argument, Mama would huff, "If they did that to me, I would never speak to them again!" She couldn't understand how I could be friends with them by the next day.

Betty Lou also told me that before I was born, she and Ida were changing out of their uniforms at the Hair and Scalp Clinic one day when Ida saw her paycheck was short. Forgetting she was wearing only her slip, she stomped into the shop to give the owner a piece of her mind. I loved that story. She had spunk like I did. In another, Ida was fed up with the advances of a boy who had tried to feel her up. She snapped, "You want them so bad, feel these." Then she whipped out her falsies (pads stuffed in her bra), and threw them at him. I would have really liked her.

Monica Hall

Not long ago, Betty Lou emailed me a black-and-white photograph of my mother, one I'd never seen before. I posted it on social media and another memoirist surprised me by colorizing it. When I saw it, my breath caught and I had to wipe away tears. Adding color brought her to life—it was the closest I've ever felt to her.

Ida 1957 is scratched in pen on the bottom of the white border. She's pregnant with me, lying in bed on her side, the striped blue ticking of a thin mattress showing around the edge of the white sheet she lies on. Her forearm is tucked beneath her turned head, and her eyes look into the lens, saying, *I see you.*

She has short, curly brown hair, the same color and shine as mine. The other hand rests on her tummy—on me. One of the buttons on her white blouse is undone, and the flesh of her swollen belly peeks through. When I look at this photo, I feel her looking at me through time.

Ida's life ended on a chilly Wednesday night in the spring of 1965 when Susan was six, Casey was five, and Gwen was three. Ida was pregnant. She sometimes gained ten pounds in a day to lose them the next day. She'd been feeling strange and had once fallen asleep in the bathtub, so she checked herself into the hospital for tests but felt foolish when they found nothing.

My siblings were on the sofa with our mother one evening eating popcorn while watching *The Addams Family*. When Susan told me the story, she said, "She started breathing funny." She puffed in short bursts, like I had while in hard labor, but the puffing soon turned into a grand mal seizure.

At first, the kids thought she was playing. When she didn't stop, they tried to get her attention by jumping on the bed. When that didn't work, Susan started calling the numbers hanging on the wall next to the phone, asking for Uncle Pat. Before long, everyone began calling each other: "Something's wrong. Try to keep Susan on the phone." My uncles told me that when help arrived, my brother was crouching in the closet. Ida died at the hospital later that night.

Tom told me he thought the doctors were covering something up.

Over the years, I made many trips to Canada and saw Tom several times. However, we never spoke about Ida again. He was done.

NIGHTMARE

As promised, my coworker Kevin introduced me to people with a solution to my drinking problem. Once I met them, I clung to sobriety like a shipwreck survivor with a life preserver. However, as I've often heard said of those new to recovery, I "wasn't wrapped too tightly" and made poor choices.

When I stopped drinking and drugging, my work attendance problems evaporated. Desperate to avoid another summer begging businesses to take my Honor Snack trays, I buffed up my resume and in a couple weeks landed a dream sales position. It came with a credit card, expense account, and company car. I parked my brown Toyota on the street and began feeling like a woman of worth.

One of the many suggestions I heard when I started my new sobriety was to focus on building a strong foundation and finding a higher power to intervene when drinking seemed like a good idea.

I was with my new non-drinking friends when I first laid eyes on Kenny. I'd gone six days without a drink or a drug. He'd been sober for a year, and I was in awe.

Practically Still a Virgin

He was the best-looking man I'd ever seen. Despite his movie-star good looks, Kenny wasn't full of himself. He had blond hair, blue eyes, a mustache, and a golden tan. My heart thumped when he rolled up his T-shirt sleeve to hold a pack of Marlboros, revealing his chiseled construction-worker bicep and a sexy blue dragon tattoo. I fell hard.

The nightly parties at my duplex tested every fiber of my sobriety. The party table was just a few feet from my room. As I tried to sleep, surges of laughter reverberated off my bedroom door. I wondered, *Who's at my table tonight?* With each intermittent slam of the dice cup, I jolted. But the worst sound by far was the once-mesmerizing tap-tap-tap of the razor blade on the mirror as they cut lines of coke. More than once, some unknown male knocked at my door. "Why don't you come out and party?" I'd watch the knob, waiting for it to turn, wishing my door had a lock.

Kenny was my savior, a replacement for the amber liquid that had once stilled my demons and inner restlessness. He became my higher power. And he needed me. Filthy work jeans, dirty underwear, pungent socks, months of discarded newspapers, and overflowing ashtrays littered his bedroom. Every dish, utensil, cup, and pan sat crusted on his countertop.

It took hours, but I washed every piece of laundry, scrubbed every dirty pot. I bought him dishcloths and even a canister for his spatulas. I imagined chipmunks and the tweet of birdies singing "Whistle While You Work." He'd be so grateful, just like those adorable little dwarves in *Snow White*. I imagined the delight and love I'd see in his eyes when he realized all I'd done for him.

In reality, he barely noticed the dishes and sparkling toilet, but his eyebrows went up when he realized he wouldn't have to turn his underwear inside out or put on crusty socks the next day.

The last time I'd done such extensive cleaning was when I washed dishes at Steven and Tommy's trailer to impress them after my "date" with Billy. It was different with Kenny, though—there'd been no joy in that trailer. That time, I'd hoped for praise and was attempting to cleanse my soul. This time, I was trying to build a foundation.

A month or so later, I woke in the middle of the night at Kenny's apartment, sobbing from a horrible nightmare. He held me, and between sobs, I told him I'd stood at the end of his bed and found him with a blonde woman. I could still see her. "Don't worry, it was just a bad dream," he crooned. "I love you and I'd never do that to you." He was so tender and sincere. I knew he'd never hurt me.

BURNING BUSH

I'd been clean and sober for two months when I discovered I was pregnant. Kenny and I were madly in love and excited to start a life together. In my naïveté, I thought sobriety would be a magic wand. Life would be perfect since I wasn't drinking and hanging around with lowlifes. I'd get to keep the baby and we'd be a real family.

By the time I was five months pregnant, I was out of the party duplex and into my own apartment. Kenny started driving my Toyota, when his pickup broke down. Anxious to impress, I'd offered it to him because I had my company car.

One evening, I was expecting Kenny for dinner. I was preparing tacos when the phone rang. I said, "How soon can you be here?"

"Uhhh, well ... I'm not coming." He sounded weird.

My mouth went dry. "Are you okay?"

"I need some space."

My heart plummeted. Not a good thing to hear when you're pregnant and the father has your car. I felt lightheaded, like I was going to puke. All I said was, "The insurance is in Mama's name. When will you bring my car back?"

"Thursday."

I hung up and immediately called the lady who was helping with my recovery. She said many wise things to me over the years, but one that I will always remember is, "We don't go looking for pain." Not chasing after him for those few days was one of the hardest things I've ever done.

Thursday came and went with no car and no word from Kenny. I was terrified and could think about nothing else. Why hadn't he called?

On Friday, I gave in. The car didn't matter to me, but it gave me an excuse to call. The phone rang unanswered all morning. Finally, I went to his apartment.

Pulling onto his street in my company car, I saw my Toyota parked in front of the complex. My heart raced—he was home and hadn't been answering the phone. I thought, *Oh, shit, he must have unplugged it.* I croaked when I looked in the back seat and saw a red-and-white ice chest, open and full of empty Almaden wine jugs and Budweiser cans.

Everything was a blur as I knocked on his door. The living room drapes were drawn and not a creature was stirring. I ran around back to his bedroom window. The curtains were closed so I couldn't see inside, but the window was open.

Bloated with child, car keys in hand, I slit the screen in one downward swipe and popped in that window, landing feetfirst at the end of his bed like Nadia Comăneci.

A blonde clutched the bedsheet under her trembling chin and called, "Kennneee! Kennneee!" It was exactly like my nightmare. No doubt the color drained from my face—between her and the empty Bacardi bottle on the dresser, I was seeing stars.

Just then, Kenny, who'd been cowering at the front door, appeared next to the bed buck-ass naked, arms hanging limp at his sides, defeated and ashamed.

I shook my head. "Why?"

He didn't answer.

Practically Still a Virgin

I could hardly see through my tears to drive home. As I pulled onto the street, there before me was the larger-than-life sign: San Juan Club, my former comrade. I thought, *I can go in and everything will be okay.*

I was scared, betrayed, and heartsick. The child I was carrying was supposed to be my second chance, but the father had left me. Once again, I was alone and pregnant. Then I remembered what I'd heard: call someone before you pick up a drink.

I turned toward a nearby grocery store, dug for a dime, and made that call from the phone booth next to the newspaper stand. I spent the afternoon crying at the kitchen table of a couple who'd been sober for years.

The next morning, a sober friend introduced me to a girl who had one day of sobriety. Gaye was my age and very pretty, although she shook so badly she couldn't hold a cup of coffee. I learned she'd made four suicide attempts. We soon became inseparable. Helping her took my mind off the terror of being abandoned, being pregnant, and being tempted to drink. She'd come over every day, spend nights on my couch, and sit in the car during my sales calls. Without her to care for, I'm not sure I'd have stayed sober.

When Kenny went for an extended stay at an out-of-town recovery house the following week, all talk of our future died. He said he was sorry. Starting a family with the woman he loved had initially sounded great, but the responsibility became overwhelming.

He was twenty-four years old but had been drinking and doing drugs since age thirteen. I was once told that people don't grow emotionally while drinking and using substances—when every feeling is anesthetized, good or bad, you can't mature or learn to deal with life. At twenty-six, I was immature, too, but I had my baby to think about.

Monica Hall

The fantasy I'd created with the perfect family, the one the nuns assured me I'd have, wasn't going to happen after all. Newly sober, I was to go it alone. I was terrified.

The day before Kenny left, we sat in my car in front of his apartment complex. I was in the passenger seat, scared and heartbroken, knowing he was leaving and we wouldn't be the family I'd dreamed of. I sobbed uncontrollably. He didn't speak, looking intently out the window as some guy went up and down the street trying to find an unlocked car.

My grief was an implosion of all my suffering. I couldn't catch my breath between sobs. I'd expected Kenny to fix me, and I was desperate for the pain to end. I wanted to die as I looked at him with pleading eyes. "What am I going to do?"

"Why don't you ask God to help you?" Expressionless, he turned back to the window. His lack of concern angered me.

I'd never prayed, unless you count the rote Hail Marys I'd said so my baby would get good parents. It seemed like something weak people did, but I was desperate for relief. I gave it a try and thought, *God, help me.* Nothing happened.

I tried again, but with more depth. *God, help me!* Still nothing.

Kenny looked out the window, absorbed in his own troubles.

Pushed by a lifetime of swallowed screams, I dug from my toes and dredged up every ounce of pain. In guttural silence, I wailed, *God! Please help me!*

I was instantly bathed in a golden warmth of indescribable peace. Cocooned by the most loving presence, I felt no fear or pain—just knowledge that no matter what, I would always be okay.

Seconds before, I'd felt the darkest despair of my life. But when the hole in my heart cracked open, I received a miracle. Kenny was no longer my higher power. I said, "It's gone."

Kenny turned to me. "What's gone?"

"The pain."

THE FARM

Ida's grandmother, Kôhkom (Cree for "grandmother"), kept a wooden box of herbal medicines. That healing knowledge had been passed down from my ancestors. But most of the elders and traditions are gone now.

In the early '90s, one of my great-aunties taught me how to make a medicine bag and decorate it with beaded five-petaled flowers in the Cree tradition. We also made dangly beaded earrings and burned sweetgrass. Another auntie showed me where to find, identify, and harvest rat root and horsetail, medicine from Mother Earth.

I have faded gray photos of my great-grandmother's small living room filled with family—Môsom (Cree for "grandfather") playing the fiddle while Kôhkom and Granny dance the Red River Jig on their toes, a dance that has a Scottish feel and combines First Nation dances with Scottish, Irish, and French footwork.

Recently, a family reunion was held at my cousin's home on a corner of the family's 160-acre property. There was dried meat, bannock (fry bread), and laughter around the fire pit. With bright-colored paint, we marked our names and handprints on a tipi erected on the property.

My cousins made gifts for reunion attendees by decoupaging photos of my great-grandparents onto wood taken from their log house.

When I first visited the farm in 2006, the dilapidated house where Granny grew up had been abandoned for years. She'd also lived there with her children for a time after becoming homeless. After a house fire, so did Ida, Tom, and my siblings.

Kôhkom and Môsom at the farm, circa 1930

Practically Still a Virgin

I collected pieces of the flowered linoleum they'd danced on and scraps of wallpaper that whispered their songs. I also gathered wildflowers from the meadow. This was where my siblings had run barefoot, spoken Cree, and spent their early childhood with our mother, surrounded by grandparents, aunties, uncles, and cousins. I'd missed all that.

When I visited, I stood in the center of the peaceful meadow, near the old well, circled by birch, alder, and poplar trees. The sun was on my forehead and I heard the gentle rustling of tall grass. I felt as if I was within an ancient cathedral, my chest full with reverence and awe. My ancestors were welcoming me home.

COLLAGE

Thirty-two years after Ida's mother passed, I dug through a box of old photos and found a letter I'd written her. I must've taken it while going through Granny's things after her funeral.

It was dated October 10, 1980, before I met her. That was three months after I married Danny and two months after I caught him cheating. He'd already moved out. I was only twenty-three.

The envelope's lining had a flower motif. The ivory stationery was decorated with a pink rose. I'd held a ruler while I wrote in straight blue script, using my best penmanship.

I am so sorry to hear that Ida died. I also gave a child up for adoption. She is seven years old now. I am counting the years until she is old enough to find me. I just hope I can live that long.

I was surprised at the reference to my mortality. Since Ida died at thirty, I must have questioned whether I could pass that threshold.

I have a wonderful mom. We are best friends. She is honest, kind, and everything Ida would have hoped for. I just hope my daughter Mary Monica's mother is like her.

Practically Still a Virgin

Mama and I were close. And although I loved her deeply, I now see my childhood and adolescence with the clarity I lacked in my twenties. It feels like a betrayal to say it, but I'd have never forgiven myself if I'd discovered Mary Monica had parents like mine.

You did a lot for [Ida] the way my mother did for me. You were her friend and you stood behind her when she needed you. Maybe I'm just dreaming but I can't imagine it any other way.

When I wrote, I assumed that like Mama, Granny had done the right thing by supporting my relinquishment. Now, I wonder if she pushed Ida to give me up, like my parents pushed me. In 1980, I didn't yet know Ida had cried herself to sleep pining for me until she died. I also didn't know about the primal wound that many believe relinquishment causes in adoptees. At that point, belonging to my new family and reuniting with my daughter were my only goals.

But over the years, I've fantasized about meeting Ida in so many different scenarios: airport, train station, restaurant. I'd spot her from the door. She'd be the pretty brown-haired lady with glasses and full cheeks wearing a floral dress, sitting in the back corner of the café. She'd rise and we'd lock tear-filled eyes. I'd make my way between tables, never taking my eyes from hers. She'd wrap her arms around me and we'd sob with joy.

After Granny's funeral, when the family went through her things and I found the letter, I asked if I could also have the framed collage of photos that had always hung on pine paneling in a black plastic frame above her velour armchair. The collage was also in every photo I'd ever seen of Granny's living room, so I imagined it had hung in that very spot since my mother died.

The collage consisted of three black-and-white photos placed atop gold paper. In the right corner was a shiny Polaroid with scalloped edges, like the one Mama and Daddy took

213

when they first brought me home. It's of Ida and Tom on a sofa; she's holding newborn Susan. Below it is a studio photo of my three siblings dressed in white and lined up by age. Susan (six) has a pixie cut and wears a sailor dress. Casey (five) scrunches his shoulders with a sheepish smile. Last is towheaded, cherub-cheeked Gwen (three). I imagined Ida combing Susan's bangs, then rushing out of the shot and saying "Kids, smile!" as the photographer snapped the picture.

A studio portrait of Ida occupies a third of the frame. Leaning into the lens, she wears a tasteful silky dress with cap sleeves; a simple rhinestone necklace rests around her neck. She looks to be about twenty, and her short brown hair is

Ida with Tom and their newborn, Susan, circa one year after relinquishing me

swept off her high forehead with a single curl at the corner of her brow.

I have her cheeks, forehead, and eyes, but her full lips are shaped like Susan's. Her smile is playful, her skin flawless. She's classy and beautiful with a kind face. I love the photo so much because it captures her sweet essence—the woman she was before she lost her baby. I imagined Granny had put the pictures together as a memorial to all her daughter loved. The only thing missing was me.

MAMA CASS

Shortly after Kenny's return from rehab, we had a shotgun wedding. I was six months pregnant and looked ready to pop on the drive to Reno. As we parked before a tacky storefront chapel, I saw our blurred reflection in the filmy window and thought, *I gotta get him in there before he changes his mind.* A little gold bell rang as we entered. Maybe I'd get my perfect fantasy family after all.

We were a pair of plastic wedding cake figurines: Big-as-a-House Barbie standing with handsome Ken beneath a rickety arbor draped with a vine of fake white roses. My hand was in his, a smile plastered on my face to trick myself into believing this wedding was the joyous event I'd dreamed of.

This was my do-over. Eleven years earlier, I'd given birth to Mary Monica and written in my journal, *It would be so much nicer with a husband to share the joy with.*

I felt the vibration of Kenny's toe-tapping through his clammy palm. He loved me but was terrified by the responsibility the day represented.

I internalized a huge sigh of relief when he squished the ten-karat gold band onto my sausage finger. I'd purchased it myself at a discount store with the last few dollars in my bank account.

I'd gained fifty pounds and was unaware that I'd developed gestational diabetes. Our daughter, Rebecca Ann, weighed nearly eleven pounds at birth. When I set her next to her Cabbage Patch doll, they matched like bookends. Her face was so bloated her eyes were slits. She would soon develop cradle cap (white and yellow scales on her scalp) and her chubby face would be covered with baby acne. Like my daughter, I resembled a squirrel with nuts stuffed in its cheeks.

I felt miserable and invisible and hoped for a quick fix. My hairstylist assured me that I just needed a fresh, new, *un-mommy* look. I agreed. I'd always been a slave to fashion, and—I'm reluctant to say—also somewhat vain.

Maybe a quick fix was all I could handle. In the back of my mind, I realized looking under the hood of my marriage would reveal more than I was capable of fixing, so I adopted the "let's put a Band-Aid on it" mentality.

When Rebecca was born, I wore my straight hair in a loose perm to give it body. But it was the mid-'80s and spiked hair was in vogue. I trusted that my stylist knew what he was doing. In my desperation, I'd clearly forgotten the pilgrim hair he gave me when I married Danny. To my utter horror, he cut off my perm and gave me a short punk style that accentuated my squirrel cheeks. Pat Benatar meets Mama Cass.

The following morning was Rebecca's one-month checkup. I jumped out of the shower and attempted to spike my bangs with gel like he'd done at the salon. I was mortified when the mirror revealed my grandad's high forehead jutting skyward beneath a wall of gel that shot straight up, like a sheer rock cliff above a sandy beach.

I thought about wetting it down like a drowned rat but opted for the cliff look. While entering the medical center, I cursed my *former* hairstylist and kept my head down so I didn't have to make eye contact. I felt the stares on the back of my neck like a cool breeze.

After my daughter's checkup, I drove home, bangs still sky-high, in what was probably the ugliest car on the planet at the time, an AMC Spirit. Not only did it resemble a space-ship but it was also oxidized beige, the color of an anemic mannequin—the most uncool color known to automobiles and the only car we could afford on our income from Kenny's framing job. My company car was gone; they let me go after learning I was pregnant. That was legal back then.

As I sat at a traffic light, probably thinking about how stupid my hair looked, I heard a ping and felt an empty pop can bounce off my car and roll across my hood.

Then I heard yelling. "Hey, you! Ugly!" At first, I paid no attention, but when there was another pop-can ambush followed by laughter, I looked over my shoulder. Behind the vehicle next to me was a car full of teenage boys hanging out the windows and yelling, "Yeah, you! Ugly!"

I couldn't believe it—they were yelling at *me*! I was incensed. How dare they, the little fuckers. I'd been a babe just a few months earlier. If they'd seen me then, they would have been gawking instead of mocking my space mobile and failed Joan Jett impersonation.

I raced home and called the police because a serious crime had been committed. A sympathetic highway patrol officer came to the house, where I explained that I had been assaulted and insulted. It must have been difficult for him to keep a straight face while looking at me in all my gel and indignation.

"They called me ugly!"

He kindly agreed that it was wrong for teenagers to throw cans at my car. After I gave him their plate number, what else could he do but assure me he'd call the little shits' parents? I think he really *did* pity me. After all, my baby was ugly, too.

BLOODY HELL

Decades after Rebecca was born, Ida's cousin Betty Lou, who was more like her sister, began sending me emails about my mother, sharing the stories I'd longed for when I learned Ida was deceased.

Betty Lou confirmed that Tom didn't show affection—and like me, Ida needed affection. She also had lots of love to give. Shortly before her death, Ida told Betty Lou that Tom would come home from work and criticize her: "What the bloody hell have you been doing all day?" Never mind that she was pregnant and had three little ones to look after.

Betty Lou wrote, *Ida came for a visit and confessed how unhappy she was, both with her marriage and still grieving you. I felt so sad for her, then and now as I recall it. Not long before her death, and the last time we were together, she was expecting another baby and was not doing well in the carrying. I asked her why she wanted another baby when she was so unhappy. She replied, "Someone else to give my love to."*

I understood this. When the nurse placed Rebecca in my arms, I thought, *No one is going to take this one away.* I wasn't desperate and anguished like I had been when I held Mary Monica.

With Rebecca, I'd have a lifetime to love her and check for similarities. But once I brought her home from the hospital, Kenny felt I couldn't do anything right. He criticized me constantly, continued to make messes, and didn't help around the house or with the baby. He also twisted everything, as if his shortcomings were somehow my fault. Even though I knew he was emotionally and verbally abusive, I defended myself as if I were guilty. I must've thought I didn't deserve better.

One afternoon, I was at Mama's. Like Ida I needed affection and had lots of love to give. I was nursing newborn Rebecca, which filled me with contentment and love. Mama remarked, "I don't know how you can do that. The thought of a baby sucking at my breast is revolting." I was stunned.

On the evening of our daughter's two-month checkup, I arrived home before Kenny and sat down to drink a glass of water. Rebecca was on the floor next to me, still in her baby carrier. Kenny, home from his framing job, entered the kitchen wearing a sweat-soaked T-shirt and dusty jeans.

Hangry, he demanded, "Where's my dinner?" I stammered, "I just got home. I haven't started it yet." He opened the refrigerator, pulled out a full gallon of milk, unscrewed the top, turned it upside down, and poured it over the floor and two counters, emptying the remainder on the linoleum in front of him. He slammed the empty jug down next to his work boots and yelled, "Now, clean it up ... bitch!"

On reflex, I threw my glass of water at him. It bounced off the counter. Stone-faced, he took three long strides and slapped me across the face.

That was the first time Kenny moved out. He left for good just after Rebecca's first birthday.

Ida and I shared the pain of belittling and unappreciative husbands. Without Kenny's income, I went on welfare. He wasn't reliable with child support and told me he didn't want the every-other-weekend visitation schedule because it felt like a chore. He said, "I'll call you when I want to see her."

Rebecca wouldn't have the stable life I'd hoped for: the covered wagon of family and a relationship with her father. At least she had her mother.

HORRORS OF BATTLE

Five years after I found my first family, Rebecca was five months old and Mary Monica would soon be twelve. I'd never stopped thinking about my little girl, but I'd also never cried for her. I tried to imagine what she was like: *Does she have straight hair? Is she strong-willed like me?* Over the years, I'd fantasized about being in Anchorage in her vicinity, maybe at the schoolyard fence so I could talk to her anonymously and hear her little voice. There was no one I could talk to who would understand—most people seemed to think I shouldn't care since I'd chosen to give her up.

A few close friends had also lost children to adoption, but we never spoke about the pain of relinquishment. It was similar, I suppose, to vets who never speak about the horrors of battle. Them: "I lost a lotta friends over there." Me: "I had a girl."

I could rattle off her birth weight, length, and time of birth. On her birthdays, I knew she'd be thinking about me. I'd sit in a quiet place sending waves of love through the cosmos, just as I imagined my own mother had done. I ached to watch Mary Monica open presents. Just peering through her window to catch a glimpse would have filled so much longing.

Since I now had my own baby, I hoped Sister Clare might be forthcoming with information and maybe even send me a photo if I asked. She'd given me a Polaroid shortly after Mary Monica's birth, but I never got the promised birth certificate. I yearned to see what she looked like as a young girl. With a nervous hand, I dialed the adoption agency's number, praying I didn't sound anxious—that I didn't seem like I was gathering information for a coup. I just needed something to hang on to.

Sister was still in Anchorage and as chatty as I remembered. In her New York accent, she said, "She's a darling, and what a little spitfire!" I learned that my daughter was bright, headstrong, and spoke her mind. I was delighted because she sounded like a miniature version of me.

I also learned her parents had adopted two other girls and no longer lived in Alaska. They'd moved to the West Coast, but not California. Her father had a prestigious job, they entertained important people, and her mother stayed home to raise the girls. I hung on every word. *Is he a judge or politician? Maybe the chief of police? Is she in Seattle or Portland?* At the end of our rushed call, Sister promised to send a picture.

I checked the mail daily, but weeks passed and nothing arrived. I thought she'd forgotten. Then, two days after Mary Monica's twelfth birthday, a tiny envelope arrived. Inside was a card:

> *Darling! In a rush–*
> *found this old picture–*
> *will get a recent one later!*
> *Love ya,*
> *SMC*

It had been cut from a family studio sitting. Like Billy and me, she had straight brown hair. She wore the same pixie cut I'd had at that age, but I felt no connection to the girl in the picture. It was oddly similar to when I'd met Chaps and hadn't felt connected to him, either. I thought, *What's wrong with me? Why aren't I flooded with emotion?*

I took the photo straight to Mama's. On the back was whited-out felt pen. Mama and I carefully scratched at it and could make out all but the third letter. Her last name was one of three possibilities.

Mama would have lost her mind if she discovered my mother had received pictures of me or sought clues to my identity. No doubt Mary Monica's mother would've felt the same.

Since her birth, I'd avoided every sad movie. I shunned tear-jerkers like I would a person with the stomach flu. I didn't watch TV shows with loss, especially loss of a child or a loved one's death from cancer. I lashed out to my friends on a number of occasions: "Hell no! I'm not watching that!" I didn't let my mind analyze why I so adamantly avoided this type of content. "Don't let the pain out of the box" was how I rolled.

Now sober, I realized I'd never mourned. I knew that couldn't be healthy—I should at least have a good cry.

I dug through my closet to find mementos from 1973 and discovered my green cloth journals. I'd never read them before—I'd been avoiding what I knew I'd omitted from those pages. I noticed I'd written daily up to the birth. Then, once Mary Monica was born, weeks passed before my next entry: *I've been away for a long while because I haven't wanted to think about it.*

My writing was immature and superficial, and I didn't feel anything as I read it. I thought that maybe Mama had been able to articulate the emotions of that day. After a quick chat, I asked, "Do you still have your journal from when I had Mary Monica?"

"I think it's in the closet with the rest of my journals. Why?"

"I thought if I read it, I might be able to cry. What do you think?"

After Daddy died, she'd told me it was important to grieve—I'd have problems later in life if I didn't. I drank and used drugs instead. Oddly, she'd never mentioned processing grief after losing my baby. I wasn't taken to therapy, nor was I asked how I felt. She probably didn't want to think of it, either, or confront her part in my loss.

"Of course, honey. I'll dig it out. And yes, I absolutely think it would be a good idea."

The next day, I opened Mama's journal. Her script was elongated and flatter than on the previous pages: *We finally told her goodbye, we would always remember her and love her. When the nurse took her away, we couldn't hold back the tears.*

I felt a swell of emotion, but just as tears came, the valve slowly...shut off. I sat empty and bereft. I'd stuffed my feelings for so long that they were inaccessible.

I closed Mama's journal, placed it in the cardboard box with my mementos, pushed it to the back of my closet, and slid the door shut.

NEARLY EIGHTEEN

Making rent had been difficult with little financial help from Kenny. I worked as a makeup artist and rented out my third bedroom to mostly unreliable roommates. When our daughter was three, Kenny moved hours away to a place where he was less prone to allergies. That was about the time I landed a job with a retirement plan and benefits. Overnight, my income more than doubled. The following year, I bought a house in an older subdivision—a white three-bedroom, one-bath with a small window air conditioner.

I planted roses and hung flower baskets off the porch eaves. In the backyard, I erected a pink playhouse with white shutters and decorated Rebecca's bedroom with a canopy bed like I'd wanted as a child. I indulged her because if my daughter had nice things, I wasn't a loser who had given up a child for adoption and married an absent father.

Shortly after we moved in, Jeff entered our lives. We would eventually marry, have our son, Quin, and divorce eight years later. With a Japanese mother and Polish father, Jeff was a mysteriously handsome deep thinker who had a clever sense of humor, yet wasn't boastful. At thirty-five, he already had salt-and-pepper hair. I loved that Jeff wore crisp white shirts, had studied art in Paris, and was employed at an engineering firm. He was told he looked like George Clooney and was even approached to play an attorney for a local TV commercial.

In December of 1990, I was seven years sober and thirty-three years old. Rebecca would soon be six and Mary Monica was almost eighteen. For almost two decades, I'd counted the years, months, and days until I could find her. When people asked how many children I had, she was always included in my answer.

As her birthday approached, I started sharing my excitement but got some pushback. People said things like "What if she doesn't want to meet you? Maybe you should wait and see if she wants to find you first." I was angry that they weren't more supportive and indignantly responded, "No! I know she's just like me. She'll want to find me just as much as I want to find her!" I considered purging the doubters from my Christmas card list.

I couldn't wait to begin searching, so I picked up the phone in my office cubicle and dialed the adoption agency six months early. My hands shook and my heart pounded. What if they turned me down or blocked my search? I asked for Sister Clare, but she'd moved back to New York. I took a deep breath and explained that I wanted to get in touch with the daughter I'd given up for adoption seventeen and a half years earlier.

Of course, the agency told me I needed to wait until she was eighteen. I could then write a letter, which they would forward to her parents. If the parents approved, the agency would facilitate our reunification. What I heard was that it was all up to her parents. They might let me meet *their* daughter, but only if they were open to reunification and liked what I wrote.

SLAPPED AWAKE

Before Ida's mother passed in 1990, I visited her several times at her house across from the old Gunn Hotel. I could see Lac Ste. Anne from her driveway. Chaps said the Cree call it *Manitou Sakhahigan*, meaning Lake of the Spirit.

When I first greeted thin, short, curly-haired Granny with a hug, she felt tiny in my arms—but I sensed she was anything but fragile. She spoke very little and seemed to be sizing me up. I wasn't sure she was as happy to meet me as she claimed. To compensate, I talked too much. Later, I realized being reserved was just her way.

Granny wasn't white-headed like I'd expected. Her short, dark hair was permed, and there were wires of gray among the curls. Her sons also had dark hair into their fifties with no obvious gray. Chaps was the same. I also inherited that gene.

As I sat in her tiny kitchen, she told me I was born with a full head of black hair. I now wish I'd asked how she knew this. Was she at my birth? Did my mother get to hold me?

When I asked Granny about Chaps, she looked like she'd taken a swig of spoiled milk. "I called him to see you in the hospital, but he never came." She didn't offer more, and I didn't say I'd heard she just wanted him to pay the bill. I wanted to

228

ask if, like Mama, she'd encouraged her daughter to give me up, but I was worried she might resent me. What could she say, anyway? "Yes, I made her give you away because I didn't want you to ruin her life"? Her quiet told me there was much I didn't know and would never learn.

Since they were raised in the same community as Granny, Helen and Chaps were polite to her, but they didn't like her. Helen told me more than once how she and Chaps thought Granny was "uppity." They said Granny felt superior because of her "white" husband and lighter offspring, and she didn't want Ida to associate with Chaps.

I wanted to ask Granny more questions about my relinquishment, but I sensed asking about her deceased daughter would bring up old wounds. I didn't want to cause her grief or make her regret meeting me—I was afraid she wouldn't want to be my Granny anymore if I did. I would've done anything to belong, even if it meant ignoring my deepest wish: learning more about my mother.

Eventually, I learned that both sides of my family settled around Lac Ste. Anne, about forty-five miles northwest of Edmonton. Ida's relations settled on the north side, Chaps's on the south.

Indigenous people have been visiting the lake for millennia due to its healing powers, and Chaps's property is adjacent to the land where the annual Lac Ste. Anne Pilgrimage is held. It began in the late 1800s and now attracts thirty to forty thousand travelers every July. The four-day event always falls on my birthday. For years, Chaps and Helen ran a large concession stand during the pilgrimage. Since 2018, when Chaps passed, my brother Darcy has taken the reins. Chaps also kept a barn-red cottage on a separate property on the southeast side of the lake, in a tourist spot at Alberta Beach. I made many fond memories around the fire pit there.

I've attended several pilgrimages, a couple with Granny, her sisters, and so many other relations from both sides of my family that I couldn't keep them straight.

Granny's parents, my great-grandparents Kôhkom and Môsom, settled in the tiny hamlet of Gunn, across the water from the pilgrimage.

Granny lived alone in a little white house not far from the farm, within a hundred yards of her sister's house on the lake's northeast shore. Whenever I had tea with Granny and my great-aunties, I hung on every story and bit of gossip. Chaps and Helen snickered when they told me they were known as the Snoop Sisters.

I called Helen in 2020, two years after Chaps's passing, planning to talk about why he didn't come to the hospital when I was born. I didn't get to ask that question, but the conversation was still revealing.

Back when we first connected, Helen knew I'd relinquished a baby for adoption but never expressed an opinion about it until that call. I asked, "Do you think Granny made Ida give me up?"

I was calling from my backyard in California. I'd just exited my garden gate when her dismay blasted through the phone like a sonic boom. It answered my long-standing question while also revealing her opinion of my mother, my grandmother, and maybe even me and my parents. She shrilled, "You don't give away your own baby! You don't give away your own flesh and blood!"

I stopped with a jerk, the gate clattering shut behind me. *Of course not! You don't give away your own baby! You don't give away your own flesh and blood!* It was as if she was trying to knock out the brainwashing and adoption normalization I grew up with. I will forever hear her ringing voice.

SPEECHLESS

A couple of weeks after I called the adoption agency, I was at work when my office phone rang. It was Elaine, the adoption caseworker. I was surprised—I hadn't expected any contact. I'd resigned myself to waiting until my daughter was eighteen, as required, to hopefully begin the reunification process.

"I'm sorry. We've been so busy that we haven't had time to get back to you, but we have a picture here."

I was confused. "A picture of who?"

"A young girl—your daughter."

Elaine said she'd mail the photo right away. She explained that within a week of my call, my daughter and her mother had also contacted the agency to start the reunification process.

I was speechless for the first time in my life. All the tears that I couldn't access for eighteen years came flooding out at once. Between sobs, I managed to get out a barely audible "thank you." I was crying so hard I couldn't even see the phone to hang it up. My coworkers rushed to my cubicle, wondering who'd died.

HAUNTING WORDS

My Rebecca was a bright, high-spirited child with an involved mother, but she was challenging for me to raise. Like me, she had difficulty focusing in school. I didn't want it to affect her self-esteem the way it had affected mine. Mama had once told me that cultivating a skill or talent builds self-worth. She'd put me in ballet, and later guitar lessons, but I was too restless to focus. Even though Mama's strategy hadn't worked on me, I followed her advice and enrolled Rebecca in dance classes, which she loved. At seven, she joined a children's dance company. I hoped keeping her busy would make her less inclined to get into trouble like I had.

Mama rarely attended her granddaughter's dance recitals or school events. I was often bitter as I watched the hall or church fill with extended family and proud grandparents while the seat next to me remained empty. It's not like Mama was angry with me or didn't love Rebecca. We still visited frequently, and she was fond of her granddaughter, but she wasn't present the way other grandmas were. I told myself she stayed at the fringe of our lives because she lacked energy due to aging and money problems. But really, I think she believed we didn't need her.

In my heart, I felt she didn't care about me or my child that much, certainly not as much as she cared about my brother— who lived with her until her death at age ninety-four.

In 2002, Becca graduated from the same high school I did—the one where I had that tasty sample of banana cream pie. She'd been a cheerleader and, like me, used school as a social outlet. But she was expelled in her junior year for truancy. She finished via independent study and was allowed to graduate with her class. It was an event to be celebrated.

That morning, I called Mama to make sure she was still coming to the ceremony. I always double-checked, even on holidays, to ensure she wouldn't back out. But she'd changed her mind. When I begged her to come, she responded in a snarky tone, "Rebecca doesn't care if I'm there." I hung up and cried.

Mama was right. Even though we lived nearby, she and Becca hadn't spent enough time together to get close. *But I cared.* I wanted her there for me! The school was blocks from her house. Although she was seventy-eight, she was still in good shape so it wasn't a physical problem. I knew it was lack of interest, and maybe vanity. She was overweight and might have been ashamed because she was once so beautiful. Or perhaps she worried about getting overheated and was too proud to tell me.

Over the coming years, she missed many holidays, birthdays, and family events. She sometimes blamed her absence on lack of funds, saying she couldn't afford presents, but I covered for her financially because I wanted her in my life and wanted to share my family with her.

For her birthday and holidays, I always prepared her favorite dishes, made sure to have half-and-half on hand for her coffee, and set a formal table because I knew it pleased her. But I was never sure if she'd contract some mysterious illness, only to recover the next day.

My children loved Mama, and she was always sweet to them, but she never forged relationships with them. She might have felt she didn't have anything to offer, or maybe she didn't want to impose. Whatever the reason, I had a hard time accepting it.

I'm like the members of Chaps's and Ida's families. For them, maintaining family connections outweighs everything else. Mama and I just weren't cut from the same cloth. Her intermittent absence from our lives continued up to her death in 2019.

In the coming years, I helped them financially. Mama said she was appreciative, but I sensed a part of her resented me for saving the day.

Rebecca's dance classes eventually paid off. At age twenty, she joined the local NBA dance team and performed on the court for six seasons. Mama and Tim never once attended a game. They also missed her wedding.

During Mama's last twenty or so years, there were many weeks when I couldn't reach her. She'd say she didn't get my messages. I once stopped by unannounced, but Tim answered the door, growled that they weren't receiving company, and closed the door in my face. Due to my brother's hoarding and fifteen-year meth addiction, their spare room was filled with so much crap you couldn't even open the door.

Not being able to see or talk to Mama was cyclical. When we were in contact, I treated her and Tim to lunch, drives, and day trips. A year or two before she died, I wanted to take her out for a mother-daughter lunch, but she declined: "I don't think that would be a good idea. I don't want to worry Tim." Time for Mama and me was running out.

Four years before she passed, the three of us went to San Francisco, her favorite city, where she'd lived with Daddy during the war. She hadn't been there in at least twenty years. We drove over the Bay Bridge as a cool ocean breeze filled the car. With her eyes fixed on the breathtaking view of the skyline, she whispered, "I have to remember this, I just have to remember this."

She was trying to imprint it to memory so she could take it back to that dark house she shared with my brother. Her words still haunt me.

CORNFIELDS AND CHEESE

On the day I expected my daughter's picture to arrive, I called my neighbor from work multiple times to see if the mail had come. In the afternoon, it had. I took a late lunch break and raced home.

Zipping into my driveway, I pulled a small gray envelope from the mailbox and dropped into the chair on my sunlit porch, which was surrounded by roses. I felt like I was about to open a hidden treasure. My heart pounded. I held my breath and, hand trembling, ripped open the envelope. It contained Elaine's business card, a note, and a photo. I was staring at Mary Monica's full-grown face. She leaned to one side, posing in a professional half-length photograph taken to commemorate her high school graduation. I was flooded with relief and elation to set eyes on my beautiful daughter. I felt like I was looking at someone familiar—someone I knew. I felt like I was looking at myself.

This was the feeling that had been absent when Sister sent that tiny photo years earlier. Later, I understood why I hadn't felt the much-anticipated rush of motherly love from the picture Sister sent me of what I thought was my daughter:

236

she had mistakenly cut my daughter's younger sister from the family photo.

In the note, Elaine said it had been good talking to me on the phone. She wrote, *I dashed a note off to your daughter letting her know of our conversation and that you would be sending a letter to her soon.*

She also asked me to prepare a letter to my daughter's parents. Finally, she said she'd suggested that my daughter write me a letter in preparation for our reunification. After we'd exchanged letters, she'd release our phone numbers. In closing, she wrote, *I share in your joy and offer you my services in making your reunification go smoothly.* I raced inside to call Mama.

I was surprised to learn that my daughter was now in the Midwest, though Elaine didn't tell me which state. It seemed silly that her location was a secret when it was clear we would soon make contact.

I'd been comforted knowing she lived in either Washington or Oregon. But the Midwest was so nebulous. I'd never been there, and she could be in a handful of different states, which made it hard to imagine her life.

This laboriously slow process of exchanging letters through Alaska would take weeks, maybe even months. I pictured a huge triangle from California north to Alaska, then down to somewhere among cornfields and cheese. Elaine explained that it was best to take it slow for a successful reunion, allowing us to process the new information and our subsequent feelings.

There were two things that I needed to do before my daughter and I spoke:

1. Watch every sad movie I could get my hands on.
2. Tell Billy he had a daughter.

SNAIL MAIL

The day after receiving Elaine's note suggesting I write letters to my daughter and her parents, I mailed them to Catholic Charities.

Dear Parents,

I'm not sure how to put this into words. Eighteen years ago, through Sister Clare, I grew to know loving parents who would adopt my baby. She spoke highly of you. I have always felt at peace knowing you are her parents. That will never change.

I was also adopted so I deeply understand what it is to have grown up with a loving family under the same circumstances. My adoptive parents are truly my parents in every way. My love for them is no different than any other close family love. When I was old enough, I searched and found my birth family, and my life became so much fuller and fulfilled a yearning that I had for a long time.

I want to express my respect for your wishes on this situation. I know so well how much it means to your daughter to fulfill that same yearning.

I also want to meet you someday, if that is possible. I pray everything will work out for the best, no matter what decisions are made. I have always wanted to say thank you. Very Sincerely,

Monica

Dear Daughter,

I have been waiting eighteen years for this moment. Words cannot describe the joy I feel. All these years I've thought of you and wondered if you were thinking about me. On your birthday I would sit still and think hard, hoping you were thinking of me too. Part of me knew you were but a small part wasn't sure. Deep down I knew that someday I would get the chance to know you.

I too was adopted and wondered about my birth mother. It was much more difficult for me to find her. I didn't have the resources that are available to you. I found my family and have a wonderful relationship with all of them, and believe me, there are a lot of them.

I have so much to share and can hardly contain myself. I have a journal I wrote the year you were born about your birth with all my thoughts and feelings. Writing helped me so much. I've kept it for you in case you ever wanted to read it. I would have loved to have something like that from my birth mother.

I've often thought of your parents and grew to love them through Sister Clare. I knew giving you up for adoption was the best for you. You deserve two parents. I knew you were getting the best, just as I did. My daughter Rebecca is thrilled to have a big sister. She is six years old and a kindergartener.

My mother can hardly wait to meet you. She was with me through the difficult times and loves you too.

239

Monica Hall

I am waiting to receive your pictures and can hardly wait to talk with you until then.
Love,

Monica

Over the next few weeks, I scanned the Blockbuster's shelves for the sad movies I'd shunned since Mary Monica's birth. After putting Rebecca to bed, I'd sit on the couch with a box of tissue and cry. At the sad parts, I leaned into the pain to purge my unresolved grief.

During my pregnancy, I'd pushed Billy to the back of my mind. I'd also said Luke had fathered my baby when he humped my leg, but I didn't believe it. It was as if she had no father. When I wrote in my journal during the last three months of pregnancy, I rarely referenced the past—including all the bad things that had happened during my teenage years, except for a sarcastic comment about the wire hanger beating: *the violet and red welts on my thighs clashed with my gym shorts.* There was no reference to Billy, but I spent a whole page detailing how sperm can swim and get you pregnant without intercourse.

When I spoke to my daughter for the first time, I knew "Who's my Daddy?" would be one of her first questions. This was the same question I'd asked Uncle Pat upon learning my mother was deceased. I knew I couldn't repeat my cocka-mamie tale about Luke, so what would I tell her? I was sure Mary would want to imagine that her parents loved each other, like I had. But what happened in that dingy apartment was far from romance.

I hadn't talked to Kelly in years, but I called to see if she could track down Billy's number. I found that she was married, had two young daughters, and still lived in Alaska. I explained that I was soon to be reunited with my baby and Billy was the father. She was happy for me but didn't recall anything about that night, not even when I reminded her that she'd ridden on Billy's motorcycle to wait at her brothers' trailer during our "date." Then again, nothing eventful had happened to her, so why would she remember? I didn't share that Billy had threatened to rape me.

She agreed to call Tommy. Within a week, I had Billy's number.

WHO'S MY DADDY?

Because I didn't want anyone to witness my humiliation, I was alone when I called Billy. I sat at the dining room table with the cordless phone clutched in my sweaty palm. I felt like I had that night when he shamed me. I'd never let myself relive the events that occurred in that apartment, but I'd fantasized thousands of times that instead of cowering in shame, I looked him in the eyes and mirrored his tone: "You fucking bastard! What do you mean, 'Next time, fuck the headlights off me'? I was a virgin!" But the thought of confronting him for real made me nauseous.

I'd imagined meeting my daughter millions of times, but I'd never once thought about telling Billy he was her father. I must have pushed him so far back in my consciousness that the obvious never came to mind. I expected him to call me a liar and hang up when I broke the news.

My hand trembled as I punched the numbers. I didn't know what I would say. I doubted he even knew I'd been pregnant. When the phone rang, a woman answered. I hung up without speaking. I'd expected Billy to answer. I assumed she was either his wife or girlfriend, and I was concerned my news could cause problems.

Practically Still a Virgin

I made three more calls over the next week. Each time, the woman answered and I hung up. I knew I couldn't keep doing that. I decided to ask for Billy if she answered the next call.

"Hello?"

"Hi. May I please speak to Billy?"

"Who's calling?" Her tone was hostile, more of an accusation than a question.

I spoke in an even, businesslike tone. "It's Monica Hall."

She spat, "Billy, the phone's for you. It's Monica Hall." I later learned his wife was religious, distrustful, and held him with tight reins. I wondered if she suspected I was his woman on the side, the one who kept calling and hanging up in her ear. That thought delighted me.

I gulped and trembled while I waited—I wasn't prepared for his warm greeting. "Hiiii, Monica. How are ya?" He spoke to me like he was a long-lost friend, not at all like the arrogant prick I once knew. I'd been bracing myself for an asshole.

I tried to keep the surprise and the nervous tremor out of my voice. "Ah ... I'm fine. I don't know if you knew this, but I moved to California."

"No, I didn't."

"Well ... I'm calling because ... do you remember what happened?"

"Yes."

I hadn't known how to word it, so I was glad he didn't need an explanation. Perhaps he didn't want to invite a more detailed conversation with his wife standing over his shoulder.

As an adult, I was aware that *what happened* wasn't consensual. I still hadn't accepted it as a real *rape* yet, though—maybe I could concede to calling it *date rape*, but that didn't feel completely right either. That seemed to lessen it although I know now that rape is rape. I wavered between my childhood memories of shame and my adult understanding. If his perception differed from mine, I didn't want to piss him off and make him deny that Mary Monica was his. So, I was vague—*do you remember what happened?*—instead of saying what I should have: *do you remember when you raped me and took my virginity?*

Since Billy had treated me like I was just another piece of ass, I was surprised he remembered. I was also confused because he seemed happy to hear from me, so polite when he came to the phone. Was he playing nice because his family was there? The last time I'd seen him, he'd accused me of lying and told me I was a lousy piece of ass.

I pushed on, trying to keep my voice steady, ignoring the quivering that had taken control of my body. "I don't think you were aware of this, but I got pregnant, and I *was* a virgin. I had the baby and gave her up for adoption. She's eighteen now and looked me up. She'll wanna know who her father is." I inhaled during the pause.

"Are you sure?" He paused. "Oh ... of course you're sure." Then, with the pride of an Eagle Scout, he said, "Well, you can tell her that her father's a ... Baptist preacher."

Those words will be etched in my mind forever. I wouldn't have been surprised if he was in prison, but a man of God? It was unimaginable. I don't remember anything else about the conversation.

I later wondered if he answered "yes" so quickly because what happened had been weighing on him. After all, he was a preacher now, and weren't they supposed to be self-reflective and repentant?

He didn't seem surprised by my call. It was as if he'd expected it. Maybe Tommy had told him I was looking for him. Or he'd heard the rumor back in 1973 and been waiting for Daddy to come knocking at his door. But more than likely, his wife had been complaining about the hang-ups and he was relieved it was me instead of some woman who could get him in *real* trouble.

He never said he was sorry.

FILLING IN THE BLANKS

L ess than a week after my conversation with Billy, letters arrived from my daughter and her parents.

Dear Monica,

What a difficult letter to write! In many ways you are a total stranger and yet through Mary, very much a part of our family. Thank you for entrusting her to us. Without your unselfish gift our family would not be.

Mary has our full support in her efforts to reunite with you. We realize how important it is to her to "fill in the blanks."

There is so much I would like to tell you about Mary but I will give you the joy of discovering her for yourself before I fill in some details from her growing years.

We look forward to meeting you in the not-too-distant future and saying "thank you" in person.
Love,

Tim & Pat

What a beautiful letter. I was touched. I must have been stunned to learn that my daughter had my same first name, but I don't recall now—probably because I was overwhelmed with all there was to absorb.

Dear Monica,

I have also waited a long time to be reunited with you and to meet the rest of my family. In your letter you said that on my birthday you would sit still and think hard, hoping I was thinking of you too. Well like you I also did, actually, I do that a lot but, on my birthdays, it's usually accompanied with a couple of tears. I am grateful for the life that you have allowed me to live, and I Thank You!

I can't tell you how excited I am. I can't wait to meet you and your family. I have fallen in love with my half-sister, Rebecca. She's beautiful! When I saw her picture, I thought it was me, then I thought maybe it was you. It took me a moment to figure out that I have another little sister. I was so excited it took me a minute before I could think or see straight.

This might sound crazy but I was almost positive that I had a sister, and believe it or not, my guess was that she was six or seven. I also imagined that she would be as beautiful as she is.

Ever since I was little, I have always loved the name Monica. I used to think it was so beautiful, unusual and yet so special. Then a couple of years ago I was asking my mom questions about you, and what you wanted to name me. She had gotten the idea from Sister Clare that you were interested in naming me Monica. Ever since then I have loved the name and have decided to name my first daughter Monica Marie. (That was my sophomore year.) I guess that you can imagine the surprise I had when my mother told me your name was Monica.

I am very interested to read your journal. I have had young friends who have gone through pregnancies and listening to their feelings has helped me understand part of what you went through both emotionally and physically but it is important to me to understand what you went through and how it made you feel.

It takes a very unselfish person to give up such a huge part of themselves and entrust it to a stranger. To me those strangers are everything and I love them very much. I hope that one day you will be able to meet them and see what kind of life you and they gave to me.

I am very excited and cannot wait to write you directly or even call you. I realize these things are supposed to take time, but for some reason I'm not feeling very patient. I figure eighteen years is long enough not to know you!
Love, your daughter,

Mary

P.S. By now I'm sure you have received my senior pictures that I asked the agency to forward to you, but I have also enclosed some with this letter.

P.P.S. I hope to hear from you soon and I am looking forward to getting more pictures. I can't wait to meet my little sister and your mom!

THE MEETING

In 1991, Elaine at Catholic Social Services released my number to my daughter, and for two nights, I waited for the phone to ring. I'd felt similar anticipation while waiting to make my second call to Uncle Pat after he confirmed there were six boys and one girl in his family, but with this call, I didn't have to wonder how I'd be received.

It was a dark, rainy evening when the phone finally rang. "Hello, Monica? It's Mary, your daughter."

I wasn't overcome with relief or sadness to finally hear her voice. I was happy and excited for her. I knew what she was feeling to talk to her mother. She wasn't overly anxious. I sensed she was dipping her toe in unknown waters. It was a friendly conversation, no flood of tears or emotion, just getting to know one another like you would a new friend.

I understood what she wanted to know and gave the information without her having to ask many questions. They were the same questions I would've asked Ida if I'd had the chance. As we spoke, I realized Elaine knew what she was doing by holding back our phone numbers. Had I not had time to process, watch sad movies, and feel my emotions, I would have undoubtedly been a blubbering mess like when I was first told the adoption agency received her photo. Because we had to exchange letters, which took time, I knew she had her parents' blessing, and she knew I wanted to know her.

We talked for nearly two hours. I told her I'd been a virgin and had known Billy, who was older, because he hung around with my friend's brothers. I said I'd gone out with him but things had gone too far—I called it a date rape. She absorbed the information but didn't seem interested in him at all.

We also talked about her friends, boyfriend, and upcoming graduation. By the end of the conversation, it was like catching up with someone I hadn't seen in years.

Mary's father had an important job; his career was in the Secret Service. Before adopting their daughters, he'd been on the Nixon detail and traveled the world on Air Force One. When they adopted Mary, he was stationed in Anchorage. Then, when she was almost three—within a couple years of my family's exit from Alaska—he was transferred to Capitol Hill, and the family moved to the suburb of Fairfax, Virginia. After that, they moved to Spokane when he received a promotion. That's where they lived for most of Mary's formative years—as Sister Clare had said, "on the West Coast, but not California." During Mary's freshman year, they made their final move to the Midwest, where her parents had grown up. In Michigan, her father headed another field office and would soon retire.

Over the next four months, we exchanged photos and many phone calls. Her mother sent a manila envelope with dozens of pictures of Mary's growing years, just like she promised. When I opened it, I flashed on the envelopes I'd received many years earlier, one from Helen and one from Ida's cousin and best friend, Betty Lou. I recalled how I'd longed to someday receive an envelope filled with pictures of my daughter, and now I had.

Mary was delighted to find we were so alike. She, too, had straight brown hair. Since it was the early '90s, we'd both chosen to style our hair in a trendy loose perm and wore it pulled back from our identical high foreheads.

Her parents agreed to fly her to California for her eighteenth birthday, after her high school graduation. Meeting her at the airport was the biggest event of my life, even more so than meeting my biological family, although I wondered if I'd have felt similar excitement had I been waiting for Ida's flight that evening. Mama and Tim were also there, and my new honey, Jeff, held the camcorder.

My nervousness is obvious in the video footage. Wearing a pastel linen blazer, I tap my foot just like I did while waiting for Chaps to arrive, but this time my anxiety is more visible. I didn't notice the outward similarity to that evening eleven years earlier. Maybe it was because inwardly, I felt different. I'd been waiting for this moment since the day I found out I was pregnant; I'd never yearned to meet my father like I did my lost baby.

I also knew how excited my daughter was. Since learning of Ida's death, reuniting with my baby had been the only thing I clung to, and the anticipation culminated at the Sacramento airport on June 22, 1991, at 10:00 p.m. I stood at the gate window and tried to peer through my reflection for the airplane's approaching lights. I sighed often and took deep breaths. I'd smile for the camera, look away, and take another breath.

Prior to Jeff moving in, I'd been raising a daughter on my own, putting her through private school and dance classes. I owned a new sporty black car with a cool car phone, and I'd even purchased my own home, but I still didn't feel like *enough*. The shame of my past wasn't done with me yet. But from all appearances, I was no longer the girl who was stupid in school, started fights, got knocked up, and had to give her baby away.

Once the plane landed, I could hardly contain myself as each passenger came down the ramp and entered the terminal. Finally, I caught a glimpse of my daughter. She looked young and had full cheeks. Her dark, wavy hair was pulled back in a stretchy white headband and she carried a couple of huge stuffed animals. When we locked eyes, my heart filled with relief and completion. She was beautiful and, like me, had tears in her eyes. We embraced in a long swaying hug, like I was rocking her. When we pulled away, she looked into my eyes, face wet with tears, like she couldn't believe it. She smiled, cried, and laughed all at once—we both did.

Rebecca approached and handed her big sister a bouquet of flowers. Mary then reached down to hug her. When they pulled away, Rebecca also wiped away tears. Then Mary embraced Mama and Tim. It was an incredible moment for everyone.

Reuniting with Mary for her eighteenth birthday with daughter, Becca

A few days later, I hosted a huge reunion and eighteenth birthday party in my backyard. Mary and I wore matching purple-and-lime tops and leggings we'd bought at the mall. Rebecca wore the same colors and had her hair in a headband, just like us. Later, I remembered these were the same "fresh start" colors we painted my bedroom in Anchorage a few days after I left my baby at the hospital.

Once Mary flew home, I eagerly developed the photos I'd taken during her visit. As I reviewed the prints, I remembered a picture of the reunion party Susan had thrown for me in Vancouver nine years earlier. Her arm is around my shoulder in a side hug. I'm wiping my bloodshot eyes and her forehead is pressed to my temple while she smiles at my tears. She holds a white sheet cake with "Welcome to the Family" written across its center.

I'd bought a similar cake for Mary's party, but from what I saw, the only tears she shed were tears of joy at the airport when we first embraced. I wondered if the tears at my reunion party were more from sadness because of my mother's absence than the joy of reunion.

Mary was close to my spitting image: same height, potty mouth, crooked teeth, mannerisms, and even the way she carried herself. We looked like twins in our matching outfits, and the attendees kept remarking that they couldn't tell us apart.

I hoped that I'd get to visit her home and meet her friends and family someday. Like me, Mary grew up in a traditional Catholic family. And like me, she's anything but traditional. Her mother told me she'd always thought nurture triumphed over nature—that people's development is determined 80 percent by their environment and 20 percent by genetics. But when she saw how alike we were, not just in looks but also in our attitudes and behaviors, she was convinced it's the other way around. When Mary's younger sisters reunited with their mothers, there was further proof. Nature trumps nurture.

Practically Still a Virgin

My daughter and I share the same first name, and her middle name is Claire. I thought her parents had named her after Sister, but her father said he just liked the name. I'd named her Mary Monica partly because I thought it might help when she tried to find me, but it turned out that wasn't necessary. Unlike me, all she had to do was call Catholic Charities. Adoption records were open in Alaska. Unfortunately, even today, most adult adoptees are still denied their original birth certificates and adoption records because an overwhelming majority of states continue to have sealed records, effectively preventing the adoptee and the biological parents from finding, or even knowing anything about each other.

MYSPACE

Mary and I had been in reunion for sixteen years when I joined her in Detroit for a conference in 2007. We settled into our room at the Hyatt early in the afternoon. Since we had a few hours before the first session, it was a good time to ask if she'd had any recent contact with Billy or her siblings. She'd been turned off when he'd written to her years earlier, a deep and heartfelt sharing about how he shunned materialism and would love nothing more than to live in the woods communing with Jesus away from civilization.

My daughter wasn't religious and, like me, she loved the finer things in life. The idea of living off-grid and memorizing Bible verses was akin to death by firing squad. Even so, I was surprised she hadn't taken more interest in his side of the family.

Years after receiving Billy's letter, she also got one from his wife. The letter, which included photos, encouraged Mary to connect with her half siblings. She felt the letter was pushy and didn't respond, in part because she was going through a breakup. But guilt and a sense of obligation eventually gnawed at her. Later, she wanted to connect with Billy and her half brothers but couldn't locate his contact information. She felt bad that he'd never reached out again.

I knew she might wish she had more information about Billy and his family someday, just like I did with mine. Since she was a mother now, I also thought she might wish to have his medical history.

In our room at the Hyatt that afternoon, I said, "Hey, let's see if we can find him." I opened my laptop and navigated to MySpace, an early social media site. At that time, social media was mostly used by teenagers and twenty-somethings, so I didn't have much hope he'd be online at age fifty-five; I only had a profile because my twenty-two-year-old daughter, Becca, had built it for me. It contained photos of my travels; Becca, my son Quin, and me at NBA games; Mary and her beautiful daughter; and, of course, only the most flattering pictures of Me, Myself, and I.

I typed Billy's name into the search bar. To my surprise, his picture came up—an old one from decades ago. I couldn't believe it.

Next, I called directory assistance for his last name and compiled a list. Then I started making phone calls. I spoke to a couple of people and left voicemails for a few more. An hour later, we were still in our hotel room when my phone rang.

"Hi, Billy. Thanks for calling back. Bet you're surprised to hear from me. How are you?"

I wasn't the fifteen-year-old who'd once felt small and anxious to impress, nor was I the woman with sweaty palms and a quivering voice who'd called sixteen years earlier to tell him he had a daughter. I'd been sober for twenty-three years, healed much of my shame, achieved material success, and had healthy self-esteem.

The cocky, boastful edge had returned to his voice. It became clear he'd exited his religious fervor stage. He bragged that he'd met his current girlfriend when she was a teenager and he was bootlegging in a remote Alaska bush village. She was now in her twenties and the curator of his MySpace page.

Later, I heard she'd met him at fourteen when he protected her from an abusive boyfriend. They began dating when she was seventeen. Clearly, he was back to his old ways. They now lived together and had a six-year-old daughter.

Mary stood at the end of the bed as I spoke with him. She seemed mildly interested, and I wondered, *Am I hijacking this from her?* I said, "Here's Mary" and handed her the phone. Later, she said she'd been curious, just not enough to find him and make the call herself.

When they talked, he repeated what he'd told me. Mary said she'd heard regret in his voice. She wasn't sure if it was because he'd returned to his old lifestyle or because he felt bad for not reaching out. She got the impression that he wanted to convince her he'd done the right thing by staying with the young girl he'd impregnated.

It didn't sit right with her that he wanted her to think he was doing the girl a favor, although Mary now suspects he was trying to justify his behavior and make himself sound like a good guy rather than a predator who impregnated an underage girl when he was in his midfifties.

Soon, Billy and I corresponded through email. He sent photos and I asked questions about his ethnicity and family so I could save the information for Mary when she was more interested.

I wrote, *BTW, I remember you saying you were part American Indian. In looking at the pictures of your parents, they don't look it.*

Billy responded, *I'm a typical American Mutt...we have German, Irish, English and American Indian; a lot of "teepee creeping" there, I think. My mother is one-quarter American Indian. My Indian blood probably bled out the first time I shaved. Thanks again for tracking me down...nice to be in touch again.*

Practically Still a Virgin

I forwarded the email to Mary, but it took her days to open it. I thought it was odd that she wasn't more interested. She was like me in so many ways, but this wasn't one of them. I'd wanted to uncover everything I could about my father, yet she didn't seem to care about hers. I wondered if she was uninterested because I, her twin, had fulfilled her need for connection. Or perhaps she was uninterested because I'd told her she was conceived in a date rape.

Eight months after the phone conversation with Billy, his girlfriend emailed to say he'd died in his sleep of natural causes. If Mary was disappointed, she didn't share it with me. I later learned that he'd returned to heavy drinking and cocaine use. Near the end, his girlfriend and young daughter moved out. He was living with one of his younger sons, hadn't been well for a while, and refused to go to the doctor. I suspected it was his liver.

THE HOLE

In 2014, Mary was struggling in her second marriage and implored me to come for a visit. She would eventually divorce. On a snowy evening, she asked if we could visit an old Catholic church across town because she wanted to pray the Rosary with me. Neither of us were practicing Catholics, so I was surprised she asked—and even more so to hear she'd been doing this for weeks.

It was cold inside the empty church as we knelt at the worn wooden pews, which smelled of wood polish. It reminded me of the small church Mama took me to when I was pregnant. Our voices merged in prayer as we repeated the string of Hail Marys. It felt oddly familiar, as if we were back in Anchorage on our knees in my living room when I'd prayed the Rosary over a hundred days in a row. I've since read that fetuses hear sounds from outside the womb and retain sound memories after birth. It's no wonder it brought us both comfort.

Earlier that week, I'd seen the gold Virgin Mary statue with the wood base, which I'd asked Sister to pass along to my baby all those years ago. I was touched to see it on Mary's nightstand and asked about it. She said she'd brought it to school for show-and-tell when she was eight to share that it

was a gift from her birth mother. Since it was a prized possession, her mother had carefully packed it in a paper bag, but it
fell through the bottom in the parking lot, leaving a small dent
in the Virgin's head. This upset her.

Mary said, "Ever since I was little, it's always been on my
nightstand." When she was worried or frightened, she would
look at it and repeat the prayer to the mother of all mothers,
the Virgin Mary. I wondered if it brought her comfort because
I'd repeated it out loud thousands of times when pregnant. If
so, I had no idea I was giving her something she would draw
comfort from throughout her life.

During early childhood, one of my adopted friends would
wake screaming from recurring night terrors in which she
heard a whooshing sound and knew something terrible would
happen when it stopped. In grade school, the whooshing
changed to counting down from ten. Decades later, when
she met her first mother, she mentioned those dreams. She
learned her mother was put under anesthesia for the delivery
and told to count down from ten. Her mother knew her baby
would be gone forever when she awoke.

This made me reflect on the shame, depression, and loneliness I'd felt while carrying Mary, coupled with the anticipa-
tory grief of knowing I would soon lose my child. Just before
her birth, I spent those gut-wrenching weeks sobbing for my
rats after they burned in that boy's garage.

I wondered if this had something to do with the intermittent depression that Mary called me about over the years. It
was as if she needed me to pull her out of a hole—the hole I
suspected I'd put her in.

WHITE CHRISTMAS

A week after Mary and I said the Rosary together, Becca flew in for our first Christmas together. We were guests in Mary's large ranch-style home, which was immaculate and stunning. Since Mary and Becca are both the oldest in their families, they sometimes butt heads. I sense sibling rivalry on Mary's part; she's my firstborn, yet Becca is the baby I got to keep.

The few arguments they've had always blow over quickly; like me, my daughters can't stay mad. Mary and I are barely over five feet, stocky, and physically strong. Becca has almost five inches on us with a thin frame and Kenny's long limbs.

A month or so before our visit, I was asked to speak about my recovery before a large group in Mary's hometown. As they say, "The apple doesn't fall far from the tree." I wasn't surprised that Mary found her way into recovery at twenty and Becca at twenty-five; they'd both be in attendance. On the night of the event, we arrived at a church and were led to an auditorium-like choir room. The coordinator told me to keep my talk to a strict forty-five minutes, ending at 8:25.

The space had two hundred or more cloth-covered seats in stadium rows. I sat with Becca, Mary, her husband, and a handful of her friends. Finally, Mary was called to introduce me. All eyes were on her as she walked toward the lectern and leaned into the microphone. She was respected, beautiful, classy, and articulate. I was blown away with gratitude for who my daughter had become.

With eloquence, she said, "I'd like to introduce our speaker for tonight. This woman has helped me over the years and I owe her my life, for a number of reasons, so here's ... Monica."

I carefully walked down the stairs to avoid tumbling like I did at that concert the night Billy arranged our date. I'd been paranoid about stadium-style venues ever since.

I took my place behind the microphone and looked up at hundreds of out-of-focus faces. All I saw with clarity were my two beautiful, sober, grown-up daughters. They had both become classy, whole women. It was surreal, like I was spinning inside a dream—the once-scared, shame-filled girl witnessing the culmination of her life.

I'd spoken to large groups many times, but never in front of my babies. As I spoke, my past flowed in one stream of consciousness and I burst with gratitude as it poured from me to the audience. I was in awe at how the shit of my past had come together in this wondrous full-circle moment. I was honored that people had come to listen and that my daughters were among them.

Mary later told me attendees were laughing, and at times wiping their eyes, while transfixed on my story. Throughout my talk, she'd held hands with Becca while they exchanged tearful glances. I sensed the effect I was having, especially on myself. I was unaware of anything other than the moment and the fruition of my journey.

As I spoke, I was aware that three parts of myself were present: the me who was speaking, the higher me who was observing, and the younger me, the little girl of fifteen watching her future unfold. She was in tears, and I sensed what she thought as I talked: *If I could've seen this incredible moment, I would have been so comforted.*

When I came to the part about getting pregnant, leading to the subsequent loss of my baby through adoption, I used the word "rape," not "date rape." It felt odd—so violent, especially in front of Mary and all those people.

My closing words were, "And the woman who introduced me tonight is the baby I gave up for adoption all those years ago."

There was an audible gasp. Heads turned toward Mary in shock. My daughters were clutching hands, in tears. Only Mary's friends knew our story. Most audience members had no idea who she was when she introduced me. I never planned my talks, so the ending came as a surprise to me, too. While audience members wiped their eyes, I looked at the clock for the first time and was shocked to see I'd ended at exactly 8:25.

ADULT EYES

One Saturday morning, about a month after Becca and I returned from our Christmas visit, Mary called. She was bothered by something and her therapist had suggested she ask me about it. "Monica, when you spoke here, you used the word 'rape,' not 'date rape.' I need more clarity around that. Can you describe what happened?"

My mouth went dry. I thought, *Oh, shit. She's talking to her therapist about it? It must have really bothered her.*

I laid it all out, even Billy's statement about never raping a fifteen-year-old girl—the reason I'd let him take me without a fight. Mary's voice came through the phone without hesitation or question. "Monica, *he raped you.*"

Her response shocked me because I still felt culpability and rape seemed so harsh. But I was more concerned with how the disclosure affected her. I said, "Are you okay?" Then I tried to soften it by saying, "He was a selfish, troubled teen. I doubt he saw it that way." She didn't say much.

A few months later, I stopped by Mama's. While sitting on the living room couch, I imagined the way it had been when we first moved in, how I loved to gaze out the sunlit picture window into the parklike yard with yellow daffodils among

263

white roses peeking up from the rock garden. In my mind, the back door was open and the sprinkler was making its familiar *chuh...chuh...chuh* as it oscillated to water the sprawling spring lawn. Pink blossoms were in a choir among fruit trees. I'd dreamed of this when I was a teenager in cold Alaska.

In reality, the lawn had disappeared years before. It was now overgrown with ten-foot-high thorny bushes and trees that had once been weeds—a haven for raccoons and skunks. The fruit trees had died long ago, the flower bed was broken up, and the daffodils and roses had been replaced by weeds and bramble bushes.

After Daddy died, Mama worked for ten years and earned a small pension. The gold and silver had been sold decades earlier, and the cash from liquidating our Alaska assets was spent on quack cancer cures, surgeries, hospital stays, and chemo. Not to mention the thirty or more boxes of dehydrated food still stacked in the garage. With Tim's bad back and the meth addiction, he didn't help much with home maintenance. The once-lovely yard had gone to shit, and the house was a mess.

Mama was in the kitchen when I started the conversation. She was on the other side of the wall fixing me a toasted tomato and cheese sandwich, just like she often had when I was pregnant with Mary.

"Mama, did you know that I used to sneak out my window in Anchorage?"

The browning butter smelled heavenly, sizzling as she flipped the sandwich. "No, honey. I had no idea!"

"I used to sneak out almost every weekend. One of those times, I got raped."

There it was again, that ugly word. It had come so easily. I was surprised because I'd rarely framed what happened in those terms—I almost always called it a date rape—but it was

264

too late to take it back. The few times I'd said I was raped, I immediately felt sheepish, like I'd embellished.

Abandoning the sandwich, Mama sat next to me on the couch wearing an expression of intense concern.

"That's how I got pregnant with Mary," I said. I stared out the window at the dried leaves and debris covering the patio. My voice was emotionless, as if I were telling someone else's story. When I told her how Billy shamed me, I choked out the words. "He said, 'You weren't no damn virgin. Next time, fuck the headlights off me.' Mama, I don't know why, but there wasn't any blood."

She placed her soft, warm hand on mine. In her sweet grandma voice, she said, "My poor darling. Why on earth did you keep it to yourself all these years?"

"I guess I just felt so much shame, like it was my fault. I've wondered why I didn't bleed."

Mama said, "There can be many reasons for that. Some women just don't."

I recounted the events. With her help, I began to see for the first time that Billy had manipulated a vulnerable girl. "But," I said, "when I think of that young girl as *me*, I feel like it was my fault for not stopping it."

I thought rape was like what happened in the movies— you were jumped and beaten by a stranger in a dark alley or abducted at knifepoint. You fought to escape. Victims had bruises, bloody lips, and ripped clothes. But I had no external marks and I hadn't fought, screamed for help, or even pro- tested. I'd only made a flimsy statement: "What if I said no!" Even with my newfound realization that Billy had taken advantage of me, I couldn't reconcile that night with my defi- nition of rape.

Mama spoke angrily, looking me straight in the eyes, like she did when I was in trouble as a teen. "Let's get this straight. There is no question of fault here. He raped you!"

Monica Hall

We talked about it for hours, and I clung to her conviction like a drowning woman struggling to stay above water. That conversation—and many more over the next months—helped me realize that much of my confusion arose from my attempt to be assertive: "What if I said no!" I'd spent years wondering if Billy had threatened rape just to scare me. "Mama, maybe I could've avoided the assault and preserved my virginity if my protest had been stronger, more confident."

"I doubt very much that would have stopped him," she said. "He all but told you he would rape you." I was shocked. At that moment, I realized that as awful as my experience was, it could have been much worse had I not acquiesced.

Mama's reaction was the same as Mary's. Everyone else saw it that way, too, but even as a woman with sixty years of life experience, I couldn't.

After I told her the events of that night, Mama patiently recounted them through a new, wiser lens. I listened with the attention of a student sitting at the foot of a scribe. I felt like a silly child as the clarity of an adult perspective washed over me. It suddenly seemed so elementary that Billy had exploited my friendship with Kelly and my reverence for her brothers, then tried to put me at ease by offering a beer and sharing a joint. He'd acted so quickly and methodically that I didn't have time to process what was happening.

Maybe the guilt had been percolating in my subconscious for so long that when I thought about that night, I only remembered feeling weak and ashamed. I had directed all the blame and judgment at myself and not the one it belonged to: my rapist.

BETRAYAL

The year after Mama helped me see the rape from adult eyes, in March of 2016, my thirty-one-year-old daughter, Becca, stopped by to visit. She was in her last month of pregnancy. As I led her to the door, she said, "Mom, I think you should write a memoir." It must have been in the back of my mind, because why else had I been lugging around boxes of appointment books and journals from as far back as sixth grade. Whenever I moved, I thought, *Why am I keeping this crap?*

The moment I opened my laptop to start writing, I knew I'd need my old friend to help me tackle *all* the dark shit that happened in Anchorage. Kelly and I had only connected a few times since I left Alaska forty-two years earlier, but I felt a modicum of hope when I heard her voice. She was still soft-spoken and patient, and, I was soon to discover, wise. Her daughters were now grown and she'd lost her husband of thirty-six years a few months earlier. She was cleaning out the forever home he'd built for her and was buying a smaller place. Kelly needed her old friend and I needed mine.

She told me all the crew had passed. Like Billy and the others, her brothers died of drug-related illnesses. She nursed

Steven first, then Tommy. I couldn't imagine her larger-than-life brothers withering away with barf bowls and bedpans. The loss devastated her.

We were on one of our long phone calls when I said, "Do you remember that I got beat with a wire hanger?"

She shouted, "Yes! I saw it!"

Her outburst was startling. She hadn't witnessed the beating, nor had she been in my PE class to help hide my thighs. Bewildered, I asked, "What do you mean, you saw it?"

She blurted it out without taking a breath. "I saw *it* in the bathroom stall. You wanted to know what it looked like. I'll never forget it. I can see it right now. It looked like you'd been beaten with a cat-o'-nine-tails. Don't you have scars?"

I froze, grasping what she was saying. "I showed you?"

"You pulled up your shirt. Monica, there were open sores on your back and shoulders! I'd never seen anything like it. I was so mad at your dad!"

My heart was hammering, and I felt lightheaded. I put "wire hanger beating" in the browser of my phone and found a photo of a child's back with thirty or more hanger scars, about four inches in length.

I didn't remember having wounds on my shoulders or my back, only those welts on my thighs. I felt sick, and my mind was spinning: *How could anyone do such a horrific thing to their child?* I texted the link to Kelly, knowing the gruesome image couldn't be anything like what she'd seen. Surely, I wouldn't have forgotten that.

I held my breath while waiting for her return text: *Yes, but not as many, and they were longer.*

She *had* seen them! My knees went weak and I collapsed on my bed. She was correct about the length of the lesions; when Daddy performed his wire-bending act, he crafted the hanger into an eight-inch length with a handle at its end. Still,

I only recalled the marks on my leg, which I'd shown Mama at my door. I also knew both thighs had welts.

I composed myself after our conversation and called Mama. She didn't call Kelly a liar, but she may as well have by her snarky reply: "He only hit you a few times and it didn't last that long. I don't remember him hitting your shoulders."

I thought, *Maybe it wasn't so bad. Have I been making a big deal out of something that was much less traumatic? Maybe he only hit me three times instead of more, like it seemed. But why would Kelly make that up?*

Mama didn't apologize for allowing the beating. Instead, she coldly rejected my flashback and minimized the horrific abuse by suggesting Kelly was dishonest and I was overdramatizing. But what really broke my heart was the thing I didn't want to admit: she cared more about her pride than healing my heart.

Looking back, I wonder why I didn't confront her right then and say, "Mama, why can't you admit you should've stopped him or never let him beat me at all? You were supposed to protect me. You'd have never let him hurt Tim. Aren't you sorry?" I was almost sixty, but I was also the young girl unable to bear another rejection.

Years earlier, when she'd confessed to seeing pleasure in Daddy's eyes, I hadn't been surprised. As an adult, I knew Daddy's feelings for me weren't right. I'd been grateful she rescued me by stopping him.

When Kelly described seeing my shoulders in the bathroom stall, it was like seeing ghost marks on a freshly erased blackboard. I felt like my memories were floating in the fog, waiting for me to grasp them. A few days later, I pulled out my laptop and forced myself back to that night by writing the beating scene for my memoir.

As I wrote, snippets of white noise began to form. I was in a time warp, screaming, twisting, covering my head as Daddy's arm came down again and again in slow motion. Searing shocks lit my thighs, bottom, back, and shoulders. He had those dead marble eyes I'd seen in the car the previous year.

Until that flashback, I had no memory of it ending, no recollection of crying in my room afterward. Revisiting that memory, I was back at my bedroom door showing Mama my welts. I hadn't recalled much about them before, only their length and shape, and that they were angry and raised. I saw myself in my panties, turning to expose my right thigh. I looked down at the vivid purple welts, the edges of which were broken open and rimmed with blood. When that memory surfaced, my stomach turned and I covered my mouth to hold back a cry. The violet injuries were so raised it looked as if caterpillars had burrowed under my skin.

Horrified, I wondered, *Why didn't I fight him off or go to the principal?* Even after gaining more clarity, my mind went back to what I'd told myself to make it tolerable: *Mama must have been horror-stricken and speechless when she saw the wounds. That's why she turned away. She'd rushed off to have words about it with Daddy.*

Maybe she didn't remember because she was so horrified by the injuries that, like me, she'd erased most of what happened from her mind. Or maybe being in the room when it happened was so traumatic that she dissociated, and that's why she thought it didn't last "that long," why she had no recollection of the strikes to my back and shoulders.

A few years later, not long after Mama died, the subject came up again with Kelly. I said, "Why do you think I wanted you to look at my back that day?"

She answered matter-of-factly. "It was probably hurting because they were beginning to scab over and stick to your shirt. They were probably much worse than your thighs because your shirt was a thinner material than your jeans."

That had never occurred to me. It was as if my mind was muffled when it came to any logic around my parents' cruelty.

After that, I saw a fourteen-year-old girl in a bathroom stall reaching out to her friend because her mother had turned her back on her. She couldn't go to the nurse to have the wounds treated because she loved her parents. I wept for that poor girl.

What loving mother could stand to watch her child suffer such pain? I certainly couldn't. Could she tolerate it because I wasn't her flesh and blood?

CURSED

I began to see the rape through adult eyes when I wrote the memoir chapter where Billy took my virginity. I wished I'd confronted him while he was alive. I thought it might help to see his face in a photograph, but I'd lost the pictures I saved for our daughter. MySpace was long gone by then, so I turned to Facebook to find one.

Levi, Billy's oldest son, was born eight years after Mary. The three of us were connected on Facebook but never interacted. Scrolling through Levi's photos, I was surprised to see him standing with a lanyard around his neck before a backdrop at the Beverly Hills Film Festival. He was in scene in another photo, fighting in battle on a set that reminded me of *Game of Thrones*. In yet another, he was behind a movie camera. Levi was an actor, producer, and director. He had a rakishly handsome smile, perfect white teeth, and the light stubble of a goatee. There were similarities to his father, but Levi had a masculine vulnerability that Billy lacked. He also had Billy's eyes, but there was softness beneath them. I was intrigued and sent him a message.

We spoke the next day. His voice was deeper than his father's and lacked Billy's sarcasm and edge. I sensed a gentle soul. He lived in Anchorage, as did his siblings, but his mom had moved to the Lower 48. He was making films, docudramas, and fiction based on his life—coming-of-age stories centered on his experiences with his father.

I said, "I'm writing a memoir about my wild days in Anchorage. I'm looking for old pictures of your dad."

"Dad told a lotta crazy stories from back then."

"I thought seeing his face might help me remember those times," I said, hoping Levi didn't detect an ulterior motive. There was no reason he would, but I felt sheepish. "What was the deal with your dad being a preacher? That was the last thing I expected."

I could hear in his voice that he was dying to talk to someone who'd known his dad in the old days. "Dad went to jail when he embezzled from a company he worked for."

I'd heard he did some sort of accounting, but I had a hard time visualizing Billy laboring over a set of books.

"He also smuggled drugs into the bush. He was dealing cocaine and drinking."

That sounded more like the Billy I knew.

"In jail, Dad got born again. When he got out, he married Christy, who was uber-religious." I smiled at the term "uber," which showed his age. I liked him immediately.

"Yeah, Christy answered the phone when I kept hanging up. She wasn't too warm, as I recall." He laughed because he'd heard about the hang-ups. Levi had only been ten at the time and lived with his mother, who had left Billy. He confirmed that his stepmom was a jealous woman. I wondered what power she had over his father. The Billy I knew wasn't the pussy-whipped type.

"Dad started getting me high when I was thirteen. He rode both sides of the line. We weren't allowed to listen to rock and roll, but he had a secret side. We'd smoke pot and he still preached."

I imagined the restriction was Christy's influence. I'd heard about some Christians denouncing rock as the Devil's music, but it seemed over the top and so unlike Billy. I pictured scrub pines rushing by as they sped down the open road, Led Zeppelin's "Black Dog" on the radio, Levi's face shining as gusts of clean air erased evidence of their sin.

"I'm writing a book about all the stories my dad told me, but piecing together his stories is kinda ... " He chuckled. "Well ... there's a lotta tall tales in there. I know some of it's based on reality, but I wonder how much of it's his own fabrication."

I felt guilty knowing I'd called to get a photo so I could yell obscenities and pull out my dart collection. But the more he spoke, the more I felt honored to listen.

I said, "It was pretty crazy back then. What kind of stories was he telling you?"

"Dad was really conflicted. He had experiences that he didn't talk to a lotta people about. He thought he was cursed and really freaked me out with his stories." I understood the hunger in his voice—he wanted to know more about his dad. I probably sounded the same way when I was talking to people who knew Ida.

"When I was thirteen," Levi said, "Dad told me he was cursed."

A knot began to form in my stomach. When he was an impressionable thirteen-year-old, the same age I'd been on that horrific car ride with Daddy, Billy told him a story. Levi said that when his dad was nineteen and addicted to heroin, he began seeing a demonic entity. A wave of nausea rolled through me. I realized it would have been around the time Billy raped me. I'd had no idea Billy was shooting smack. One night, Levi said, Billy offered the entity his firstborn son for the power to quit. He never used heroin again.

Practically Still a Virgin

My daughter's father had not only seen a demon but prayed to it. Horrified, I stared out my living room window and into the darkness. The hair on my arms stood on end. I quickly closed the blinds and locked the doors.

I was also sickened for Levi. Being told such a thing by the father he idolized, true or not, was gut-wrenching. "I thought my dad was crazy, but at the same time, I put him on a pedestal. After he died, I started making films." There was pain in his voice, and I realized why I felt so connected to him. We were attempting to heal from the same man.

"I'm so sorry, Levi."

"Yeah, it was a confusing way to grow up. Dad wanted to be a good man but struggled with his past and was tormented by guilt for the things he'd done."

I wondered what other *things* he'd done. Given Billy's thirst for virgins, I wondered how many girls shared my fate.

Levi was quick to tell me his father had helped many people in the church and worked with addicts to free them from drugs. I understood his conflict. I'd put Daddy on a pedestal, too, and loved how people respected him.

Levi's story helped me understand why Billy became religious. It was still a stretch for me to picture him praying on his knees, but I could see him preaching from a pulpit. The Billy I remembered was charismatic and liked attention.

"Dad helped a lotta people. Even after he left the church, if someone at the bar couldn't make rent, he'd pull out his wallet. At the end, he was mournful. He felt alone and went back to drugs and alcohol."

There was hopefulness in Levi's voice when I told him I was writing about my experiences in Anchorage. He was working on a docudrama and was interviewing people who'd been at the middle of those wild '70s. He must've been trying to prove that his father's stories were true, that Anchorage really was crazy back then. In telling Levi these stories, Billy must have also been trying to heal from Anchorage.

"I'd love to hear anything you've written about my dad," Levi said.

I'd been dreading the request. I didn't want to cause him more pain but knew I couldn't deny him. I'd also yearned for any little scrap about my mother. I hadn't cared what I found, even when Helen told me Ida slept around. It was better than nothing.

I said, "Well, I don't know if you know this, but ... it wasn't consensual."

"Yeah ... I wondered."

"It's not pretty, but I can read it to you if you want."

"Yeah, I'd really like to hear it."

I read the draft while I stood at my kitchen bar. As the words came out, I knew they probably drove daggers through his heart. When I finished, I waited for his response with every fiber at attention. Would he hang up on me? Would he believe me? Had I harmed him? Did he think I was at fault? I'd felt connected to Levi and could tell he reciprocated. I didn't want to ruin it—at some deep level, our alliance was important. He finally said, "I'm not surprised. My father could be a wicked man."

I took a big breath and relaxed. I knew something important had happened. Levi said, "You know ... I don't understand. Even after all the horrible things he told me, I still cherished visiting him. I idolized him."

"Yeah, of course you did. He was your dad."

Even though Daddy had abused me, I still loved him. I wanted to be smart and good in business, just like him. I wanted him to be proud of me. I wanted people to shake my hand and respect me like they did with Daddy. Levi and I were both stuck between the love and idolization we had for our fathers and the unconscionable boundaries they'd crossed.

Based on what Levi told me about the demonic apparition, it seems Billy's surrender had given him the power to quit heroin, just as my surrender had given me the strength to quit alcohol and cocaine. The difference was that I reached for a higher power and Billy reached for a lower one.

For the three years I'd been hanging around with Kelly, Billy had treated me like I was Tommy's kid sister. The person who growled at me in the schoolyard, and later the apartment, was not the Billy I'd known. It made sense now. The demon must have been the darkness I saw in his eyes when he threatened, "I've never raped a fifteen-year-old girl."

I no longer needed to confront Billy. I needed to meet Levi.

RUBIK'S CUBE

Mary's video-chat request came in May 2016, a month after I'd talked with her half brother Levi. I was lounging in bed when my laptop rang. When Mary's face popped up on the screen, I saw that she, too, was in bed. My granddaughters were with their father for the weekend, giving us an opportunity to have a long chat—a rarity because her girls required so much attention. Sometimes we'd go months without a call.

"You on your laptop or phone?" I asked.

"Laptop.'"

"Me too."

We talked about everything, quickly jumping between topics. Two years earlier, Mary had divorced her second husband, and she'd just begun online dating. I offered advice—I'd also experienced online dating at her age.

I also read to her from my memoir manuscript and the journal I kept while I was pregnant in Alaska. She could listen to my stories for hours. I'd occasionally glance up to catch a warm, contented expression on her face as she looked down at the scarf she was knitting. It was the same look I imagined she might have had if I'd read to her when she was little. Seeing the comfort my words brought her both filled my heart and broke it.

When she needed to change rooms, she carried me with her to the kitchen and propped me against the backsplash while she rummaged for snacks. I also accompanied her to the patio where she swung on the hammock. That day, I was always with her.

Mary and I had been video-chatting for about five hours when our conversation switched to our ethnicity and our 2007 phone call with Billy the day we found his MySpace page. Opening a file on my laptop I said, "I saved those emails Billy sent. According to this, he was German, Irish, English, and some American Indian."

We'd recently sent saliva samples to Ancestry, a company that analyzes each customer's DNA, provides an ethnicity report, and uses an online platform to suggest likely relatives (others who have submitted DNA) based on their genetic makeup. Because we had long since found each other and knew our origins, the DNA results hadn't been terribly interesting, and neither of us spent time studying them. I'd reviewed mine a few months earlier; the report said I was mostly French and Aboriginal[2] with some English and Irish, as expected.

"Monica, that doesn't make sense," Mary said. "My DNA shows me to be exactly half the Native you are. So, if Billy had Native American like he claimed, I would have more Indian than I do. Billy can't be my father."

I explained that DNA isn't always pulled equally from each parent. I also told her that a lot of people claimed to have American Indian heritage—especially in the '70s when it was

---

2. At the time, Ancestry listed "aboriginal" but after additional updates to their DNA ethnicity updates, it lists "Indigenous Americas—North." Updated Dec. 13, 2023. https://support.ancestry.com/s/article/List-of-AncestryDNA-Regions?language=en_US

cool—but Native American heritage often turned out to be family legend rather than fact. Such was the case with Kelly. Still, Mary wanted to take another look at the DNA results.

I was stir-crazy after being in bed for half the day, so I dragged my laptop into the dining room. Just as I got situated and logged on to Ancestry, there was a knock at the door.

"Crap! I didn't realize how late it was. Hold on. I think Becca's here with the baby." As they came in, I called, "Say 'hi' to Mary! We're on video." Becca was with her wife and my one-month-old grandson, Miles. They said their hellos and sat across the room. I could see Mary on the screen and Becca feeding Miles on the couch. They'd come for movie night.

I clicked on my DNA matches. At the top was Mary, showing a parent/child relationship with an *extremely high likelihood*. "Ha! It says you're my daughter."

She laughed. "No shit. I'm practically your twin."

I scrolled through a list of other matches, but the closest after Mary were second cousins.

She said, "Okay, this is what mine says." She read her percentages. "English, Irish, French, aboriginal, Scandinavian ... "

My eyes widened. *Scandinavian?* I wondered if I'd heard correctly.

I asked, "Who are your other matches?" I looked at Becca. She mirrored my surprise.

"It shows a cousin here. She's got to be on my father's side because there's no DNA connection to you. There's an extensive family tree with over seven hundred people, but it's all blacked out. I wish I could see it."

I said, "Send her a message. Request to be added to her tree."

I stared at her high forehead and wondered what she was writing as she typed a message. Later, she gave me her password so I could read the conversation.

Practically Still a Virgin

Hi, Mary wrote. *We're cousins. I'm adopted and have known my birth mother for many years but I'm unsure about the paternity. It looks like we may be a match on my birth father's side as my birth mother has also done the DNA and the lineage doesn't match hers. Any information you have would be helpful.*

Her cousin immediately asked for more information. While Mary typed, I looked over the top of my screen at Becca, who had deer-in-headlights eyes. As she burped Miles, she mouthed, "What?"

Mary's second note said, *There were two possible birth fathers. My birth mother was raped at age 15 by a Billy Mawson but had also dated a Luke Travers. This would have been in Anchorage Alaska in 1972. I've spent all these years thinking I was a product of this rape, but now based on the DNA I'm not so sure.*

Mary looked up after reading her cousin's response. "She says there are Traverses on her grandmother's side. Monica, do you know Luke's parents' names or when he was born?"

My head spun. Dazed, I sent a Facebook message to Harrel, one of the boys Daddy thought I'd been with on the night of the wire hanger beating. Harrel was good friends with Luke's brother, and he replied almost instantly. I relayed the information: "Luke's father's name is Harris."

Becca's brows arched. She was grinning.

"Monica," Mary said, "she's calling her grandmother right now."

I was dumbfounded. I held my breath as Mary silently read the cousin's reply. Then she looked up. "Harris is her grandmother's brother. His family lived in Alaska in 1972. *So, Luke is my real father.*"

Still holding my breath, I stared through the lens frozen with astonishment.

Becca and her wife looked at each other in shock, then at me. I'll never forget their gaping mouths and wide eyes.

Becca said, "Oh my God! I can't believe I was here to witness this!"

Almost instinctively, I got on social media to look for Luke. In seconds, I found someone who might be his daughter and sent her a message: *Are you by chance Luke Travers's daughter?*

Within seconds, she responded.

I am.

I'm an old friend from Alaska. Do you happen to have his number?

He's standing right here, she wrote.

Within minutes of the DNA discovery, I had Luke on speakerphone. Unbeknownst to him, Mary was still on my computer screen. She could hear the conversation and see my face when I blurted the news with zero tact. Luke immediately burst into tears. I was surprised by this show of emotion—he was such a self-centered kid back then.

"I knew it," he said between sobs. "You disappeared and I couldn't find you. You were gone. I knew it!"

"We moved to California a few months after she was born and I've been here ever since," I said. I remembered sending him away when, in the last months of my pregnancy, he'd come to my window to talk about the baby. I'd thought he was a kook.

Eventually, I told him that Mary was listening to our conversation. I introduced him to his daughter, and they exchanged hellos.

He later said, "All the men in my family have swimmers." Mary was the oldest of Luke's eleven or twelve children. All but two were girls. Trying to extricate an exact child count was frustrating. He estimated seven different mothers, but when I pushed for clarification, he texted, *You might as well run an ad in the Anchorage newspaper to find out.*

I can remember that afternoon on Luke's bed with clarity when I let him hump my thigh gap. It was the only time we'd made out with my pants down. I can still hear his pleas, can feel the pressure with which I locked my legs together. Luke and I now laugh about the irony of it because had I not been raped by Billy, it would have truly been a virgin birth.

Since it was at Becca's request that I'd begun documenting our adoption story, it was incredible that she arrived within minutes of the discovery to witness the unlikely sequence of events leading to its culmination.

Had Mary not been home alone, had I not been lounging in bed with no plans for the day, had her cousin not been on Ancestry, had my friend in Alaska not answered my message immediately, had Luke's daughter not been looking at her phone when I contacted her, and had Luke not been standing next to his daughter ... It was as if the stars were perfectly aligned, and it all happened within ten minutes.

Even so, I was twisted up for weeks. The lie I'd told Sister forty-three years earlier was actually the truth. I was relieved Mary wasn't conceived through rape, influenced by what I now believe was demonic possession, but I was too disoriented to be joyful. My brain felt like a Rubik's Cube trying to put the last forty years of shame in right order.

For over four decades, I'd accepted that the rape had been necessary to result in Mary's life. But with that off the table, I didn't know how to process it. I could see no light in that event, no purpose, no silver lining. It was just a humiliating experience that stole my virginity, my crutch to self-worth—and it caused me to punish myself for decades.

When I think about the rape and pregnancy, my mind still defaults to the old story of Billy being Mary's father. Although it's now been over seven years since we learned the truth of her conception, I lived with a different story for more than four decades. Mary experiences the same thing when telling her adoption story. She has caught herself still sharing that she was conceived by rape. That also makes sense; we made the discovery twenty-five years after our reunification, so rape had also been her truth for a long time. It's hard to rewrite the narrative.

Eventually, I met Luke when I was visiting Washington, where he'd lived for years. During that trip, we video-chatted with Mary. I took screenshots and sent them to her. A few weeks later she was talking to a new friend and told the story of being adopted. She pulled up the photo and said, "These are my birth parents." To most, having a picture of their parents isn't a big deal—but to an adoptee, it's everything. She enlarged the photo and said, "I can't believe it! These are the people who made me, and they're together in one picture." I wish I had a similar photo with Ida and Chaps.

With her dark hair and features, Mary looks nothing like Scandinavian Luke. Still, when I showed her his picture, she said without hesitation, "Yep, that's my father." She just knew. Much like Luke knew when he came to my window that I was pregnant with his child—bizarre, given that we didn't have sex. It also explains why Mary never felt connected to Billy or desired to pursue a relationship with him or his family.

The final message Mary sent to her cousin on Ancestry read, *Thank you for the information. My birth mother is in tears. Crazy story but she and Luke never truly had intercourse, so all these years she thought my father was the man who raped her.*

ANCHORAGE

I'd been working on my memoir for three months when Anchorage began calling. In June of 2016, I disembarked an Alaska Airlines flight and was embraced through a panoramic wall of floor-to-ceiling windows, by the breathtaking Chugach Mountains. Their enormity brought me to tears. I'd seen them every day for sixteen years, but viewing them again in such splendor induced an overwhelming flood of nostalgia.

I yearned to run my fingers along their slivers of white, as if doing so would transport me back to the court as Tim and I leapt through the icy sprinkler, cold wet grass between our toes as a prop plane purred overhead. As I walked to baggage claim, my heart sang and I had a smile so big, I knew I looked crazy. I was home.

Kelly drove three hours from her house in Soldotna to meet me at the airport. We picked up our friendship right where we'd left off—it was as if we'd never been apart. We spent a few days tooling around our childhood homes and haunts, then headed to her house where we spent two days lounging in our jammies. It was comforting being with my old friend again.

When we returned to Anchorage, it was overcast and chilly for our meetup with Levi. I'd had many phone conversations with him, but I felt guilty that he still thought Mary was his sister. Reality sounded like a *Jerry Springer* episode, and I needed to look him in the eye while breaking the news so he could see I was sane. I'd also be able to gauge his expression and do damage control if needed.

Levi towered over us by more than a foot. He was handsome and polite, but his wheels were turning as he sized us up. We exchanged hugs and slid into a booth at the taqueria. He looked vaguely like his father but was much warmer. He had Billy's sharp, intelligent eyes—not the cold eyes that had stared me down the night of the rape, but the ones I remembered from before.

We talked for at least two hours and sat at the table long after we finished our meal. Then, Kelly abruptly said, "I gotta make a phone call." She walked outside to avoid the awkward conversation.

I began with the leg hump and then how Mary and I had been video-chatting all day. When I finished, Levi's expressionless eyes pierced mine. He said nothing. I held my breath and met his stare, hoping my discovery wouldn't change our friendship. Finally, he said, "That's some crazy shit." I smiled in relief, adoring him even more.

A few years later, I asked what he was thinking immediately after my confession. He said, "It felt weird when I found out I had an older sibling, but when you told me it wasn't true, I felt like, *Oh yeah, I'm still the oldest.*" We cracked up.

GUTTURAL CRY

A year before I began writing my memoir, when I first told Mama about Billy, she helped me realize I wasn't at fault for the rape, but my guilty feelings resurfaced.

On a stormy winter evening, I was revising the chapter I'd written about my "date" with Billy. Each time I worked on it, I cracked open more memories. That night, as gusts of wind blasted my house, I was transported deeper into that time and place—and to my teenage mindset. I examined Billy's smell and his threats, the way the room looked, the physical pain I felt, his shaming comments when he felt cheated because I didn't bleed.

I'd been trying to recreate the innocent feeling I'd had in Mama's living room when she walked me through that night with adult eyes. It had made so much sense then, but now I felt at fault when I looked back on those memories.

Why can't I see what everyone else sees? I wondered.

I video-called Mama. Her smile lit up my screen and I could see she'd been reading while sitting on the couch.

In her sweetest voice, she said, "Hi shuga... whatcha doin'?"

"Remember when you went over the rape with me so I could see it wasn't my fault?"

"Yes, of course."

"I'm feeling guilty about it again."

"That's no good. I thought we got that all cleared up."

"Yeah, but it's back. I think you can help."

"Of course, honey. What can I do?"

"Could you go through it with me again, like we did last time? You know—break it down, how he manipulated me? I'm going to record your voice so I can play it back and hopefully reprogram my brain."

I'd done this when Becca was a child, when I listened to parenting audio tapes on repeat so parenting with thoughtful consequences became embedded in me, instead of the raging I grew up with. Again, here, I needed to hear Mama's words and see the truth in her eyes as she broke it down for me. I began recording.

Her voice was patient but firm, just like when I was little and woke from a nightmare to hear her sweet voice hushing my fears. I felt like a blind person being led through a mine-field. I could see Billy's premeditation and manipulation as she spoke, but I feared it wouldn't stick. Over the following months, I played the recording repeatedly and rewrote my account multiple times. I also had a dream where I was drinking alcohol, my first drinking dream in over thirty years.

During many calls, Kelly also walked me through my innocence. I was concerned she might have mixed feelings because Billy had been like a brother to her. She was silent the first time I read her my memories of the rape. I held my breath, waiting for her reaction, worrying she might think me culpable.

Like always, Kelly picked her words carefully. Finally, she said, "Monica, he threatened to rape you for gosh sakes. What more do you need?" I needed to hear that from her more than anyone.

Practically Still a Virgin

If I imagined a different girl in the scene, I became enraged and could clearly see that it was rape. In fact, I would have loved nothing more than to string him up by his balls and beat the living shit out of him. But when I pictured myself on that filthy sofa, I was still washed through with guilt.

I'd been at it for weeks. Then, something shifted. I saw the inside of that apartment with more clarity and felt my humiliation in every cell. Billy had just gotten off me. He was turned away, buttoning his jeans. The room was shadowy and dim. I rose from the sheets, desperate to cover my nakedness. I had one leg in my panties when his enraged pupils bore into me. "You weren't no damn virgin! Next time, fuck the headlights off me!"

I remember thinking, *Next time? I'll never look at your face again, you fucking bastard.*

For the first time, I realized he didn't crave sex—it was power, the power of breaking a virgin. I was enraged and screamed into the empty room, "Fuck you! Fuck you! I hate your fucking guts, you fucking bastard!" I pushed back my chair, stood, and screamed a guttural cry. Then I wept.

CONDOLENCES

In 2017, I opened the old green box with "Mary Monica" written across its front. Inside were the treasures I'd carted from Alaska to California and through eleven additional moves over forty-some years.

I pulled from the box a vintage-looking hospital menu, my patient wristband, the black-capped pen I'd used to sign the adoption papers, and the Catholic holy cards the sweet little French nun had brought when she visited my room. There were also greeting cards from my parents, brother, and Paula's mother. I wondered what had gone through their minds when choosing cards. Congratulations weren't in order, nor were "Get Well" wishes. "Our Condolences" would have been more apropos, but no one had the guts to give me that card.

My twelve-year-old brother's card featured a seagull's silhouette. Inside was printed, "Miss You." Beneath it, he wrote, *From Tim.* My sweet but annoying and mostly adoring little brother had been torn apart by the impending adoption.

There was also a card from Mama. It was white with a tasteful, artsy line etching of a sleeping baby in a flowing gown. It was titled, "An Unspeakable Joy." Inside, it said,

Practically Still a Virgin

"Your brand-new baby." The card was signed, *From her loving grandmother*. My artist mom may have thought she picked it for the lovely drawing, but I wonder if it was also a subconscious choice. It had been, after all, an *unspeakable* pregnancy.

Paula's mother also sent a card, which I had no memory of. She'd blamed me for every little trouble her daughter got into, which wasn't much next to my shenanigans. When I was in the hospital, Paula told me her mother had said, "It's too bad for the baby." For decades, I hadn't been able to forgive her for that. What was too bad? That my baby was born? That she was going to be adopted by a loving family? And what did that say about Tim and me? We'd been adopted, too. I'd pictured Paula's mom shaking her head in reproach while standing before the card rack, picking through them as she might when removing lint from an unkempt sweater.

When I dug through the box of keepsakes decades later, I saw her card for what felt like the very first time. Maybe I'd never opened it because I disliked her, or maybe I didn't believe the sentiment behind it. Whatever the case, it seemed brand-new to me. The front showed a charcoal sketch of forget-me-nots paired with an Abe Lincoln quote: "The better part of one's life consists of his friendships." Inside, she wrote, *Dear Monica, We truly respect you for the heartache you have had to accept. May God bless you always.*

The card softened me. How could I have missed it back then?

Ever since I left Alaska, Paula and I had talked every five years or so to catch up. During our conversations, I always asked if her mom still felt the same about me. Paula had conveyed to her mother that I turned out to be a good person, but her mom never stopped disapproving of me.

After looking at the greeting cards, I dug deeper into the box. Sister Clare's business card caught my eye. As I held it, I could clearly see the Catholic Charities parking lot, thanks

291

to my shameful memory of that drunk man. I remembered it was close to the Cook Inlet, but I could barely bring the lobby and building to mind—curious, since I had been there so many times.

I sensed there was more to uncover in Alaska, and Catholic Charities was the key. I booked another flight.

UNSHACKLING

In August of 2017, I returned to Anchorage. I grabbed a rental car and picked Kelly up—she was in town visiting her daughter.

The phrase "There's no place like home" rang in my ears as we cruised through our old neighborhoods while I once again soaked up my beloved town. There's something magical about Anchorage on those rare sunny summer days with a vivid blue sky and the majestic crown of mountains bordering the city—warm sun on your cheeks, cool fresh air, and lush midnight-sun vegetation.

I stopped the car because I'd forgotten to bring Sister's card with me and didn't have the address for Catholic Charities. I used my phone to search for directions, and a telephone number popped up. I dialed. As it rang, I wondered why I was calling.

With Kelly in the passenger seat, I told the receptionist I'd relinquished a baby for adoption forty-four years earlier and wondered if I could visit the building to look inside. She said their offices had moved.

Minutes later, I received a call back from Lisa, who didn't facilitate adoptions but was the organization's director. She was gracious, even honored to talk to me. She invited me to come over, then thanked me and told me I was an incredible woman.

I was embarrassed by her praise. I still felt shame for the pregnancy and having to give my baby up for adoption. I thought I'd be interrupting by showing up at the office—I certainly didn't imagine I'd be welcomed like a visiting dignitary.

My weekly counseling with Sister Clare hadn't been effective in helping me with my guilt and shame about Billy, my delinquent behavior, Daddy's abuse, the pending adoption, and so much more because I wasted the time with meaningless chitchat and told her only what I thought she wanted to hear. I don't remember much about what I said during those sessions. The only thing I truly recall is the lie about my baby's father—which, it turned out, hadn't been a lie after all.

I pulled into the parking lot and grabbed my handbag, preparing to go in. Kelly announced that she would wait in the car.

I panicked. "Get your ass out of the car. You're coming!" Being an introvert, she was reluctant—but I wasn't taking no for an answer.

As we entered through the glass doors, I didn't know what I was doing there—I'd wanted a tour of the old building but had no interest in the new location. It felt so different with its wide halls and shiny tile floors, more like a school. A minute later, Lisa greeted us. She looked to be fortyish, conservatively dressed with chin-length brown hair, a sweet face, and kind eyes.

While she led us to a meeting room, she told me about the many programs Sister Clare had founded, like the adoption program, Head Start for low-income families, home placement for unwed mothers, and refugee programs for the Alaska bush. She'd visited the previous year for the fiftieth-anniversary celebration. I'd just missed her.

Lisa led us down the hall to a large room with six-foot-long tables positioned in rows, like a school cafeteria. She offered us seats at the table closest to the door. I sat before her, facing the windows with Kelly on my right. I wondered if her reverence for what I'd done by giving my child a better home was contrived, like a funeral director's sympathy.

Lisa sat up tall, her hands clasped. She looked so good and wholesome with perfect white teeth, no makeup, and ungroomed brows. I laid my hands on the table and straightened my spine.

"It's an honor to have you visit us today. What an incredible woman you are." Lisa had said something similar on the phone, but looking into her eyes, I could see that she meant it.

I knew Kelly, feeling awkward, wondered what she was doing there. I wondered what I was doing there, too. This woman wasn't Sister Clare, and we weren't in the building where I'd had my counseling sessions. I wasn't sure what I hoped to gain by meeting Lisa. Without knowing quite what to say, I thanked her for taking the time to see me and said, "I was fifteen when my mother used to bring me for weekly counseling sessions."

I knew this was somehow important. Like a prisoner of war who had been shackled for forty-four years, I felt I was about to be rescued, my freedom so imminent I could hear a team of soldiers rushing through the dark corridors to release me. My voice broke when I said, "I never told her anything real!"

I told Lisa I'd lied about my baby's paternity because I was ashamed of the truth—that, as far as I knew, my pregnancy had resulted from being raped when I was a virgin.

I also told her my dad had beaten me with a wire hanger and had raged at me about what sluts and whores do as if I was one of them. I told her that as an adoptee, I'd felt the only person in the world who would be a part of me was the baby whom Sister and my parents wanted me to give away. Unchecked tears flowed down my cheeks.

Lisa and I never took our eyes off each other. It was as if the outside world didn't exist. Her blue eyes filled with tears, and I felt like I'd known her forever. I could see I'd brought up something personal for her, yet I kept going, aware that she was the catalyst I needed. Somehow, I knew I was hers, too. I sensed Kelly next to me, also in tears as she witnessed my history come full circle.

I was aware of everything in that moment: the secrets finally escaping, the white cafeteria room, bright beams of sunlight streaming through the cathedral windows and illuminating us. My regret rose, lifting a thousand-pound robe from my shoulders. I was in the midst of a miracle.

When I finished, I took a deep breath and wiped my face with my palms. Lisa's compassionate gaze felt like that of a mother tending to her feverish child, her gentle expression was as comforting as a cool cloth. We sat in silence, then I thanked her. She thanked me, too, and I knew she meant it.

I was spent, maybe even in shock. I cried on and off for a week without provocation. It was as if I were acclimating to a new reality, one without secrets and shame.

When I talked with Kelly about that day three years later, she remembered the space as a small conference room, not a cafeteria. I thought she must be mistaken, so I asked Lisa to send pictures. It *was* a small conference room, not big and bright like my memories. The ceiling was low and acoustic. There were no cathedral windows—just small ones set near the floor. It would've been impossible for light to shine down on us.

I'd needed to tell the truth at the adoption agency. That day, I did what I didn't have the courage to do at fifteen. I'd worn a brave face back then, but I was just a scared little girl alone with her shameful secrets.

HIS RELUCTANCE

In 1992, the year after my reunification with Mary, we were excited to plan my trip to her hometown. She wanted me to meet her friends and family, see the home she lived in, and visit the schools she'd attended. It would be my chance to fill the blank pages of the childhood scrapbook I'd imagined while trying to picture her life during our years apart.

Mary's family had a lot going on with three teen daughters, so I thought nothing of it when they kept postponing my visit. The reason for the final delay was, "My mom says it would be better for you to come after my dad's retirement party."

I didn't know it, but her father was the one who'd been stalling. Mary and her mother thought he wasn't so gung ho on the reunion after all, but they didn't share that with me. Unbeknownst to him, Mary and her mother were tired of rescheduling and told me to book my flight.

Years later, Mary shared the story. She was waiting at the kitchen table while, upstairs, her mom broke the news to her father that I was to arrive the next day. When her mother came downstairs, Mary knew something was wrong.

Practically Still a Virgin

Pat slowly pulled out a chair and studied her daughter's face. Mary found this odd—her mother was usually quite animated. Mary feared her father was angry and might refuse to meet me. Bewildered, Pat said, "He's up there crying."

They'd assumed his reluctance meant disapproval of my intrusion. But they were wrong. Meeting me face-to-face meant he'd have to confront his internal conflict, his guilt, knowing that he'd only gotten to experience the joy of loving and raising Mary because I hadn't.

It was almost verbatim what Mama had said. She'd teared up back in 1973 when I told her someone from the state adoption agency had visited my unwed-mother school. Many years later, I finally had the courage to ask her about her reaction.

She said, "Oh, honey. I was sad that while I had the joy of being your mother and loving you all those years, my joy brought your birth mother pain."

Like Mama, Mary's father didn't want to confront me—or his feelings—out of his compassion for my loss.

MY EVERYTHING

When perusing my pregnancy journal, I discovered many things I'd forgotten. For instance, our family went to the Fourth Avenue Theatre to see *Fiddler on the Roof* instead of going to the Fireweed Theatre, which was closer to our house. This minimized our chances of seeing someone we knew—the Fourth Avenue Theatre was patronized mostly by people living in West Anchorage. We sat in the back row so I didn't have to parade my adolescent pregnancy down the aisle. Before the movie, I spotted Sister Clare sitting in the middle of the theater with a couple. I wrote, *They were probably the parents for my baby.* I felt like I was sitting in the cheap seats. My instincts could have been correct; Mary once told me that although Catholic Charities limited adopting couples to two babies, her parents received three. They'd buttered up the nuns, and Sister Clare once took out their mailbox after too many hot toddies.

I was also shocked to learn that all along, I'd had all the information I needed to sneak a peek at my daughter.

I'd journaled that while visiting me in the hospital, Kelly had been near the nurses' station and overheard them reveal that my baby's parents lived in the Oceanview neighborhood.

She'd also heard their last name. Mary's mother would have been horrified had she known how careless the nurses had been, putting their family's anonymity at risk.

This matched what Father Hornick had told me when he visited my room. Excited to be in the know, he said, "The couple who are adopting your baby attend my new parish." His church served Oceanview, the upscale neighborhood that overlooked the inlet. I noted in my journal, *The families in Oceanview live in real nice, classy houses, so they must be rich. They have everything.*

The nursing staff must have had an exciting three days while I was on the ward—the priest and visiting nun in and out of the nursery, the intrigue about the adoptive parents, chatter about the adoptive father's prestigious job, and the fancy neighborhood where they lived. Yet all the while as the nurses bubbled with excitement, a nearly forgotten young girl sat at the far end of the ward, fulfilling her duty to give birth, say goodbye, and try to forget she'd just become a mother.

WILD COLTS

A year after my reunification with Mary, I finally booked my flight to Michigan. When my daughter picked me up at the airport, I yearned to brush her shiny brown hair from her high forehead and temple, which matched my own. But I held back because I sensed the affection would make her uncomfortable. I was more like an auntie she shared secrets with and sought advice from on boyfriend issues.

Even with our Catholic upbringings, Mary and I were both as untamable as wild colts. For instance, the nuns had let her out of class to smoke rather than suffer her disruptive and inattentive behavior, and we'd both gotten in trouble for fighting. Her parents weren't always sure how to handle her, so they often gave in to avoid her outbursts. It's not surprising that my daughter and I sometimes clash because we're both headstrong.

As we rode from the airport to meet her parents, I asked, "Who's at your house?"

"My *babcia* is visiting." I broke into a cold sweat. Weeks earlier, Mary had told me her maternal grandmother didn't approve of the reunion because her daughter was Mary's *only* mother and I shouldn't be interfering in her life. Meeting her parents was terrifying enough. Having her disapproving grandmother there to judge me would be mortifying.

Mary pulled into the driveway of a large Tudor home in a neighborhood with wide streets and groomed yards, a place where I'd have loved to grow up. It was so different from my home in Anchorage, and it was a mansion next to Chaps's small house with lava-rock siding. I trembled with anxiety. I was normally confident, but when I followed her up the walk, I reverted to that knocked-up, shame-filled fifteen-year-old who had to give her baby away.

I had newfound sympathy for Chaps, who'd been so uncomfortable and insecure when he met Mama and Tim. Maybe he'd felt similar shame.

The door opened to Mary's six-foot-four teddy bear of a father wearing a lumberjack shirt and overalls, but it was her mother who first enveloped me in an uncomfortably long hug, joined next by her father. It came in the form of what they called a "Mary Sandwich." This was a thing in their family, except I was in the middle this time instead of their daughter. I couldn't wait for it to end.

I felt unworthy of such warmth and was embarrassed to be greeted with a graciousness I didn't deserve. This "sandwich" lacked the joy and belonging I'd felt when receiving bear hugs from Ida's family members at my reunion party in Vancouver.

Feeling like sour cream instead of icing in an Oreo, I remembered what her parents had written in the letter they sent through Catholic Charities: *Without your unselfish gift our family would not be. We are looking forward to meeting you in the not-too-distant future and saying "thank you" in person.*

At the time I couldn't put my finger on why I felt so squirmy and chalked it up to shame, but it was more complex than that. It took years until I could see why. I think the "adoption gift concept" had been normalized for me because growing up I'd heard it a lot, but as I writhed inside this Mary Sandwich, something just felt wrong.

Over the years on birthdays, Christmas, baby showers, I have always given gifts with a joyful heart, and it felt nothing like relinquishing my baby. I know my daughter's parents meant well and yes, I've heard that children are gifts from God and such, but I never intended my daughter to be a gift I gave to her parents. *They* were the gift I gave to *Mary*. It was always for her.

The only thanks to be had were from my daughter, which I'd received in her letter when we first made contact.

I am grateful for the life that you have allowed me to live, and I Thank You!

DROWNING

When I looked through the window of Mama's car in 1973 as the hospital disappeared from view, I imagined Mary Monica's new parents sitting by the phone, waiting for the call: "The coast is clear. The girl has exited the building. You can pick up your new baby now." I pictured that scenario for decades.

But not long ago, Mary texted me a photo of her parents posing on a tweed sofa at Catholic Charities, where they picked her up. When it came up on my screen, tears filled my eyes and I grabbed my heart on reflex. I could almost hear Sister Louise's voice, *Say cheese!* as they popped their heads together. In the photo, my newborn looks vastly different than she did when I held her in the hospital, hours before, and repeated, "Oh, she's just so beautiful, she's just so cute. So beautiful."

Mary sits in her new mother's lap, her head cocked at an uncomfortable angle. Her eyes appear crossed. The *perfect parents* each grip a tiny hand. The new mother is beautiful and fair-complected, just like Sister told me. Her eyes sparkle with elation and her lips are parted in a gasp of joy. As the new father's arm wraps around her shoulders in a hug of shared euphoria, his round cheeks, face, and forehead glisten with pride.

Their unmistakable joy hit me like a tidal wave and shot me back to my bedroom on June 26, 1973. I had just arrived home and was sitting on the edge of my twin bed, my upturned palms in my lap, drowning in grief that far eclipsed their feelings of elation that day.

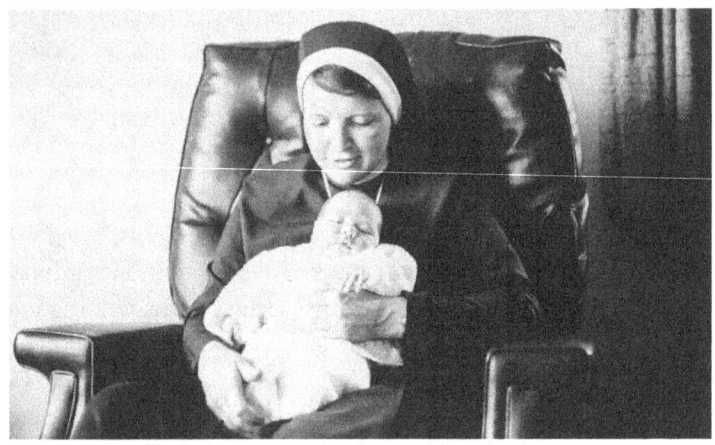

Sister Louise and baby Mary on the day she was delivered to her new parents. Photo taken by the adoptive father.

I was still overcome with loss three weeks after Mary Monica's birth, when Father Hornick dropped by. I was at the end of the cul-de-sac with Paula and the other neighborhood kids. When he pulled me aside, I assumed he'd come to check on me. He casually said, "I was mistaken when we talked at the hospital. The couple at my parish didn't adopt your baby after all. Theirs was born at Community Hospital." He must have realized he'd made a mistake by giving me information that could help me find her and disrupt her life.

I was disappointed. I'd felt comforted knowing where she was. I'd pictured her at his church, in the arms of her new mother. That had been better than knowing nothing at all.

Practically Still a Virgin

Had he not told me of his "mistake," I would have made excuses to attend mass at St. Benedict's so I could scan the attendees to glimpse my daughter in the arms of a light-haired woman. I might even have walked through the crowd outside the church to get a better look and catch her little eyes. It would have been torture if I'd found her, but I wouldn't have cared. When Father took it back, I wiped the information from my mind. For forty-three years the truth was pressed in the pages of my journal, but cracking it open would have been like opening Pandora's box.

MOTHER'S GUILT

On a cool fall day in 2021, around the two-year anniversary of Mama's death, I was revising what I'd written about her rejecting me at my bedroom door after the wire hanger beating. The longer Mama was gone, the more clearly I could see her culpability. Her betrayal was wrecking me.

One Saturday morning, I was crying when Kelly called. Between tears, I asked, "Am I ever going to get mad about this and stop crying?"

"Monica," she said, "you always made excuses for your mom." I was beginning to see what I had felt since adolescence but never identified: Mama had been jealous of me.

Mama was the disciplinarian. If she wasn't in on the pre-planning, wouldn't she have pulled Daddy out of the room to ask what he was intending with the wire-bending act? I thought, *Did she stop the beating because she realized I was giving him pleasure, not because he was causing me pain?*

While trying to absorb this possibility, there was a horrific moment when my mind flashed on an image of Rebecca at fourteen taking my place in the beating. She was flailing on the bed with coltish legs and long hair, like a wild animal shrieking and screaming with tears of heartbreak, pain, and betrayal. I wept with a depth I hadn't in years. *I would have fucking killed anyone who would dare hurt my daughter like that.*

That was a dark week. When I cruised Costco, handles of Johnnie Walker Black jumped out at me across the aisle like in a cartoon. I thought, *Wouldn't it be nice to not feel today?* I clung to a Winston Churchill quote: "If you're going through hell, keep going."

The day after I sobbed to Kelly, Paula called. She'd retired to Arizona. We'd grown close again, visiting each other and talking often. My voice cracked when I tried to articulate my grief about Mama's part in the beating. She was shocked and maybe a little hurt because I hadn't confided in her when it happened. We'd been friends since early childhood, but I'd only known Kelly for three years.

I tried to explain that I'd probably been too ashamed to share, but Kelly had said it better: "Broken kids understand broken kids."

Paula asked, "Do you think writing is doing you more harm than good?"

I thought, *She doesn't get it.*

"I wondered that at first," I said. "Now I see that when I was young, I internalized the bad things that happened as 'something must be wrong with me.' Now that I'm writing, it's become clear that really, my parents were the sick ones."

Kelly affirmed. She said, "It wasn't you—it was them! They were sick sons of bitches. If they tried to adopt today, they could never pass a psych eval or background check."

The following week, even my son Quin, then twenty-seven, weighed in. "If you or Dad had done that to me, I'd have run off and reported it. It sounds like you had Stockholm syndrome."

I thought, *Wow. That's harsh.* Later, I did some research and found many articles supporting the theory that abused children can, in fact, suffer from Stockholm syndrome.

In January of 2022, I was with Gaye, the sober friend I'd helped in her early sobriety, on one of our road trips. I shared the chapter where Mama made Daddy stop beating me when she saw pleasure in his eyes. She said, "When you were reading, you know the first thing that came to my mind?"

I thought, *What insight could she possibly have that I haven't already dissected?*

Gaye said, "I wondered … would she have let him keep beating you if he wasn't enjoying it?"

I asked Tim if he remembered the beating. He didn't. Mama must have sent him to a friend's house when I didn't arrive home on time so he wouldn't be traumatized by my screaming. I can hear Daddy saying, "We need to teach her a lesson she'll never forget."

I sometimes wonder if the memory of lifting my shirt for Kelly in the bathroom stall will ever resurface or if I'll recall the examinations that I must have given the lesions over the weeks they would've taken to heal. Or maybe the wounds were a reminder of a betrayal that was too much to bear. Maybe, like how I had erased Billy, I refused to acknowledge they existed.

I wish I'd had the courage to push Mama to talk it through. I know she loved me. My heart wants to believe she repressed those memories and was telling the truth when she said she didn't remember. But my gut says she suffered with years of guilt.

When Mama passed in 2019, Tim, two years clean and sober, moved in with me and wept for months. I cried, too, but nothing like my brother did. I realized I'd already been grieving her for decades.

REAL

It wasn't until 2022, when reading Mama's journal entries from the time when I'd first contacted Uncle Pat, that I realized the depth of her struggle.

Mama wrote, *Monica's relations want to express their gratitude to me for raising Monica so well! I don't appreciate having expressions of gratitude as if I were just a caretaker. They must be stupid to say such a thing. Monica defends them and that hurts too. I'm not so sure I have a daughter. We shall see.*

Being raised well had been a compliment to me, too. It felt good when Uncle Pat was impressed with how I turned out, but Mama's anger deflated me. I told her he was just trying to be nice. In early reunion, I felt she was being irrational and mean-spirited.

As I read those sections of Mama's journal to her, Kelly reminded me that, like Uncle Pat, I'd also thanked Mary's parents in the letter I sent when we first made contact. As far as I know, they weren't offended. At the time it felt right to say thank you.

Reading how angry Mama was made me curious how she would've acted had she met Ida. I remember back in 1973 when Mama pulled my adoption papers out of the safe deposit box, she told me that she'd like to meet my mother someday. Years later, she expressed the same sentiment to my brother. Was she just curious to see what her children's mothers were like?

After being released from the "Mary Sandwich" on the day I met my daughter's parents, I was ushered into the kitchen where her disapproving grandmother waited. I was relieved that she was polite, even if it was insincere. I suspected she didn't approve of my interference but didn't want to hurt her ecstatic granddaughter.

Reading Mama's conflicted feelings stabbed my heart: *I fully believe that there is enough love for everyone to have a full measure. It's only in my moments of self-pity that I feel she owes it all to me.*

I was shocked by Mama's feelings but not by Mary's grandmother's attitude toward first mothers. We are often expected to shrink back into the shame from which we came. But being an adoptee, I understood the protectiveness Mary's grandmother felt for her daughter; I, too, felt Mama was my real mother.

I used to get angry when someone ignorantly referred to her as my stepmother or foster mother, and not my mother. She was the only mother I knew, the mom who comforted me as a baby, the mom who brought me Seven Up and soft-boiled eggs when I was sick. She was also my companion when I hid in the house once my pregnancy became obvious.

She let me win at gin rummy and she prayed the Rosary with me so my baby would be healthy and have wonderful parents. She rubbed my back while I was in labor and held my daughter when she was born.

For a long time, I didn't realize the word "real" could be so nuanced. The dictionary definition makes it seem so obvious: "Something that is real actually exists and is not imagined, invented, or theoretical."[3] Mama was my real mother, just as Pat was Mary's real mother. But I had another *real* mother. She was the mom who carried me in her womb, whose voice I heard in utero, who had labor pains and loved me enough to give me what she thought would be a better life. Didn't that make *her* real, too? Wasn't I real to have done the same? How could carrying my daughter for nine months, imagining every milestone, and missing her for eighteen years make me anything but a being with actual existence—not imagined?

For over forty years, I've had an orange bumper sticker stuck to my ALMA search binder. It perfectly expresses my thoughts: "Adoptees Have Mothers Two."

Both of them are real.

---

3. *Collins English Dictionary*, "real (adj.)," accessed January 17, 2024, https://www.collinsdictionary.com/us/dictionary/english/real.

COMPLEXITIES

We were five years into our reunion when Mary called to announce her engagement. We chattered like girl-friends about wedding dress shopping and the venue tours she'd done with her mother, events I longed to be a part of. She didn't mention my role. Would I get to attend? I was happy for her, but our conversation reminded me of all I'd missed through the years and the loss I would continue to feel for the rest of my life. I hung up and wept.

I was elated when the invitation arrived in the mail. For eighteen years, I'd pictured the events I'd missed—but this time, I wouldn't have to imagine. I didn't know in what capacity I'd be attending, but I didn't care. I'd be content to hide in the back row or peer through a window.

Before our reunion, every imagined scenario had included a window or fence. I'd become so acclimated to being invisible that lurking in the shadows was the only vision that came to mind. I knew my place.

As the usher showed me to my seat that day, I was confused when he walked past all the guests, then stopped at the front row and gestured to the open seat between Mary's parents. I gulped back a sob. As they each took one of my hands,

Practically Still a Virgin

I realized they'd been saving me a seat. At the end of the cere-mony, my eyes pooled with tears and the guests were a blur as the three of us followed the bride and groom down the aisle, her parents' warm hands holding mine for all to see.

Our daughter chose a cream-colored gown with bell sleeves, empire waist, and full-length skirt. Roses circled her crown like a flower child. I thought she'd pulled the dress from a Goodwill bag; later, my suspicions were confirmed. I was disappointed her gown wasn't as elegant as the venue, which was out of a fairytale. The white mansion was separated from the courtyard by a garden of boxwood and rosebushes along a network of brick walkways. I'd never seen a more beautiful wedding.

Clearly, she had the budget for a new dress. My daughter could have been Cinderella had it not been for that hideous gown. But like mother, like daughter. Even though Mary and I have champagne taste and don't favor thrift stores, that's where we both purchased our wedding gowns—years before repurposing was trendy. We were drawn to dresses that had been in style when we were born.

While guests gathered around the brick terrace for the father-daughter dance, I found my seat on a raised ledge at the far end of the courtyard. I had a good vantage point away from the guests, some of whom Mary had warned me about and who didn't think I had a right to be there. But her parents made it clear that I did.

Mary and I have grown close over the years, but our rela-tionship hasn't been without complexities. Mary's first mar-riage was nearly as brief as my marriage to Danny. On her second marriage, when her first child was born in 2004, I visited for a week. It was a dream come true to be at her side helping with my new granddaughter, just like a *real* mother would be. But in her eyes, I couldn't do anything right, even simple things like making coffee. I fumbled around, trying to

315

use the fancy coffeemaker, cringing that I had to ask how it worked.

She snatched the pot out of my hand and barked, "Never mind. I'll make the fucking coffee."

The guest room was in the basement, and although the space was beautifully decorated, I felt banished to the dungeon. I sobbed every night and longed to go home. I couldn't understand why she treated me like a gross inconvenience.

Months later, I asked if she'd been angry with me. I wondered if, having felt a new mother's love for her daughter, perhaps she couldn't understand how I'd parted with her. Did she subconsciously feel that I couldn't have given her away if I'd loved her? But she said she didn't think that was it. She blamed it on the hormones.

DEEP WELL

On a Sunday morning in 2018, almost thirty years after our reunion, Mary called me on video. I could see that she was on the verge of tears and asked, "What's wrong?"

"I'm really sad but I don't know why."

I sensed the underlying cause. I had dreaded the day she would realize her pain comes from being relinquished at birth. I'd seen her get like this many times since having her first child, and always felt that I was largely responsible.

On the outside, ours looked like a normal long-distance mother-daughter relationship. Yet we'd only seen each other in person a dozen times in fifty years.

I tried taking her mind off her sadness by asking about her recent trip to the zoo with my granddaughters. When she inquired about my favorite features on the smart home device we both owned, I thought she seemed to be feeling better. She also wanted to know the best way to dispose of spoiled chili. She said, "Garbage disposal or trash?" I recommended not putting so much down the drain for fear of clogging, but she felt bad contributing to our landfills.

She turned away and began to weep. I felt as if my presence had increased her sadness. I think the warmth of our conversation reminded her of the miles between us. She can't drop by when she needs me. We can't have coffee, go for a mani-pedi, or grab lunch. Guilt washed through me. She needed me to comfort her, an act that fulfilled a longing I've had since leaving her at the hospital. As I indulged my maternal instincts, she suffered.

"I'm making you sadder," I said.

She sobbed. I'd seen that look in her eyes before. It was like she was hanging in a dark well, clinging to a rope, beseeching me to pull her up. One might think Mary wouldn't miss me since she didn't know me while growing up. But she did.

On a few occasions she's told me how, as a child on her birthdays, she'd sit by the window, crying, waiting for me to come for her.

I wanted to teleport to her side, tell her I was sorry for relinquishing her, and explain that I understood her sadness. That all my life, I'd also yearned for connection—but to what, I didn't know. Although I deeply love my adopted family, something has always been missing, like a shirt held together with just one button. It doesn't quite fit and will never be whole.

When she called, I'd been doing the deep work on myself, trying to heal from my own relinquishment. I was painfully aware that surrendering her had created the same wound my mother had left in me, a wound so deep, no amount of therapy or writing will ever fill it. It's the ultimate betrayal—a betrayal that adoptees are expected to be grateful for. I worried that taking the blame for her suffering would cause her to resent me.

I forced back my tears and listened to her weep. With her head still turned, her cheek and right ear filled the screen.

Practically Still a Virgin

When I'd held her in the hospital, I'd noticed that unlike mine, her ears were asymmetrical—one had an extra ridge.

Staring at it on my screen, I had the strangest feeling, as if I had one foot in the present and the other in that hospital so long ago, studying cheeks and temples to find similarities to my own, to confirm that she was truly my flesh and blood. Just then, Mary's nine-year-old daughter rushed to her and said, "Mommy, why are you crying?"

Mary embraced her daughter. "I just miss Grandma." That was the first time she named her pain. I wanted to cry, too, not for my loss but for hers. She'd called me on and off over the years with an unidentified sadness, but until that moment, she'd never said what I always suspected. She missed me.

I knew how she felt. Meeting my first family had filled much of that hole, but it also created a different kind of emptiness. There are no words to describe the deep ache and longing I feel when I see social media posts and photos showing Ida's large family coming together for hockey games, concerts, and celebrations. I feel the same longing when I see Chaps's family gathering in the cottage or at the pilgrimage, bonfires, baseball games, and parties.

My home is in Sacramento with my children and grand-child and, now that Mama is gone, my brother. I could never leave them, and I wouldn't want to.

Being on both sides of adoption, I know some schisms are invisible until they're filled. Mary once visited when Quin was a baby and Rebecca was nine. One night, while all my children were sleeping, I slipped out of the house for a late-night walk. The air was brisk and cool, the moon was bright, and the streets were still. But something was odd—a feeling of contentment. This particular feeling was something I'd never experienced before. I felt complete, like a missing piece had clicked into place. For the first time, all my babies were together under my roof. I hadn't recognized that particular emptiness until it was filled. I'd lived with that hole for so long, it felt normal.

THE DANCE

I'd arrived at the venue early on Mary's wedding day so I could assist her bridesmaids. A steady stream of girl-friends passed through the bridal suite, and my daughter introduced me to each one as if I were a celebrity: "This is Monica, my birth mother." Her friends gasped when they saw me. "You look so much alike! You could be twins!"

Not long ago, while looking through pictures of the wedding ceremony, one in particular caught my eye. In it, I stand next to Mary's mother. We wear matching blush rose corsages and she's in a tasteful beige mother-of-the-bride dress. Her hair is short and curly, her eyes dry.

By then, Pat and I had developed a relationship. I loved it when she'd call in the early years after Mary came out to meet me, to say in pretend shock, "Do you know what *your* daughter did today?" She was so kind and treated me as an equal. She must have sensed I needed that. We've had many long talks over the years, and I felt Sister couldn't have picked a better mother for my daughter.

In the photo, I'm still plump from Quin's birth and wear a forest-green dress with an empire waist. I'm wiping tears from my face, and my mouth is in that unfortunate twist one makes when trying not to cry. As I looked at the photo, I noticed the vacant seat next to me and realized I was witnessing Mary's father give her away.

During the father-daughter dance, Mary's commanding dad towered over her. This was the man who hadn't wanted to face me because of the pain I'd felt while he experienced the joy of raising Mary. At barely five-foot-two, she was so tiny in his arms. When he looked down at her with pure adoration, through her crown of blush-colored roses, my heart burst and I openly wept.

That dance was proof that all I'd prayed for had come true. I cried as I thought, *If I'd had a glimpse of this moment, it could have spared me so much suffering. It could have given me such peace.*

My daughter looked content in her father's arms, taking his love and adoration for granted—proof that my pain had been worth it. My intention with over five thousand Hail Marys had been granted and was playing out before me. At fifteen, I had no example to measure "good parents" by. Even so, I knew I didn't want my daughter to receive a family like mine. She hadn't.

As I watched my daughter dance with her father, unchecked tears rolled down my cheeks and my shoulders heaved with silent sobs of gratitude. I was witnessing a miracle, the most beautiful sight of my life. It was even more incredible than when she was first placed in my arms, more wonderful than when she walked off the plane to meet me.

The six-foot-four retired Special Agent in Charge, the man who had been personally thanked by presidents, this teddy bear who cherished his little girl—this was the father I'd prayed for, to stand watch over my baby. I had no idea what strong and loving parents would be like, but God did.

I wept with both gratitude and sorrow. She'd received the exact parents I wanted for her, the exact parents I'd needed for myself.

TURN THE PAGE FOR A PREVIEW
CHAPTER OF BOOK TWO
COMING SOON

PREVIEW OF BOOK TWO

Practically Still a Virgin: The Rest of the Story

(WORKING TITLE)

DADDY'S GIRL

It must have been midwinter because the sky had already been dark for a few hours the evening I followed the narrow-shoveled path down our driveway to visit my neighbor friend. Missy lived in the house behind us with her foster parents for a short time. She'd come to my school late during our sixth-grade year. We were both eleven. When I first tried to talk to her at recess, she shuffled while studying her snow boots. Her blonde hair was often matted in the back, and although she had bright eyes, she didn't seem very smart. I got the feeling that Missy was unhappy, although she didn't tell me so.

She'd invited me to keep her company while she babysat her foster parents' toddler. The baby was already asleep when I arrived. Later that night, the police would pay us a visit when they traced our prank phone calls. Between these calls, Missy told me what she'd been doing with her foster father. She mentioned it more in passing than in confidence.

"Me and Ray have sex in the bathroom."

I was shocked and grossed out, but I didn't let on because I didn't want to make her feel bad. Her foster father was a creepy old man (maybe all of thirty) with sideburns and greasy hair. I couldn't fathom how she could stand him touching her. And how could this even happen in their tiny bathroom?

I remembered when some cheeky kid had told me about sex on the way home from the baseball park. He'd said, "They do it laying on top of each other." So I thought it must happen in the yellow tub behind the water-stained shower curtain, and I couldn't imagine how awkward that would be.

I don't know why I wasn't more concerned with her confession. I knew it was against the law for a grown man to be having sex with his foster daughter, but I took it in stride, as I would many other disturbing things.

I didn't breathe a word about Missy until that summer break. I stepped out of the bathroom one morning, my head wrapped in a towel. I had just zipped into my green velour robe when I heard Daddy call from the kitchen, "Sweetheart, can you come here for a minute?"

It was the middle of the week. Normally, he would have been at the office but because he was self-employed, he sometimes took the morning off, so I didn't give it much thought. I towel-dried my long hair, then rounded the corner in my robe, my hair smelling of Johnson's baby shampoo. He was dealing a game of solitaire with a lit Salem hanging from his lips.

"Get ready, I'm taking you out to lunch."

I wondered what was up with the special occasion but knew it would involve showing me off to his business friends, and I loved the attention they gave me. Although spending time alone with Daddy felt yucky, I had yet to understand that such feelings weren't normal in a healthy father-daughter relationship. I pulled my shiny brown hair into a headband and put on my best paisley-print dress, the one I'd gotten for Easter.

As a family, we often ate at the busy café in the Westward Hotel, which later became the Hilton. This was where Daddy networked with potential investors for his real estate deals. Everyone seemed to know him.

He pulled out my chair, and I sat with a straight back like I'd learned in charm school. The waitress brought us water. "Oh Howard, who is this lovely young lady?"

Daddy introduced us. "I'm very pleased to meet you," I said.

While waiting for our lunch, Daddy introduced me to business acquaintances who dropped by our table in a conveyor of expensive suits, firm handshakes, and pats on the back, including a multitude of compliments just for me. I smiled sweetly, just like Daddy taught me.

I'd beamed under his tutelage while he schooled me on the importance of integrity, how he'd earned his excellent reputation because everyone in town knew Howard Hall was a man of his word. Daddy's handshake could seal a deal, he said, because he was honest and highly respected. This seemed obviously true. Even the waitress fawned over him like he was a celebrity. That was probably because he was a big tipper and huge flirt, I later realized.

Decades after this lunch at the Westward, I asked my brother if he remembered Daddy schooling us on his excellent reputation. Tim said he had no recollection of such lectures. It seems likely, then, that Daddy was trying to groom me for the move he was about to make while I ate my sandwich.

"Sweetheart," he said, "now that you are so grown up, I'd like to teach you about business. I'm looking into an apartment building I'd like to buy for you." He told me how he would teach me to collect rents, take calls from tenants, and order repairs. As he spoke, I began to panic. I'd been gobbling up the public attention, but the idea of having to spend extended time alone with him made me sick inside.

Even the lunch was a trade-off because, while I reveled in sharing the spotlight with the famous Howard Hall, at

327

the same time, I felt icky, like I was too close to him. I didn't understand these feelings. To avoid disappointing him, I nodded at his offer but really, I was hoping he'd forget about the apartment building.

What he said next seemed to come out of nowhere. I guess there wasn't a way to ease into it. I remember him shaking his head for emphasis when he said, "I can't believe how disgusting it is when fathers have sex with their daughters."

I'd just taken a bite of my club sandwich. Horrified and confused, I could barely swallow. I hid my shock because I didn't want Daddy to feel bad. To save him from the awkwardness, I added, "My friend who lives behind us has sex in the bathroom with her foster father."

Daddy didn't ask me anything more about it. Nor did he act surprised or repulsed. He also never brought up the apartment ever again.

Decades later, when I repeated his words to Mama, she said that around the same time, he mentioned to her how some of the men at the card table talked about having sex with their daughters and how he found it so disgusting. "I wondered why he would tell me such a horrible thing," she said.

For years, I was confused by that lunch conversation and tried to figure out what his purpose could have been for telling his pubescent daughter about parental incest. I would find out but it would take decades. Regardless, a part of me died that afternoon, the part that had been proud to be Daddy's girl.

 Use the QR code to visit my website (monicahall.com) and subscribe for book two release date, cover reveal, and an occasional newsletter, along with bonus content from *Practically Still a Virgin* and reunification videos.

Look for *Practically Still a Virgin: The Rest of the Story* (Working Title) to be released in 2025.

Leave a Review: Help others find this book by sharing your thoughts on Goodreads, Amazon, or your favorite retailer's website. You can also post a review on your blog.

Spread the Word: Gift a copy to a friend or family member who might like the memoir.

Share online: Pose with the book and share your experience on Facebook and Instagram. Tag @monicahallauthor and use the hashtag #PracticallyStillAVirgin. Connect on X: @monicahallwrites.

Advocate for Wider Access: Encourage your local bookstore and library to carry the book, making it accessible to a broader audience.

Explore Further: Visit monicahall.com for information on speaking engagements, coaching sessions, podcast guest bookings, and additional resources for book clubs.

Connect Personally: Monica is available for virtual or in-person meetings with book clubs. If you're interested in having her as a guest, connect with her through MonicaHall.com.

Suggest for Book Club: *Practically Still a Virgin* is a great choice for book club groups. It can spark important discussions. See Discussion Questions that follow here.

DISCUSSION QUESTIONS

Please be aware that, to provide reading groups with questions that are both insightful and thought-provoking, certain key elements of this memoir, including its surprises, will be disclosed. If you haven't completed reading *Practically Still a Virgin*, consider postponing your review of this guide to avoid spoilers.

1. Discuss the traumatic events that Monica experienced in her early years. How did she cope with these childhood events at different life stages? Have your own coping methods changed over time?

2. In the chapter "Car Ride," Monica describes the car ride with Daddy that ignited her juvenile delinquency and pride of her virgin identity. Why do you think her experience in the car had such an impact?

3. Why do you think Mama and Monica's perspectives on Daddy's wire hanger beating differed so much? How should she have handled Monica's questions over the years about that beating? In what ways did Monica's view of her mother change over the years?

4. Monica struggled to define what happened between her and Billy as rape. Is this a common struggle of victims of

sexual assault? How do you think society defines rape? How does this definition affect us?

5. In the chapter "My Everything," Monica sees Sister Clare at the movie theater with a couple while Monica and her family sit in the back. Why do you think Monica felt like she was sitting in the "cheap seats"?

6. Why do you think Monica was unable to write her baby a letter even though she knew having a letter from her own birth mother would have "filled an immense longing" and that she wanted such a letter "more than anything in the world"?

7. As a child, Monica was frequently told that her own birth mother was "selfless" for giving her up for adoption so that she could have two parents. Did this narrative affect Monica's own decision to relinquish her baby, and if so, how?

8. In the chapter "Signing," Mama sends a message to Monica through Sister Louise that she doesn't have to give the baby up. What do you think motivated Mama to send this message? Should Mama or Sister Louise have handled the situation differently?

9. Monica explains that she later discovered Mary's family was able to adopt three children instead of two after entertaining Sister Clare. How do you feel about what is described?

10. Does society view adoptive parents as superior to or more deserving than those who relinquish their children? If so, why, and is it understandable?

11. In the chapter "Edmonton," when Chaps and Helen learned Chaps's child had been born, he refused to pay the hospital bill and claim his daughter. How did learning about this affect Monica? What do you think was behind his decision?

12. In the chapter "Vancouver," Monica learns that her mother gave her up for adoption because she was treated badly at home and didn't want Monica to have a life like hers. How did it feel to read this revelation? Did it raise any thoughts or reflections?

13. If Ida had been successful in reclaiming Monica when she went back to the adoption agency, who would have raised Monica when Ida died? Was Monica better off being adopted into the Hall family?

14. In the chapter "Wild Colts," where Monica squirms in the "Mary sandwich," the adoptive parents thank her for the gift she gave them. Why does this make her uncomfortable?

15. In the chapter "Eeyore," Monica repeated the Rosary thousands of times while she was pregnant. She later discovered that her daughter Mary drew comfort from praying to the Virgin Mary when she was troubled or worried. Is it possible that these two are related? If so, what other effects could a mother have on her child while in utero?

16. Monica experienced a lot of grief in her life, including grief for what she lost culturally by being adopted into a white family. How did this grief reveal itself during her

life? Have you ever had a loss that took years to process and understand?

17. In the chapter "Elephant-Sized Tears," Monica felt Mama's love was conditional after reading her journals. Do you think Mama's love was conditional? If so, what conditions did she place on it? Have you ever experienced a love that felt conditional? How about unconditional? Do birth parents have the capacity to love their children more unconditionally than adoptive parents have to love theirs?

18. In the same chapter, Mama has complex feelings about Monica's growing relationship with her birth family. Do you think Mama's feelings are understandable?

19. Do you believe Monica's DNA surprise at the end of the story? Why or why not?

20. Helen was the first person in Monica's life to tell her that "you don't give away your own baby! You don't give away your own flesh and blood!" How did this affect Monica? Have you ever been slapped awake by another person voicing their truth? What did they say? How did it change you?

21. What was the impact of Mama giving her journals to Monica years before she died even knowing she was writing her memoir? Did it help her come to a deeper understanding of the complex mother-daughter relationship? Was it more hurtful than helpful?

22. In the chapter "Real," Monica explores the definition of "real" as it relates to motherhood. What do you think

makes a mother "real"? Are birth mothers more or less real than adoptive mothers?

23. In the chapter "Complexities," Monica visits Mary in 2004 to help with her newborn. Mary treats Monica like she is a gross inconvenience, that she can't do anything right. Why do you think this behavior continues over the years?

ACKNOWLEDGMENTS

I want to express my heartfelt gratitude to numerous friends and family members who gave their support, and the many who patiently listened as I delved into my memories while working on this book for over seven years. Mary, if it weren't for your interest in this story, I would never have tackled this memoir and experienced the healing it brought me. A loving thanks to my daughter Becca, who not only suggested that I write this memoir but also got me out in nature and stepped up with companionship and support during the dark years of writing and Mama's death. Thank you to my dear son, Quin; because of your depth, sharp mind, and ability to see beneath the layers, you provided me with perspectives I wouldn't have discovered on my own.

Without Betty Lou's stories, letters, emails, and photos over the last four decades, I would have never fulfilled my deepest wish—to know my first mother. Gaye, when I asked if you knew of a ghostwriter, you gave me the confidence that I could do it myself, without which I may never have undertaken this arduous endeavor. To Maxine, I'm eternally grateful for your wisdom, guidance, and emotional support in the early years of my spiritual journey. You will always have a special place in my heart. I also want to thank my community and my spiritual mentors, Gwen and Pauli, who have self-lessly offered their time, guiding me toward a principled life.

I'm deeply grateful for Mama's support, her willing-ness to hear about painful events, her assistance with reconstructing memories, and her enduring patience and selfless spirit. I extend my love and thanks to my sweet brother Tim, whose eidetic memory helped jog mine regarding events and details. To my longest friend, Paula, your loyalty and compassion have meant the world to me. I am indebted to Kelly, my dear friend and midnight sun comrade. Thank you for your wisdom, guiding me to see things for what they truly were. Levi, your courage, friendship, hours of phone calls, and support have been invaluable. Melanie, you have become like a daughter to me, and I can't thank you enough for the many hours of help you gave me with the final touches, for your compassion, perspective, and friendship.

To Kim Rich, a kindred spirit, thank you for your unwavering support and encouragement, for believing in me from the beginning and assuring me that I could do it. Thanks also to Amy Seek, who helped me gain clarity on some of the most difficult elements of my story. Erin Wilcox, thank you for your input and copyediting. Thanks to Sharon K. Miller for designing the book layout and endlessly Zooming with me to discuss it. Signe Jorgenson, your developmental editing over the entire seven years has been invaluable. Your advice to show, not tell, and your guidance in mining my memories essentially taught me how to write. Each one of you and many others have played a crucial role in bringing this memoir to fruition, and I am profoundly grateful for your contributions.

ABOUT THE AUTHOR

Monica Hall was born in Canada, adopted by American parents, and raised in Anchorage, Alaska. She spent the first sixteen years of her life there and had many of the foundational experiences that drive her writing during that time.

In addition to working as a business consultant, Monica has founded several successful companies and has worked in advertising and marketing for more than twenty years. She's also a self-taught writer and is telling her life story to provide others with understanding, courage, and empowerment. She wants readers to realize that no matter the difficulties they face, it's possible to heal and succeed.

Monica is a speaker, life coach, and mentor. She has three grown children and lives in Sacramento, California.

MonicaHall.com

WORKS CITED

Ancestry LLC. "Indigenous Americas—North." Updated Dec. 13, 2023. https://support.ancestry.com/s/article/List-of-AncestryDNA-Regions?language=en_US

Collins English Dictionary. "Real (adj.)." Accessed January 17, 2024. https://www.collinsdictionary.com/us/dictionary/english/

Reamer, David. "A 1944 Contest Asked the Question: 'What's Wrong with Anchorage?' This Was the Winning Response." *Anchorage Daily News*, Sept. 6, 2020. https://www.adn.com/alaska-life/2020/09/06/a-1944-contest-asked-the-question-whats-wrong-with-anchorage-this-was-the-winning-response/.